The
Daughters
of
Madurai

RAJASREE VARIYAR

ORION

An Orion paperback

First published in Great Britain in 2023 by Orion Fiction,
This paperback edition published in 2024 by Orion Fiction,
an imprint of The Orion Publishing Group Ltd,
Carmelite House, 50 Victoria Embankment
London EC4Y 0DZ

An Hachette UK Company

1 3 5 7 9 10 8 6 4 2

A CIP catalogue record for this book is
available from the British Library.

ISBN (Mass Market Paperback) 978 1 3987 0728 3
ISBN (eBook) 978 1 3987 0729 0

Typeset by Input Data Services Ltd, Bridgwater, Somerset

Printed and bound in Great Britain by Clays Ltd, Elcograf S.p.A.

www.orionbooks.co.uk

To Acha, for his storytelling, and Amma, for her strength.

Prologue

2019

A girl is a burden. A girl is a curse.

I read this in the articles and reports and books I've downloaded onto my phone.

There are a dozen reasons why so many families in India don't want a girl. Reasons rooted in India's centuries-old pastiche of traditions.

When she gets married, her parents pay a dowry to the husband's family. It's supposed to be her inheritance, her share of their parents' wealth. It's illegal. It has been since 1961. But they don't call it dowry anymore. They are 'gifts', ounces of gold, white goods, land, piling high on her parents' shoulders, driving them into the dirt. More than one dowry can leave families destitute.

She doesn't carry the family name. Without a boy, the family dies.

She has no independence of wealth. Until recently, she couldn't have a bank account without a husband or a father. She could not own property. In the records, in history, she doesn't exist.

Her education is basic. She struggles to earn income.

She can't perform her parents' funeral rites. And without those rites, her parents will never reach nirvana.

In some places, up north, there are so few girls now that

they're kidnapped from other states, sold into marriage in families whose language they don't know. Sold into slavery.

The flights, the hops from Madurai to Chennai, Chennai to Sydney, bring me no sleep. Instead I read until my eyes ache.

Chapter One

Madurai, India, 1992

Almost two months before her conception

She does not exist even in thought.

Janani knew, the minute the midwife placed her naked, squalling, soft-as-silk daughter in her arms, that she couldn't lose this one.

An image came to her mind, burying a bundle gone cold and still in the dirt by the young coconut palm. Her hands drew the hated little body closer.

Tiny limbs moved in fitful pumps as Janani looked down into a face as round and purple as a mangosteen. The baby's mouth shifted over the swollen skin of her breast, and her plaintive wail died as she found the nipple and began to feed. Her minute fingers rested against the skin over Janani's heart.

Janani watched her in the light of the oil lamp, her eyes trailing along each line of her body, trying to find something that made her less than perfect.

'*Rock, my little peacock.*' The lullaby escaped through her lips, the first words she'd managed since that last, pain-riddled push.

Hands were fussing around her, tender and papery – Kamala, the old, strong midwife who had delivered most of the rest of

Usilampatti district, over what seemed like centuries. Janani barely noticed, until someone spoke.

'Give her to me.' Pain and weariness turned what should have been a familiar voice into a half-recognised echo.

No, Janani tried to say. It stayed a tired whisper in her mind. She wanted to hold this new life for as long as she could.

There was a rough fumble, nails scratching against her forearms, and the warmth of new-born, new-drawn skin was gone. Her daughter began to cry again. The noise stuttered into existence like a steam engine's chugs. The door closed, muffling the sound.

Was it Shubha? No, no it couldn't be. Her friend was gone, pushed out, a long time ago, before the pains became so strong Janani forgot what was around her.

Get up, you idiot, she thought. She raised herself on to one elbow, then rolled on to the other.

Kamala loomed over her, hands on Janani's shoulders, gently urging her down onto the thin pallet. Her wrinkles had reshaped themselves into grim worry. 'Rest now, child.'

Janani's arms were shaking beneath her. She collapsed back on the bed. One hand came down on the mat with an angry thump. She'd lost track of the hours she'd lain here, but exhaustion was drifting over her like fog.

Sleep dragged her down, blanketing the echo of the baby's cries.

Janani woke.

The shutters had been opened, letting bright sunlight and the heat of the day pour through the bars on the window. Light extended in strips over the room, reaching up onto the bed and over her ankles. Her feet were as warm as though they'd been lying on coals. She lifted them, drawing them up into the shade. The smell of blood and must had dissipated, carried away by fresh air laced with the familiar aromas of the village – chickens, the tamarind and tomatoes in simmering rasam, ground rice, cow dung, motorbike fuel.

For a moment, she lay staring at the roof thatching, dis-oriented by dreams, blinking in the broken darkness. There was a plastic pitcher of water on the tiny round table by the bed, crowned by an upside-down steel tumbler. It woke her thirst.

She sat up, tensed for the sharp shoot of pain she remembered even from that first birth, Lavanika's, five years ago. When there was nothing but a dull ache, she shifted her legs over the side of the bed, the cement floor cool against her feet.

The water was already warm. She drank anyway, cup after cup, until she became aware of the low hum of voices beyond the door.

The tumbler abandoned, she pushed her fists against the pallet to lever herself to her feet. A fresh sheet had been laid under her as she slept, and she noticed for the first time that her nightdress, sticky with the wetness of fluid and blood and piss, had been changed.

Kamala's bag, with its lotions and powdered herbs and roots, had disappeared. The tiny room which held everything Janani owned was as cramped but as tidy as ever. She had managed to finish folding her fading saris during the earliest pangs of her labour pains. They were stacked as she'd left them, on top of the squat, splintering cupboard that housed her husband's clean lunghis. Her ancient sewing machine sat nestled in a corner.

The straw mat that Lavanika sometimes slept on when the heat was unbearable was rolled and leaned against the wall, and Janani felt a deep, desperate yearning for her, to bury her face in her soft curls. But she'd sent Lavanika away with Shubha, away from the pain and blood of birth.

And the room was empty, but for her.

The baby.

A memory, of that petal-soft skin.

She staggered forward.

A glint in the sunlight caught her eye, drawing it to the gold-framed picture of the goddess Meenakshi Amman that had been her mother-in-law's wedding gift. Janani stopped, her hand on the door latch and her womb throbbing, and stared at the perfect, peaceful face. It's all OK, it seemed to promise her. She fought the urge to kick it to the floor, feeling sick.

She took a half-step and, when the pain didn't increase, continued towards the door. Pushing it open, she found herself facing her husband and mother-in-law.

Darshan and Vandhana stood in the other room of the house, the one room that made up the kitchen, living area and the draped-off nook that was Vandhana's bedroom. The midwife had gone.

They'd been speaking in low voices, but both looked up as Janani entered. There was no sign of a baby.

Instead, a few plates painted with the remains of idli and coconut chutney were stacked on the step of the open back door, ready to be washed. Janani felt a sudden stab of surprise that her mother-in-law had prepared breakfast. She hadn't had a choice, of course. Vandhana's only exception to her rule of minimal housework was when Janani was barely able to stand.

The smells of roasted onion, ground coconut and hot, sweet tea still lingered, and Janani was suddenly aware of the new ache of hunger in her stomach. She thought of her daughter nuzzling for her breast and looked instinctively around the room.

'You should eat,' Vandhana said. 'Go and take a bath first, though. You stink.'

Janani's mouth felt parched again. She took another step

forward, craning her head around Vandhana to look in the corner of the room, searching for a small bundle of legs and cloth. 'Where's my baby?' she asked.

Vandhana stepped towards her. Her husband remained where he was, head down but eyes on her like a sullen child, his mouth thin and almost hidden by the thick black forest of his moustache.

'You stupid bitch,' her mother-in-law said.

Tiredness had made Janani slow. She blinked. It was Vandhana's voice she'd heard, Vandhana's fingers she'd felt, pulling her child's warm weight from her arms.

She raised her hands, palms open. 'Where is she?'

Vandhana slapped them away. 'The useless thing,' she said, voice sharp with disgust. 'Just like the last one. It's not worth any more thought.'

Darshan looked down and away, and that was enough.

Is it for the best? Janani thought. It was a flash of a thought, hot and grimy and she'd heard the answer a thousand times, but . . . *No. No, give her back. I want her.*

She couldn't force the words through her lips.

Through watering eyes, she saw Vandhana turn and walk towards the back door.

She couldn't let it be too late.

Janani took a step forward and then another, her arms outstretched.

'No!' she said. 'Where is she?'

A second later, Darshan was a wall in front of her, hands on her shoulders. He manoeuvred her back towards their bedroom. She scrabbled at his arms, but thin though he was, she was still so tired. Before Janani could form a thought, she was half-sitting, half-lying on the unforgiving mattress in their bedroom, Darshan standing over her.

'It's easier,' he said. 'We can't afford another girl, you know it.' Her placid, inert husband sounded as angry as she'd ever heard him. 'What are we going to do? Even if we stopped eating, we couldn't pay another damned dowry.'

Janani didn't realise she was crying until she felt the pounding sign of too little breath in her head and the taste of salt at the corner of her mouth. *Dowry.* She thought of the golden jewellery she'd worn on her wedding day, locked away in the chest at the foot of the bed.

From beyond Darshan, she could hear water being sloshed from a bucket behind the house – Vandhana, washing the plates as though nothing had happened, and she hadn't held her new granddaughter hours ago.

Janani tried to get up, not caring if he hit her, but Darshan's hands were on her shoulders once more, holding her down.

'Just trust Amma,' he said. 'Rest and I'll bring you some food. You need to build up your strength. Hopefully you can be back working by the end of the week.' At the door, he turned, his face seeming softer in the dappled gold of late-morning light. 'You're well enough, aren't you? The next one will be a boy.'

'I don't want the next one!' she said, but the door had closed, muting the sound beyond it into a frustrating wasp's hum.

Pushing herself off the bed, Janani ran to the door, her stomach muscles groaning in protest. Hard as she pushed, it wouldn't budge.

Maybe it's for the best. Maybe it's easier.

A memory filtered into her mind from another life, of sitting on her father's lap and listening to the low rumble of his voice as he told her the story of the birth of the baby god Krishna. Krishna's mother, Devaki, had seen her brother, the doomed king Kamsa, dash six of her newborn children against stone in front of her eyes, their little skulls smashed like pomegranates trodden underfoot. The seventh, the only girl, had slipped from his grasp as he swung her at the wall by her little feet. She had transformed into the mother Goddess in the sky above his head, and cursed Kamsa, reminding him of the prophecy that Devaki's eighth child would kill him. There was no escaping fate.

Leaning against the door, Janani imagined her baby slipping away into the air, shining in triumph against the stars.

She burrowed her wet face into one arm as she pounded the door with the other, and her breasts cried tears of milk into her nightdress.

Chapter Two

Sydney, Australia, 2019

'Your achacha is quite ill.'

It's the first thing my father says to me when I get home from work.

Everything I was going to say slips away.

The unusual March heat has my trousers sticking to my legs, but I haven't had time to change – only to pour myself a glass of ice-cold water from the fridge and worry about my father's pinched expression. I'm light-headed after the journey home. The bus had become an oven in the sun, struggling to navigate the quagmire of Sydney's peak-time traffic. But still, I'd been distracted at the thought that now, this sun-baked weekend, is the time to tell them.

Acha's announcement strips that thought from my mind, makes me forget the commute entirely. I've never seen him look like this, my easy-going father with his wry, always-on sense of humour. He looks older than I've ever seen him. He's cradling his phone. In his other hand, his pruning shears hang like a dead bird.

'I'm sorry, Acha,' I say.

Amma's standing beside him, by the dining table, part-hidden by a vase of Acha's roses. She begins to fuss with the edges of one of the rolls of fabric on the table. I'm not sure if they've come from the shop, or if they're for her college students. Her fingers are small and slim and nimble, but they fumble with the soft material. I find myself looking for signs of pain, of the early arthritis I'm worried is beginning to creep through her joints.

'I am going to go to Madurai.' He clears his throat. 'I would very much like if you all came too. He's an old man now, your achacha.'

Madurai. India. My heart misses a beat. How long has it been? Twelve years? Thirteen? My memories of the place are dominated by squat toilets and awkward conversations with older relatives.

I can't help but look at my mother.

Amma's still silent, but her forehead has wrinkled like cellophane, into delicate little frowning folds. Her hands come together in front of her, fingers intertwined, squeezing into a single fist. That's when I realise that they've talked about this. That they might have fought about this.

'All of us?' I say. I don't know what's thrumming through me more – dread or excitement. I don't want to go, but I do.

Amma looks as though it's her father who's ill. Her eyes, dark as mine, watch me over the steam spiralling above the mug of coffee on the table in front of her. Just looking at that steam makes me sweat. It's never too hot for coffee for Amma, an impressive attribute melted into her bones through half a lifetime in steaming Tamil Nadu. As always, a red pottu separates her carefully filled-in eyebrows. Those eyebrows usually make me fight a smile – they're one of the very few little vanities she gives in to. Not that she needs much else; her skin is still as smooth as a child.

'It might be too hard,' Amma says. She sounds tentative, gentle. 'I have work, Nila has work, Rohan has his classes . . .'

I feel the scratch of irritation. Frustration. Again, Amma's speaking for me, just as she's always done when it comes to India, as though I'm five, not twenty-five. She's got no right now. It's her past and her family she avoids, that she fights to keep away from us, not Acha's.

Even though she's never come back with us, she's grudgingly let our father struggle with Rohan and me and too many suitcases for the few trips we've taken back. His family, she says, we should know. Hers isn't important. Nothing about her past is. I don't need to know about what her school was like, the games she liked to play, if she'd always wanted to make clothes, to teach others how to make them too. What her parents are like, or her sister. All I know is that they exist, or existed. That they're Tamil, not Malayali. That their caste was not one that was acceptable to Acha's family, and that was why we left, why Amma will never go back. What's important is the future, not the past, she says. And then she's back to her bubbly, beautiful self.

It took me a long time to realise that that life, that place, must hold something too painful for her to ever return.

And yet, it's her past and it won't let her go. She's prayed for every exam I've taken. Every karate competition I've entered. Every birthday, as though without a mumbled plea to the goddess Lakshmi, I might not make it to the next one. Every priest at Helensburgh temple knows my birthdate by the solar calendar, my birthdate by the lunar calendar, my star sign.

I wait for Acha to take her side. He always does when it comes to Amma and Madurai. He's more tight-lipped about it than she is.

'It would be nice . . .' My father stops, clears his throat. 'It would be nice if you all were there.' He looks at Amma. 'Deepa can look after the shop, can't she?'

My mother hesitates, then nods.

'And the course you're teaching ends for the Easter holidays, no? In a few weeks? We'll go then.' Then to me, 'Can you get some time from work?'

He's just come in from the garden. The smell of it still lingers – roses and soil and bushfire smoke. He's wearing his Akubra, the wide brim shading his face, as though he's a Bendigo cattle farmer. Under it, his eyes and mouth are wilting, sinking towards the floor.

Love for him tightens my chest.

'Sure, Acha,' I say. 'I'll come.'

Amma sits down. A calculator balancing on the edge of the table clatters to the floor. She ignores it, her gaze trained on me.

'You don't have to,' she says. 'If your acha needs company, I'll go.'

As she finishes the sentence, her mouth twists. Both Acha and I look at her. I can see my disbelief reflected in my dad's face. Amma, offering to go back to India? She sounds about as enthusiastic as Frodo announcing his trip to Mordor. We've gone other places – Southeast Asia, the Americas, Europe. There are photos of the four of us smiling in front of the Colosseum, the Washington Monument, the Eiffel Tower. Not one of the four of us in India.

'Janani . . .' Acha says.

Her eyes flash towards him. There's a flicker of the relaxed melted-chocolate smile she wears just for him.

I find it awkward and embarrassing and beautiful, their love for each other. But I have no patience for it now. Looking at it reminds me of the conversation I had planned to have this weekend. The conversation I can no longer have, not now.

'It's not a two-person plane, Amma. We can all fit, with about five hundred other people.'

She ignores me. 'Rohan will not be able to come,' she says. 'He has his exams. Who will look after him?'

'He's twenty-two,' I say, letting myself drop onto the edge of the sofa. 'He can look after himself.' She's never as worried about him as she is about me, and though she won't admit it, I know it's because I'm the girl. My hands squeeze themselves into sweaty fists.

'How will he eat, wash his clothes . . .'

'That's what YouTube is for.'

'Ha.' She shakes her head. Her fingers are writhing, interlocking themselves, unlocking. 'You don't need to come. It might be upsetting. Stressful, with your achacha sick.'

I stare at her. My temple's throbbing. I rub it with the heel of my hand. 'You do realise that's why I should go, right? Just because you don't want me to have anything to do with your family doesn't mean you can keep me from Acha's.'

There's silence. Amma looks as though I've slapped her, and the expression on her face, eyes wide, lips parted, melts my irritation into guilt in one breath.

'That is . . .' She stops, and looks at Acha. 'That is not what I am doing.'

Acha holds up a finger, then disappears into the kitchen. We listen to the clatter of glass on granite. A moment later, he re-emerges, balancing three tumblers of orange juice. Water condenses on the exterior of the glass, leaving a trail of drips behind him. He places one next to Amma's still-steaming coffee, presses the other into my hand. The cold is reviving, although the juice will be warm in moments – summer heat snakes in despite the air conditioning. Sweat glues the end of my ponytail to my back.

My parents are looking at each other.

'It is entirely up to you,' Acha says quietly. 'I do not want to pressure you. But it would be . . . good, to have you both there, even if Rohan cannot come.'

I rarely see him this serious. His speech has lapsed into Indian formality, still entrenched despite almost a quarter of a century in Australia. That perfect grammar they taught in Indian schools in the seventies, the Austen and Dickens he's read, is irreversible.

Amma looks torn. My breath feels trapped high in my throat as I try to predict which way she might go. She might speak, her voice performing a crescendo that ends in panicked shouting. She might shut down, as she has done before when I've pushed her on this, when I've asked one question too many. I have a horrible memory of the aftermath of our worst fight. It didn't seem possible to live in the same house as someone and not speak to them for a month, but Amma's the most resolute, persistent, bull-headed person I've met. I've almost resigned myself to the thought that I might never know, that I'll live my whole life hovering near the black hole of Amma's past, too close to escape it, too far to get sucked in. But maybe someone else will. Someone in Madurai. Someone who was there. My uncle. My grandfather.

An old memory filters into my mind, of Acha holding Amma as she cried in the sitting room. It had been raining outside, the type of exciting, drilling rain that seemed like the droplets were being hurled straight down at us, almost as heavy as hail. The sound had drowned out Amma's gentle sobs. What happened? I'd asked, and Amma had looked at me and her face had contorted into the most terrible grief I have ever seen. I'd watched, terrified, as she sank to the floor even as Acha tried to hold her, her head buried in her hands.

'Your amma's acha has gone back to Bhagavan, Nila kutty,' Acha had said. And I'd felt a sadness that was just the straining edge of my mother's, spreading out from her like an ink stain.

I ran to my room and cried too, my tears soaking the fur of my soft tiger toy.

The next day, I'd crept to Amma and asked, 'I call Acha's dad Achacha. What do I call yours?'

She'd looked at me. A hint of the sadness remained in her closed face, her drawn mouth, but the anger was stronger. It hurt like a slap. She was never angry at me.

'Don't worry about it,' she told me. 'It doesn't matter.'

It did matter. It's mattering more and more, every day. I want to know my family. And I'm not a scared, sad ten-year-old anymore.

So I break the silence.

'I'm going, Amma,' I say. 'I'll get leave. It'll be OK.'

A fly's made it through some gap in the defence of our window screens. It buzzes around my face and I slap at it. It's as futile a gesture as my words.

Because – and the thought makes me even angrier – if Amma asks me to stay behind, I might have to. It's so hard to say no to her, her hand on my arm, her pleading smile. Which is why I'm still here, twenty-five and living at home, why every second Saturday is family dinner, why I let Acha pick me up from every party, even at three a.m., while Amma lies sleepless in bed.

Why I haven't told her what I thought I'd be able to this weekend.

There's something about my mother that lies behind the light in her eyes, behind her ready laughter. Something fragile, something frangible, that I've always felt I need to protect.

I'm starting to hate it.

And then, finally, Amma nods.

There's a feeling of pressure lifting from the room, as though a thunderstorm's decided not to break but to wander off to another neighbourhood instead.

Amma looks so wilted that I can't stand it anymore. I push myself up, my legs peeling away from the sofa. 'I'm going for a run.' It's still swelteringly hot outside, but I don't care. I need space.

Five minutes later, I'm out in heat that feels solid, sweat already beading on my face and the end of my ponytail whipping me in the eyes. The smell of eucalyptus and wattle is everywhere, natural aromatherapy.

I like to run. It's precious time alone, uninterrupted time. My mind focuses with pinpoint precision, as though I'm in a moving meditation. I can never drift too far from awareness. The rhythm of my breathing and the strain of exertion makes me hyperconscious of my body.

I dodge the hoses of people watering their dying lawns and replay the conversation. I'm still angry. I can feel it pushing me into spurts of speed. But I know it's not just Amma's reaction that's making me angry. It's guilt, too. And that makes me angrier. I don't need to feel guilty. I keep secrets because she does. I haven't told her, because why should I? It's not because I've imagined her reaction, and Acha's, the tears that she rarely sheds, his quiet, confused disappointment, and I'm afraid of it. It's not because she might never speak to me again.

My feet seem to be burning through the soles of my trainers. I can almost smell the rubber melting. The Hills District is aptly named and my quads and knees are on fire as I pound up one incline to fly down the other side. By my fifth kilometre, my mouth is sandpaper-dry, my legs are screaming and I realise that I'm punishing myself. It reminds me of something Murakami said, true as a well-shot arrow, in the book Iphigenia gave me for Christmas. 'Pain is inevitable. Suffering is optional.' I feel like I've earned this suffering.

The sun's sinking down to bleed into the horizon by the time I get home, exhausted. Rohan's back from university. He sprawls on the couch with a bowl of ice cream, his phone and an unopened law textbook. Colin is curled up alongside him. Rohan gives me a wave and Colin wags his tail, his cocker spaniel fur drooping; neither moves another muscle.

Amma and Acha are chopping vegetables in front of the television. The air conditioner blasts cool air that ruffles the tendrils of hair that have escaped Amma's bun. She's laughing at something Acha's saying.

She looks up and her face relaxes with familiar relief when she sees me. 'Nila kutty? It is almost eight-thirty. Why do you go running so late?'

I ignore her and head upstairs, let the water run cold enough to bite, and stand motionless as it washes my sweat and sins away.

'Shame I can't come,' Rohan says the next evening, leaning back in his seat. 'How unwell do you think Achacha is?'

I've asked him to escape out into the city with me, to Darling Harbour, for a drink, for a debrief. We're in Cargo Bar, sprawled in a couple of wooden chairs at the edge of the beer garden, looking out over the water. From here, I can see the lights from the buildings opposite – hotels, restaurants, the Maritime museum – ripple over the otherwise pitch-black harbour. I imagine if I look closely enough I can make out the stars in the water, pinpoints of light dancing, elusive.

The wind is warm against our skin and my muscles ache from a day kneading out cable-tight hamstrings and making back adjustments. I feel an urge to dive into the dark depths of the harbour. These days, it's clean enough for the sharks to return.

'I don't know,' I say. 'He's quite old now.'

A tension headache is tightening its net around my head. Now I've made the decision to go, I can feel anxiety beating its wings in my chest.

I look away, searching for distractions. There are plenty – further down King Street Wharf, dinner cruises are pulling in, spilling their well-heeled, well-watered occupants out in front of the bars and restaurants. Above the water, Pyrmont Bridge stands illuminated by a promenade of lights, the multicoloured flags along its length playing in the breeze. It's in moments like this that I remember I do love this city, no matter how close and small and cramped it sometimes feels. I wonder what my life would have been like, had we stayed in India.

'He's had a good life,' Rohan says. He looks at our glasses. 'Hang on. We're empty.' He gets up and walks quite steadily to the bar.

I watch him go with a smile. It's always so nicely comfortable, hanging out with him. We're only two years apart, but I think our closeness is because we have no family here aside from each other. Or maybe it's all the untold stories Amma and Acha keep, the ones we see in their glances at each other, the ones we try to guess at from their careful words. But that's never seemed to bother Rohan as much as me. He's always been comfortable with himself, with his friends, happy to belong to the present. I wish I could be like that, that I didn't think so much. Chewing on fears like a cow on cud.

He returns with a glass of wine for me and rum for himself.

'You shouldn't be drinking so much,' I tell him. 'You're a baby.'

He ignores me blithely. 'Do you think you'll tell them, Chechi?' he asks instead. 'About . . . you know. You're planning on doing it soon, right?'

I feel my mouth curl, half-grimace, half-smile. It's hard for

Rohan to understand. For him, the news about my romantic life was a happy, awkward non-event.

'What, you mean when Acha's already worried about his dad? And Amma's worried about him, and this India trip, and you being all alone?'

He makes a face. 'I mean before they pair you up with some nice Nambeesan doctor. Or engineer. Probably distantly related to us. They might find one in India.'

'She wouldn't do that,' I say, because we both know he's talking about Amma.

'She would,' Rohan replies. He raises his chin and when he speaks his voice has risen two octaves and taken on an atrocious Indian accent. '"It's the best thing for you."'

I have to chuckle, but I also feel a bit sick. She's talked about it forever, as though finding a good husband was a sacred duty.

Raucous laughter sounds from the other side of the hedge blocking us off from the public. I watch a group of teenagers meandering along, the boys in ripped jeans and the girls baring their bellies and most of their legs to the summer night. All of them hold cans of cheap beer. For a half-second, I wish I were that young again.

'You can find out more about Amma's family,' Rohan says. 'From the cousins and ammayis and ammamas and whoever else is there. We were too young to ask before.'

'Do you think I might get complete sentences out of them?' I ask.

'Maybe.'

'About what the story is with Amma's side.'

'What her problem with India is.'

'What her problem with me is.' I take another sip.

'She doesn't have a problem with you.'

I snort, and almost choke on my wine. The sleepovers, the holiday camps, the nights out, the contact sports – Rohan's never had to fight for them like I have. Hasn't had to endure the silent treatment after those fights. What, I think, will she do when I tell her about . . . *this*? My eyes water as I cough the Pinot Grigio out of my trachea.

Rohan chuckles. 'OK. What Acha's problem with Achacha is.'

'Yeah, that's not likely. Not now.'

We're quiet for a moment.

'I barely remember Achacha's face,' Rohan says, looking at his hands interlocked on the table before him.

Do I? I remember an impossibly tall, severe figure looking down at me with something I think was disgust. That last visit, for the fortnight we stayed in his home, he'd ignored me and fussed over Rohan. Told him stories, laughed at his jokes. Even at twelve, I had known there was a wrongness in that. Even then, I'd thought, *It's because I'm a girl.* The prospect of seeing him again . . . But maybe I'd misunderstood, all those years ago. And he's just a sick old man now.

Rohan's phone rings. He looks at it, then at me. He rolls his eyes with his whole head.

'Hi Amma,' he answers the phone. 'Yes, we'll come home soon. No, don't stay up. Just try to sleep, OK? Yes, Chechi's fine.' He hangs up and takes a sip of his drink. 'Look, Chechi.' That sweet term, *older sister.* He never calls me that when we're with anyone outside the family. 'Just try to have a good time, OK? And whatever you want to do about the parents, whatever they say – well.' He looks down. 'I'm here, you know?'

My throat closes up. I can feel my heart, accelerating as though it's sliding downhill.

I focus on the sound of Rohan's voice as he says, 'Do you have to, Chechi?' His voice is gentle. He was always gentle, even when he was little. A sweet, sensitive boy. At least I'd been able to speak to him about this. About everything. 'Do you have to tell them?'

'Yes,' I say. 'Yes.' I have to force the words out. There's a band around my ribs and my breath shortens. 'How can you be with the person you love if you can't bring them into your family?'

Chapter Three

Madurai, 1993

One month before her conception

Now she is something that cannot happen.

Janani sat on the step outside the front door. The sun was just beginning to stretch its rays over the rice fields. She leaned her head against the doorway as she ground the rice and lentils for the morning's dosas.

She loved this time of day, the freshness of it, the new-birthed feeling of potential. The day's heat was barely stirring. Usually, she'd be humming, bhajans, film songs, anything, pitched low to avoid waking the family. Today, she let it sink into her, the sense that she was the only human in the world. In this quietness, she felt as though she could feel spirits lingering, hear little feet on the hard dirt.

She had to force her eyes away from the coconut palms, standing tall over to the left. The thought of them gave her strength to think about what she'd decided to do this day.

By the time she'd finished, the village was beginning to come to life. Across the street, Janani watched the door of her best friend's house open. When Shubha emerged, knuckling her lower back over the hair that still hung loose over it, arching to try to ease the pressure of her growing belly, Janani waved.

Shubha's pretty face, framed by the thick dark hair she hadn't yet pulled back into its braid, broke into a smile that couldn't hide the concern in her eyes.

Janani wanted nothing more than to go over to her. Shubha had been there from the beginning, from the day after Darshan had led her around the smoky marriage fire smouldering in the decorated, dilapidated marriage hall in Usilampatti. Shubha had arrived the following morning with a plate of laddoo and that never-fading smile. Janani had met her in the doorway of her new, unfamiliar home, still shocked and sore from the pain of her wedding night. The beaming face, almost as dark as the kohl that outlined her eyes and smooth as chapatti dough, had been not much older than her own – maybe eighteen or nineteen. Janani could still remember the surge of utter relief that had rippled through her chest when she had first looked into those welcoming dark eyes. She'd almost embarrassed herself by crying.

Now Shubha was beginning to walk towards her, but Janani shook her head and pointed back into the house. She wasn't ready yet to talk and, in any case, time was like gold, today. For everyone, not just her – there were only two days to Pongal, and every household was scrubbing and washing and shopping for rice, moong daal, jaggery, flour to draw their kolam.

Shubha nodded, but she stayed standing as though poised to take another step forward. They hadn't spoken since Janani's labour pains had begun.

Janani picked up the steel pot. Her arms were sore from the grinding. Two weeks of little movement had softened her muscles. She was glad she was becoming strong enough for her usual chores. The itch to get back to work was growing every day she spent trapped with Vandhana's discontented muttering, with her own thoughts, with the milk that still stained her clothes.

Carrying the dosa mixture, Janani nudged the door open with her elbow and stepped back inside. Morning light was beginning to filter in through the windows. The flame she'd lit in front of the altar cast a halo in which she could just make out the faces of the gods. She tiptoed her way past Vandhana's curtained-off bed to the back door.

Outside, she lit the gas stove and began to heat the water for the sambar. The lentils were soft and the sparse vegetables added by the time Vandhana emerged from the house, her hair damp from her bath.

'Isn't it ready yet? We're hungry.'

'Soon, Mamiyar.' Janani turned to find the dosa pan, rolling her eyes the minute she was out of her mother-in-law's eyesight. She lifted the pot of sambar inside, into the kitchen, the smell of turmeric, ground lentils and mustard seeds making her stomach grumble. Setting the pan down, she went to wake Lavanika.

Her daughter lay on her sleeping mat, flushed with warmth and sleep. Her little pink lips were parted and her curls were a tangled mess, a storm cloud around her head. Kneeling beside her, Janani slipped a finger into one slightly cusped little palm, just as she'd done when Lavanika had been a baby. Her first baby. The one tiny girl she was allowed to keep. What would the other two look like now, if they had been allowed to live?

She was surprised her heart could still ache like this, that this much love and grief and guilt could live within one person.

'Lavi?' She kept the tremor out of her voice. 'Wake up, little one. Time for your bath.'

Darshan had already arisen, bleary-eyed and blinking, rubbing his hands over his hair. He had a full day of driving today, thank Bhagavan. She needed him gone.

'Another day of you lazing in the house,' Vandhana muttered as they finished breakfast.

'No, Ma,' Janani said. 'I'm going to the Nambeesans' house. I'll tell them I'll start work again tomorrow.' Her mother had always told her she was a terrible liar. Hopefully that had changed since her marriage. She had already gone to the Nambeesans' house, had told Parvati Ma that she would be back after Pongal. She was looking forward to it, to being away from this place. She loved Parvati Ma in a way Vandhana would never allow herself to be loved. It had been that way ever since she was a little girl. Growing up with Sanjay, with bookish, quiet Vijay – the Nambeesans' house had seemed almost as much of a home as her own, with Amma and Appa and Rupini Akka.

Until the day came when she realised it wasn't. That that life didn't belong to her.

But now she was back there, the only way she could be.

'Finally,' Vandhana said. 'You're getting older, girl. You didn't take this long to recover after the last one. I had eight children, and after each one I was in the rice fields four days later.'

Janani bit her lip. 'I'll take Lavi with me. It's Sunday, after all. She has no school to go to.' She turned to Lavanika, who'd looked up from the scratched rubber ball she was rolling from one hand to the other. 'Do you want to come, Lavi?'

'Yes, Ma,' Lavanika said, at the same time as Vandhana spoke, 'Take her. Out from under my feet, for once.' She flapped one of her scarred hands towards the door.

Janani finished the dishes and waited for Darshan to leave, without a farewell, before she rushed Lavanika off to get ready. She wanted to be gone before any more questions were asked. She wanted to be back before Vandhana noticed her afternoon chores hadn't been done on time.

Her sari seemed to take forever to tie, as Lavanika spun around on the spot, watching her red, gold-hemmed skirt flare out around her.

'I'll see you soon, Ma,' Janani called as they stepped through the door.

'Bye, Patti!' Lavanika shouted.

Vandhana stirred herself enough to raise a hand and grunt after her granddaughter.

'Janani.'

They were halfway down the street when the voice called out from behind them. Janani was tempted to keep walking, but she heard her name a second time, enough to confirm who it was.

She turned.

'Kamala Amma,' she said.

The old woman was carrying a clump of dried coconut palm leaves, slung over her shoulder. The stalks were almost the same thickness as her arms. Some of the fronds were sliding into the dignified grey bun of her hair, as though seeking shelter from the sun. Her face, lined but unweathered in a way that made her impossible to age, showed no strain. As usual, Janani was drawn to those unusual eyes, a pale golden-brown, that made her seem younger than she could be. Kamala was old, older than anyone in Usilampatti, older than anyone knew. She was as much a part of the village as the old banyan tree beside Santhana Mari Amman's temple. Everyone knew her – she'd delivered them, or their children, or their husbands. She was respected, and, though the men wouldn't admit it, a little feared.

Janani hadn't seen her since the night of her labour. Now, under the blue sky, the crispness of morning not yet faded from the air, that night seemed to have happened in another world, in a nightmare. She wasn't sure she wanted the memories Kamala brought with her. The midwife had been there, every time. She'd known what would happen, and done nothing to help. But what could she have done, this old kind-eyed woman with her gentle hands?

'I'll walk with you, girl,' Kamala said as she neared Janani. 'Keep moving, you seem in a rush.' She waved away Janani's offer of a helping hand. 'Where are you going, with the little one dressed so prettily?'

Lavanika had slipped to Janani's other side and was peering at Kamala from around Janani's body. Janani had dressed her in her favourite pattu pavadai. The iridescent green of the blouse glowed in the sun. Janani had stitched it herself, on the old Singer sewing machine, worried as always that the needle would sputter and stall.

'The temple,' she answered.

'Ah.' Kamala looked at her and back down the road. Her lips curved up into a smile. They were walking in a direction that would take them nowhere near any of the local temples. This road would take them into the warren of streets at the heart of Usilampatti and directly towards the bus station. 'How are you feeling? It's been two weeks. Has your pain gone?'

'Mostly, yes,' Janani said.

'Good. You shouldn't travel long distances until you're recovered.'

Janani shot her a quick sideways glance, but there was no change in the old woman's expression; she just repositioned the coconut palms and swatted at a dried frond that tapped at her forehead.

'I won't,' she said.

Kamala hesitated, glancing down at Lavanika. Her daughter was walking ahead, a little skip in each alternative step, singing to herself. 'The baby,' Kamala said quietly. 'Your mother-in-law didn't say . . . didn't ask me . . .'

Janani shook her head, quick, hard. 'She did it herself. I don't want to talk about it.' She had to bite down on her lip to force the tears back. She felt Kamala's hand on her arm, squeezing once, gently.

They walked in silence for a few moments.

'You know,' Kamala said, her voice once more brisk and sure, 'you have to be careful what you pray for. Some places are powerful enough to pick the thoughts out of your mind. Before you enter a place such as that, you need to be sure of what you want.'

Janani cast a startled glance at the old midwife.

'I'll remember that, Kamala Amma,' she said.

'Good,' the old midwife replied. Her steps slowed and she came to a stop. 'I'm glad you're feeling well enough to be out. And,' she looked at the ground, then back up, her strangely pale eyes glistening, 'I'm sorry, child. I'm sorry.'

She raised a hand and began walking, back the way she had come.

Lavanika trotted beside Janani. 'Everyone says she's a witch, Amma,' she said.

Everyone did.

She must be a witch. When Manasi's husband came home drunk and beat her, a stone fell on him in the quarry the next day and broke both his hands.

When the elders curse her, the monsoons are so bad the canals burst and the village floods.

Murugan didn't pay her for the delivery of his second girl, because Kamala refused to use the poison. But then he got sick. He couldn't work for months.

Gossip to break the boredom in the ration shop queue, waiting for the government-provided rice and lentils.

'She's a wise old woman, Lavi, that's all.'

Lavanika tilted her head, a curl falling over her eyes. 'You said we were going to the temple,' she remarked. 'Why are we going this way?'

'I'll tell you on the bus,' Janani said. She stopped and turned to squat down to Lavanika. Dull pain rippled through her stomach. She ignored it and cupped her little girl's face in her hands. 'Lavi, you have to promise me something. This is a secret trip, OK? A secret that's mine and yours only. You can't tell Appa. You can't tell Patti.' If they realised she'd gone so far un-accompanied, even Darshan would beat her.

Lavanika nodded, dark eyes wide and solemn, and Janani kissed her forehead.

'Good.'

They walked on towards the chaos of the bus station.

'Look, Ma!'

A man rode by on a bicycle, balancing five sacks of rice on his head with one hand.

Janani gripped Lavanika's upper arm. The traffic ricocheting through Avani Moola Street felt as if it were an inch away from her face. Trucks, buses crammed with shoppers and temple-goers on their way home, autos, cars, motorbikes – they were travelling much slower than they did on the highway, but there were so many of them.

It was rare that Janani came into the teeming heart of Madurai. It felt like stepping into a disturbed anthill. It was busier now than usual, of course. With Pongal came people from outside Madurai, sometimes from outside Tamil Nadu. There were as many crowding the streets as there were vehicles. She heard languages she recognised – Hindi, Malayalam – and many she didn't. People from Karnataka and Andhra Pradesh, clogging the markets, crowding into the restaurants where the cooks made masala dosa after masala dosa, their arms moving in lithe, practised circles, their faces gleaming with sweat. So many people, it felt as though she'd be smothered.

But she could see Lavanika loved it. As the bus had trundled along, she'd pressed her little face against the window, watching places she'd never seen rush past them. She'd turned in circles as they'd jumped from the bus, gazing at the hordes of people. It was delightful to watch, but the sharp fear digging into Janani's chest demanded her focus. Her daughter's head barely reached the top of the wheels of the oncoming lumber trucks, but she didn't seem to notice as she twisted around, her eyes huge to trap all the sights within them. Janani imagined her vanishing beneath those trucks, never to be seen again, or some strange man striding past and scooping her up. She couldn't – *wouldn't* lose her. Her fingers were sweaty on Lavanika's skin.

'Yes, Lavi, I saw,' she said, answering the impatient tugs that threatened to loosen her sari. 'But see there?' She pointed up. 'That's where we're going.'

Lavanika's head dropped back, the curls tied up in their red-ribboned pigtails just brushing her shoulders.

Above the sounds of the horns and the slight haze of dust that hovered over the road rose the tiered spires of the Meenakshi Amman temple. The five towers they could make out stood in coloured splendour against the grey-blue sky, uncaring of the madness teeming around their base.

A gap appeared, a heartbeat wide, and Janani stepped into the road, her hold on Lavanika's arm tightening. They scurried across under a barrage of horns, stopped in the middle of the road to let a lorry with a picture of Ganesha painted on its side race past, and ducked ahead of a young family on a scooter. The woman on the back looked Janani's own age. The pallu of her sari flapped behind her in the wind. Her little son sat in front of her, her arms wrapped around his chest.

Across the road, everything seemed to slow down, just a little. The streets were still seething with people, people coming to shop, or worship, or both, but at least the street leading to the temple was too narrow to allow anything but pedestrians, cycles and scooters past. Janani's chest loosened. They hurried past jewellery stores and shops for sari material, much faster than Lavanika seemed to like.

'Amma, I want to see!' she shouted, pointing at a shop window adorned with gold chains and elaborately decorated, silver-belled anklets.

'We don't have much time, Lavi,' Janani said. 'We don't want Patti to become angry.'

There seemed to be a hundred shrines here, to saints and deities, for every prayer. As they passed a minor temple to Hanuman, Janani looked in to see his statue carved in loving detail, his tail flowing to curve just above the floor in a graceful arc.

And then they emerged into the road encircling the grandest temple in the city.

Here, so close to Meenakshi Amman, the street was lined with shops selling lamps, incense and flowers. The scent of jasmine overlayed the dust, cow dung and fuel. Market stall holders displayed their trays of plastic bangles and packets of pottu.

Lavanika shouted and pulled away from Janani's grasp, sprinting to the nearest stall, the golden hem of her skirt fluttering at her ankles. She passed right over the plain traditional red circle pottu and pulled out a packet that glittered like jewels.

Tense though Janani was, she had to smile. They'd look like coloured stars on Lavi's smooth sun-darkened forehead. But she shook her head. 'No. You're always losing them. It's a waste of money.'

Lavanika's brow wrinkled. She opened her mouth, but Janani got in before her.

'Where's the one Patti gave you this morning?'

One hand went to her bare forehead and a grin leaked back onto Janani's face.

'When you come home from school with your pottu still where it's supposed to be three days in a row, I'll buy you some that sparkle like diamonds,' Janani said. She didn't mention the new pottu waiting to decorate Lavanika's head on Pongal morning. 'Now, let's keep walking. We don't have much time.'

Lavanika was pouting as Janani pulled her along, but there was too much around her to distract her. Even Janani's eyes were drawn to the hundreds of brass lamps, the women in silk saris that paraded in and out of the jewellery stores, and the stalls selling pictures of gods gazing with idyllic calm from their painted gold frames.

They followed the crowd around the side of the temple to the main entrance. The sun was hanging well above it now. The arched gate rose above them, now close enough for Janani to make out the vivid blues and yellows and reds of the paint that adorned the hundreds of carved figures around it. Demons and gods, animals and humans, all frozen in moments of frantic activity as though time had stopped still halfway through their lives.

Just outside, an old woman, her legs and arms barely wider than a broomstick sat with her wares – strings of brilliant flowers only just beginning to wilt in the heat – watching the stream of people pass her by with the indifference of years. Janani noticed the moment the rheumy old eyes alighted on Lavanika. They brightened and drew at the corner of her lips until the two of them were exchanging jarringly similar gap-toothed smiles.

Janani, smiling herself, handed a few paise over to the old lady and selected strings of jasmine flowers to twine through their hair. Lavanika's she wrapped around each pigtail so the soft petals brushed against her neck.

'God bless you,' the old woman said.

The temple itself was swarming with people. Janani couldn't believe that it would be even more crowded on Pongal morning, but she'd seen it once before, the lines of devotees streaming out of the temple's mouth like an undulating tongue, heads craning up to the pillars, children bouncing on their toes.

She led Lavanika through the east entrance, towards the beautiful square pond where other worshippers were congregating to wash the dirt of the streets from their skin before they entered to pray. She'd forgotten how huge it was, more a lake than the tiny ponds built into the fields behind the village temples hundreds of years ago. All four sides were formed of steps leading down towards the blue-green water. On three sides, rows of plants created a barrier between steps and water; on the fourth, people were descending to wash their hands and face and feet.

For a split second, Janani was tempted to walk straight on and save precious time. They'd already bathed this morning, and if she didn't return in time to start the evening meal Vandhana would . . . She had to stop her hand lifting to her head. But the sweat dampening the hair at her temples swayed her towards the steps down to the water. She felt too grimy to enter after the jolting bus ride with the exhaust fumes blowing back into their faces. And she didn't want to take any chances. It would be a long time before she'd be able to come back here.

As they splashed water over themselves, Janani told Lavi the story of how Meenakshi had descended from heaven to earth here, on this very spot. 'There are lots of miracles that happen when you pray here,' she said. 'Babies born, marriages made, sicknesses cured.' Maybe an evil mother-in-law dead, she didn't say, and pushed that thought to one side.

'I'm praying for you and Appa and Patti and my pottu,' Lavanika said.

Janani kissed her wet forehead.

They moved through the pillars, carved with image after image of gods and goddesses, nymphs and celestial beings, the demon asuras and rakshasas. The crush around them became a constant pressure as they moved through the open archway of the main complex, men and women all mingled together. Janani kept Lavanika close, pressed into the folds of her sari, her arms around her chest to create some semblance of personal space.

A colossal golden statue of Ganesha stood guard at the inner shrine, surrounded by flickering clay lamps. Janani touched her hand to her ears and bowed three times. Lavanika copied her movements, a tiny, delayed reflection.

'Keep moving!' barked a stern-faced pujari, sweat glistening on his face.

They shuffled into the inner rooms and the heat intensified. Not the heat from the outside world – that was kept at bay by the cool grey stone. This was the living heat of bodies pressed against each other, a devout, desperate heat. Janani was conscious of her tongue, dry as stale idli in her mouth, tasteless as paper.

They crept forward like prisoners in the darkness. Lavanika's body was rigid and she was moulded against Janani's legs. Janani could feel the growing tension in the room as the breathing, sweating mass around her inched closer and closer, until finally, just a few steps ahead, in the tiny alcove of the innermost shrine, she caught her first glimpse of what she'd risked coming to see.

The smell of ghee and incense engulfed her. Janani breathed it in and closed her eyes for the briefest of moments. The room wasn't quiet – with this amount of people flowing through it, it could never be – but Janani ignored it. She pulled out her prayer from the dark recess in her mind, from the black solid mass that her grief had become.

Anything. Please, Bhagavati, I'll do anything. Just give me a boy. Another baby I can keep.

With Lavanika pressed against her, the prayer felt like a betrayal. She pushed the feeling away.

'Keep moving!'

Around her, people being propelled past the goddess craned themselves backward, hands reached above their heads with palms pressed together, their lips moving in frantic last-minute prayer.

She was swept away, clutching Lavanika to her and shuffling to keep her footing, leaving the goddess smiling mysteriously behind her.

Janani's lungs felt lighter the second they emerged into the main hall.

'There are too many people, Amma!' Lavanika said. Her round cheeks were flushed a dark red, the curls at her temple sweat-flattened against the skin, and her eyes were wide.

'I know, little one,' Janani said. 'We're going.'

They lined up for prasadam first. Janani had to admit the thought of food that she hadn't had to prepare or pay for made her stomach clench and her mouth water shamefully. Yoghurt rice, jaggery and rice payasam, ghee-roasted sweet appam – Lavanika was scooping up balls of rice the size of her palm and forcing them into her mouth. Her mouth was ringed with yoghurt and she had a piece of pappadum stuck to one cheek. Janani was caught between laughing and scolding her, but she didn't think she looked much better herself.

She was aware of some tightness leaving her shoulders as she left the temple. Around them, the crowd broke apart like a torn necklace, people scattering like loose beads in a hundred directions. Lavanika had recovered almost as soon as they had stepped outside.

'Amma, let's look at the shops now!' She bounced along, hanging off Janani's hand, her jasmine flowers shedding petals onto her blouse.

'No, Lavi,' Janani said. She needed to get home. There was rice to be cooked, water to be pumped and carried, and she had to bring in the clothes before the rain came. Vandhana would sit and watch them soak, and wring them over Janani's head when Janani got home. And tomorrow was the first day of Pongal. She would clean the house, top to bottom, and walk to get the rice and jaggery and milk she would need for the day after.

She so badly didn't want to go back, didn't want to drag Lavanika away.

What choice did she have?

'Lavanika, it's time to go.'

They were caught in the traffic on the bus ride home. It was packed full of people, like chickens in crates, limbs and heads hanging out of windows. The two of them sat tight against their own window, Janani keeping a firm arm around Lavanika's waist, as two more women piled onto the seat beside them. The bus stood with a herd of honking others behind cargo trucks full of timber and quarried stone. Fumes the colour of ash engulfed them. Janani made Lavanika hold a piece of her sari across the lower half of her face. Although she did the same, there was a thick, rancid taste in her mouth.

Thankfully, the bus's lingering effects had faded by the time they reached home because Vandhana was waiting for them.

'Where have you been?' Vandhana asked, her voice quiet.

'Lavanika, go and wash your hands,' Janani said. When her daughter had gone, she faced her mother-in-law. 'They wanted to speak to me, Mamiyar,' she said. 'Tell me about some changes around the house . . .'

Vandhana slapped her across the cheek. The blow wasn't hard, but the old, bony fingers left Janani's skin stinging. 'What will you feed your husband when he gets home, useless girl? And clean that mess up.' She pointed behind them and Janani turned to see a trail of jasmine petals, already yellowing, marking where Lavanika had stepped. 'Wasting money on flowers.'

Janani managed to finish the cooking just as the sun sank beneath the horizon and mosquitos began to gather around the oil lamps. Darshan still hadn't appeared. The three of them ate together, accompanied by Lavanika's aimless, soothing chatter.

Afterwards, Janani took Lavanika outside for a bath, pouring jugs of water over both of their bodies, and the grime of the road sluiced off with it. When they returned, Vandhana had already retreated behind the cloth curtain that hid her sleeping mat. Her snores bounced around the tight walls.

They slipped into their room and settled together on the bed.

'Amma, can you tell me a story?' Lavanika asked.

'There was once a prince named Prahalad,' Janani whispered. Light flickered on the walls above their head. 'His father was the demon king Hiranyakashipu.'

Darshan's voice floated through the window. *Aahaa kannan thunai raadhae raadhe . . .'*

His voice was an atrocious attempt at Ilayaraja's. Janani wondered if it were her imagination, or whether the cheap whisky on his breath really was being carried through the walls.

Janani ignored him and continued. 'Hiranyakashipu was a very rich king with a rich kingdom, and he was very proud of his son. But there was a problem.'

The singing was getting louder.

'That's Appa,' Lavanika whispered, a moment before the door slammed open.

'. . . *nenjellaaaaaam*,' Darshan trailed off.

For a brief moment, there was little more than the heavy sound of his breathing and the rumble of a scooter passing in the street. Then there was his stumbling footsteps, and the sound of the door banging.

'You might have to sleep with Patti tonight,' Janani murmured, heart sinking.

'Again?' Lavanika said. She frowned. 'She snores louder than Appa.'

The bedroom door opened with more force than was necessary and they both turned to face it. The stench of whisky, harsh enough for tears, rolled off Darshan as though he'd bathed in the stuff.

'Wife,' Darshan slurred. His head lolled to one side and his body leaned in the opposite direction. It made him look like he'd been assembled wrong. 'Janani. My wife.'

Quiet and unnoticed, Lavanika rolled off the bed.

'It's time to sleep, husband,' Janani said. She moved to the side of the bed furthest from him and eased her feet onto the floor.

'Sleep!' Darshan said. He chuckled and lurched another step into the room. 'A wife should be asking for sons, not sleep.'

Janani felt a sinking feeling in the pit of her stomach. The thought of him on top of her made her feel nauseous. At least it would be quick, if it happened at all.

Lavanika was inching her way towards the door. Darshan caught the movement and gazed through bleary eyes. 'Little bird,' he said. 'Look how big you've grown.'

'Yes, Appa,' she said, still moving. 'But you stink.'

'Yes'. His head swung back around to Janani, standing motionless at the foot of the bed. 'No sons tonight,' he added. 'I've already . . .' He thrust his hips forward, once, twice. Laughed, a horrible wet laugh. 'Next time.'

She couldn't believe it. Of course, she knew what he did, with those others, while he loitered around the car, waiting for hours for an employer. But that he would come back to sleep unbathed beside her, covered in the dirt of another, unknown woman . . .

Darshan took a few more unsteady steps, angled his body slightly and collapsed, fully dressed, across the bed. In seconds, he was snoring.

Lavanika had frozen in the doorway. Janani beckoned to her.

Together they rolled the bamboo sleep mat out at the foot of the bed. Janani lay down beside Lavanika's warm little body and stroked her hair, watching her eyes getting heavy.

Janani's nightdress was damp from her leaking breasts. It was almost dawn before she was able to shake off the thought of her achingly empty arms, of the memory of soft newborn warmth against her chest, and fall asleep.

Chapter Four

The piles of paper had slid in an ever-growing circle over the glass-topped table in the hours Sanjay had sat before them. He was suddenly aware of an ache in his tailbone. The straight-backed mahogany chairs that had cost a fortune decades ago looked glorious. They impressed the guests and the extended family and were comfortable enough for a one-hour meal; he'd been sitting here all morning.

'What are those?'

Sanjay was startled enough to slide the piles of paper towards him in pure reaction. He'd expected to be alone. He certainly hadn't expected the man standing in the doorway, tall and imposing, almost skeletally thin except for the slight swell of his belly. For the thousandth time, Sanjay wondered if he might end up looking like his father in his old age. He was lanky enough, had the same long nose, the same thick hair, although his remained black as a crow's wing. For the thousandth time, he wondered why, if he looked like Acha, he couldn't be like him.

His father shouldn't have been back so soon. *Damn*, Sanjay thought, but he hadn't prepared a lie. 'I'm looking at job applications,' he said.

'Why?' his acha asked. 'What's wrong with the job you have?

The pay is good. You seem to be doing well.' He said this last as though he didn't quite believe it.

Although Radhakrishnan Nambeesan had lived in Madurai for almost three decades, he only spoke Tamil when he had to. All conversation in the house was in a combination of Malayalam and English, depending on whether his father wanted to impress or not. It kept, he said, gossip from the servants. As though the servants couldn't understand at least a little Malayalam. As though anyone cared what went on in this house.

'It's fine,' Sanjay said. 'But too bureaucratic for me. Any government job is. It's time for a change.' Tamil Nadu Electrical Distribution was hierarchical and arcane. The name perfectly captured the tedium. He hated calling his dull superiors *sir*. The building itself was old and decrepit, the grey smog of Madras traffic seeping into every crack and pore, turning even the carpets a lifeless, elephant-skin grey. He hated the rattling ceiling fans. He hated sitting at the tiny booth-like desk he'd been given, and the view he had out of his window onto a dirty alleyway full of scraps and rubbish from the restaurants and cheap diners backing onto it. He hated that even though he was an IIT graduate, men ten times less competent were simpered at and bowed to because they were twice as old.

He hated how close it was to home.

And yet, here he was. At home. Every weekend. Because where else could he be when his mother might be dying?

Acha had moved into the room and was casting his eyes over the mess of paper. Dressed in a beige suit that seemed to hang off him even though it had been tailored, his tie was perfectly cinched. With the thick-rimmed glasses resting halfway down his long nose, he looked like a tax officer sniffing around suspect accounts. Sanjay willed him to lose interest and go away.

'You're home early,' he said. This time on a Saturday,

Radhakrishnan, the perfect, dedicated doctor, should still have been in the surgery.

'My last patient cancelled,' his father said. He picked up one of the sheets of paper. 'This firm is based in Hyderabad, I see.' Dropping it, he moved onto another one. 'Bombay.'

Sanjay stayed quiet. It was easier.

'So you want to leave Madurai again.'

Sanjay closed his eyes and ran a hand through his hair, hoping when he opened them he'd be alone. 'Maybe.' *God, yes.*

'When even your Priya Ammayi has returned.' Radhakrishnan threw the paper back onto the table. 'Even though you have just come back, when Monday to Friday, you have your freedom in Madras.'

'It's not freedom, Acha.' Sanjay couldn't help the words escaping. 'It's work.' *Shut up, you idiot.* He bit his tongue to cage his irritation and stop himself talking. All Acha would do would be to twist his words.

The corners of his father's mouth tightened. Sanjay knew what he was thinking. As far as Radhakrishnan was concerned, Sanjay wasn't a doctor and so he couldn't be working hard enough. His gold medal from IIT meant little. It wasn't a medical degree.

'I suppose an electrical engineering position will not just appear here,' Radhakrishnan said. 'Priya has left that big accounting firm – now she is paid almost nothing by that charity, or whatever it is.' Scorn dripped from the word *charity* like acid.

'She doesn't need the money,' Sanjay couldn't help replying. His aunt had made her money. She'd got more in the divorce, although nobody but she spoke about that. For the rest of the family, it was as though she'd never been married in the first place.

His father ignored him. 'Go wherever you want,' he said.

'When we find a wife for you, you'll come back here to get married and raise your family. At least Vijay is here to look after your amma between now and then.'

Sanjay felt the sting of the last comment, but ignored it. 'I don't need you to find me a wife.'

'Is that because you were so successful when you tried? That Gujarati girl who is still failing to be a film actress?'

The familiar flare of anger. Sanjay was aware of the tension in his shoulders, the unconscious tightening and shrinking whenever he was in his father's presence. It had become a habit now. One more thing that Amma's illness had brought.

He opened his mouth to retort, when a noise interrupted them. Someone was rattling around beyond the back door which led into the kitchen.

Leaping at the excuse, Sanjay pushed away from the table, stood and walked through into the kitchen. The back door handle trembled and turned. The door opened, creaking inward, and revealed Janani, standing on the doorstep with a pail in one hand and a pile of cleaning cloths. The morning light illuminated her face, glinted from her silver nose ring.

This was how it had been when they'd first met, Sanjay remembered suddenly – except that day, they had both been peering, shy and unsure, from behind their mothers' legs. He couldn't help but take a step backwards. For a moment, they were both frozen, staring at each other, but then Janani said, 'Vanakkam,' and stepped into the house. The bells on her silver anklets chimed.

His father had followed him in. 'Ah, Janani. You're back. Good.' He spoke in Tamil, although Sanjay was sure her Malayalam was better than passable. She'd begun to pick it up from that very first day, soaking it in without fear.

'Yes, sir,' she said.

Before you start,' Radhakrishnan said, 'could you make me a coffee?'

He turned and walked away without waiting for a reply.

They were left with each other.

'Do you need anything?' Sanjay asked, as he always did now.

'No, sir,' she replied, as she always did now. 'Do you?'

'Don't call me that.' It grated, that respectful 'sir' she'd insisted on using from the first day he'd returned to Madurai three months ago. It had thrown him a step back, that day. He hadn't been back since Geeta Ma had retired, since Janani had taken her place. Seven years in Bombay, and he had come home to find his mother unwell, Geeta Ma retired and Janani taken her place cleaning the home. Sir, she'd called him. As if they hadn't grown up together and called each other names that had them both doubled over in fits of laughter.

She was already moving towards the counter, reaching for the cleaning liquids in the cupboard below the sink. Her arms, slender and small-boned, didn't seem strong enough to be carrying the pail of water she set down on the floor.

She'd had the baby, of course. The last time he had seen her he had wondered at her ability to move, swollen as her belly was. It was a Sunday, and he had been packing his few things to get ready for his flight back to Madras when he'd overheard Amma tell Janani to go home, to not come back until after the baby, heard the rustle of paper and Janani's protests as his mother had pressed a wad of cash into her hands.

Now he had a thousand words, but they were all crammed together and not a single one seemed ready to go first.

'Did you have a good Pongal?' was what finally came stumbling out of his mouth. Pongal had been a week ago. He could feel his face burning.

Finally, she looked up at him, and nodded. 'It was nice. There was a parade in Usilampatti.' He thought he saw the quirk of a smile at the corner of her mouth. 'Lavanika loves her book. She barely puts it down.'

He smiled. She had brought her daughter with her the day before she'd left to have the baby. The shock at seeing that bright-eyed little girl had been almost as strong as that first sight of Janani in more than a decade, rounded with pregnancy. He could still remember when they were children, when they were Lavanika's age, playing hide-and-seek around the house, and now here she was with one of her own. He'd given the little girl an *Amar Chitra Katha* of the goddesses Durga and Saraswati and Kali.

'I'm glad. It was one of my favourites.' A brief pause. 'How are you?' He tried not to look at her stomach.

She nodded, head moving side to side, but her eyes were hooded with tiredness. 'I'm fine.' Turning, she opened the cupboard under the sink. 'I'd better start.'

Sanjay backed out of the kitchen. The door closed behind him.

That night, Sanjay went to the opening of a new hotel bar in Madurai. He left Vijay at home – his younger brother was studying for his first surgery exams and seemed constantly on the edge of explosion.

Walking through the door, Sanjay was confronted with a seating arrangement of soft couches encircling black marble tables that formed a horseshoe around an indoor garden. A fountain bubbled in the middle of a cluster of gardenias. Miniature palms splayed out under the soft lighting of the overhead candelabra.

'Sanjay!'

There he was, his best friend. As usual, Praveen was wearing a suit he must have paid far too much for. He could it afford it, though. Rather than riding the wave of prominence his Minister for Labour father was floating on, Praveen had been one of the hardest-working boys in the school. He was an investment banker now, flitting between New York and Bombay in business class. His hair was swept right to left and gelled into what was likely whatever style Shah Rukh Khan was wearing at the moment.

'What have you done to your hair?' Sanjay asked as he reached Praveen.

'I'll talk you through it,' Praveen said, grinning. 'Trust me, we'll get yours to the point where some other poor girl will like it.'

Sanjay punched him in the arm, lightly, just enough to dent the sleek black material of his jacket. He found himself wondering whether Janani liked Shah Rukh Khan. Liked that hair.

Praveen's smile faded. 'Seriously, though. I'm sorry to hear about Diya. Although I never thought she was good enough.'

Sanjay looked away, not wanting to see the sympathy in his friend's face. 'Ha. Thanks, Praveen. It's old news now.'

Truthfully, Diya had begun to fade from his mind. They had met at a time when they were both different people. He couldn't imagine what they'd say to each other now. Still, something lingered. The loss of the warmth of having someone to share his days with. Someone to listen, to listen to. To plan and dream with.

Praveen clapped him on the shoulder. 'Come on. We've ordered whiskies.'

It was past midnight by the time Sanjay stumbled out of the bar. He was far too drunk to ride his motorbike home, so he left it in the hotel car park and hailed an autorickshaw. Madurai flashed past him in a rush of brilliant light and car horns. He extended his head as far as he dared outside the rickshaw, hoping the relatively cool stream of air blowing into his face would sober him up. As they hit the highway, a lorry passed close enough to quash that idea. Resting his temple against the inside of the rickshaw, Sanjay closed his eyes.

It seemed like seconds before someone was shouting, 'Ey! Sir!'

Sanjay jolted awake, almost smashing the back of his head against the rickshaw, and slid groggily outside. The familiar shape of the front gate loomed before him. He handed the man a twenty-rupee note, ignoring the part of his brain that screamed at him that it was too much, and wove his way to the gate without waiting for change.

The latch seemed inconsiderately difficult to operate, but after much fumbling, he was inside, up the steps and unlocking the front door.

Darkness had seeped throughout the house. Sanjay knew his way around without a light, but alcohol had drowned his memory. He bumped into a side table at the entrance to the living room and set a mahogany lamp wobbling; he watched it sway for a few seconds before he was able to put out a hand and still it.

Stepping into the room, he immediately stubbed his toe on the leg of a sofa.

'Ah . . . ouch.'

Something in the darkness moved.

Sanjay froze, his gaze fixed on the thing on the far sofa. It sat up slowly, a wispy halo around its head picked out in some of the street light slipping through the shutters.

'Sanjay?'

'Amma?'

Worry took the place of fear. Staggering over, he dropped down to kneel beside where his mother lay on the couch. She'd pushed herself up on one arm, off the cushion that had been propping up her head, her fine hair creating a silver-black cloud around her face.

'What are you doing sleeping out here?' he asked.

'I was too hot to sleep,' she said.

'Are you feeling sick? Should I call Acha?' The paleness of her skin was enough to sober him up substantially.

'I was,' she replied. 'A little. I had some water, I feel much better now. No need to disturb your acha. He had a tiring day. He's snoring now.' She settled back against the pillow. Her olive nightdress seemed to engulf her.

'Good.' He sat down on the tiles, his back against the sofa and feet extended under the Taj Mahal coffee table, wrinkling the Kashmir rug beneath it. By turning his head, his cheek against the edge of the sofa, he could look straight into her eyes.

'Go to bed, kutty.'

She always called him that, even now when he was years past being able to be called a child.

'Can I sit here with you for a little while?'

'Of course.'

They sat in silence. He wondered if, despite how hard they'd fought to keep it from her, she knew. If she was hiding the pain, ignoring it, to keep the lie alive for them.

He took her frail, soft hand in his and kissed the back of it. 'I love you, Amma.'

He felt her hand on his hair, felt it move in gentle strokes, until he fell asleep.

The next morning, Sanjay woke from broken sleep to his alarm with a thankfully mild headache. Forcing himself out of bed, he repacked the bag he'd take back to Madras tonight.

As he made his way down the stairs, the sound of the television told him Acha had returned from the temple. He'd be sitting there, barely listening to the TV, thumbing through the *Hindu Times*. Sanjay could just make out the excited voice of a reporter shrieking about Jayalalitha's descent upon some electorally advantageous village in the middle of nowhere. The Chief Minister already had the rich and the middle classes at each other's throats and in the palm of her hands. Now it was promises of a better life to buy the poor, the crowds of Dalits and backward castes, the masses who had the power of the swing vote. 'Amma', they all called her, the miserly and miserable and every idiot in between. Jayalalitha, the ex-actress, the 'Mother of Tamil Nadu'. Sanjay had a cold respect for the shrewdness behind that benevolent, round-faced smile.

He had to get out of here.

Bangalore, Hyderabad, Delhi, Calcutta – he was starting to feel a sinking certainty they weren't going to be far enough. And Bombay was out of the question. *She* was in Bombay, slinking around with her B-list Bollywood star of a fiancé. Yes, the hurt was fading, even the memory of her, of the two years their lives had been intertwined. Still, the thought of being in Bombay, surrounded by places they'd loved, people they knew, always at risk of stumbling into her, was nauseating.

So . . .

He'd managed to hide them thus far, the forms tucked between his university textbooks upstairs. Immigration forms: India to the United Kingdom, India to the United States, India to Australia.

If they didn't work, perhaps he'd try Germany, or the Netherlands. He'd heard they spoke excellent English there. And what a novelty it would be, to learn another language that wasn't an Indian one.

He thought about Amma and about how long it would take

him to get back to her if he moved to one of these places. His headache seemed to grow.

The door to the dining room opened and Sanjay almost fell down the final two stairs.

Janani appeared, holding a steaming tumbler of coffee in one hand and a plate of biscuits in the other.

'Sorry,' she said, moving past him.

The door to the living room was ajar. He watched her walk through and disappear from sight, heard her say 'Here, sir,' even heard the plate click down onto the marble of the coffee table. It had always been his favourite table, a round-edged rectangular beauty in grey-veined white, mined from the same quarries as the marble of the Taj Mahal, inlaid with semi-precious lapis lazuli and tiger's eye, jade and mother-of-pearl, by workers whose ancestors had slaved on that absurdly grand tomb.

He didn't hear his father say a word.

Janani reappeared in the doorway empty-handed. 'Breakfast?' she asked him.

He wanted to tell her he'd get it himself. Being served by her seemed alien, uncomfortable, as though the world had shifted around them. But then again, maybe it had, with the turn their lives had taken.

He nodded. 'Please.'

She glided back into the kitchen without looking at him.

Sanjay sat down at the dining table with a sigh.

He must have drifted off, to the sound of running water and the scrub of cleaning brushes, the whisk of dried coconut palm leaves against the tiles, the smell of fresh dosa and lemon.

It was the silence that woke him. He'd been dozing for twenty minutes, and there was no sound from the kitchen.

Pushing his chair away – it made a stubborn, unfriendly scraping nose – Sanjay stood and made his way to the kitchen door. Laying his ear against it told him nothing, so he turned the handle, pushed it open and stepped through.

A container full of dosa sat by the stove, beside a dish of onion chutney and a pot of steaming sambar. The coconut palm broom was resting against the back door.

Janani was sitting on the tiled floor, her back against one of the cupboards, eyes closed.

Shit.

'Janani?' Sanjay said. 'Are you OK?' He stepped forward, afraid to touch her.

Her eyes opened as though she'd been burnt, head snapping towards him. She was struggling to her feet before he'd finished speaking, although when she managed it, she had to lean against the cupboards for balance.

'I just needed a rest for a minute,' she said.

Sanjay hurried over to the fridge to pour her a glass of water. 'I'm sorry,' he said. 'I didn't mean to startle you.'

'No, no, I'm fine,' she replied, but she took the glass. He watched as she drained it, her throat moving as she swallowed.

They hadn't had much of a chance to speak alone in the months since Amma had become ill, since he'd moved back from Madras to Madurai. It wasn't a complete move. Monday to Friday, he was in Madras, in a dingy apartment in Balji Nagar, walking to work every morning past the Zambazar market and a dozen temples and mosques. On Friday night, he was on a plane or a train to Madurai, stumbling exhausted into the house by midnight. The two precious days of the weekend, he spent as much time with Amma as possible – and when he wasn't with her, there was nowhere he'd less rather be than in this house, claustrophobic despite its size. He was almost always out when Janani arrived mid-morning.

And before that – it had been years. Even now, as she stood

in front of him, he still thought of her as a loud little girl, her hair tamed into two swinging plaits tied with red ribbon. He remembered the skinned knees earned playing tag with him on the concrete driveway. He remembered yanking at those plaits during those rare times they'd fought, until their mothers – the mistress of the house and the cleaner – separated them, trying to look stern through their laughter.

She'd begun to change into the adult she was now a lot sooner than him, and then she had stopped coming to the house with her mother. He'd asked Geeta about it the first time she'd appeared without Janani.

'She needs to take care of the home now,' she'd said to him as she swept the floor. 'Her sister is married, and soon it will be time for Janani's marriage too. There is a lot for her to learn.'

He remembered the grief of that moment, stabbing through him. Even then, at fourteen years old, he knew that something had come to an end that day. He barely saw her in the four years before he'd left for university in Bombay, but he asked Geeta about her regularly, and kept asking, through his mother, from his dorm room on campus. He learned that she was engaged, then married. The news of her first daughter's birth shocked him – he hadn't even finished his undergraduate degree – but these things happened much earlier for village girls, his mother told him. Thinking about it now, he wondered how he could have accepted it as easily as he had. Maybe it was because everyone around them had made it seem natural. A Kallar village girl was never going to have the same life as a Brahmin-born son of a doctor. But it hadn't made sense to him then. Why couldn't she, his smart, funny, spirited friend, have the same life as him?

And now, here she was, cleaning his house. It was wonderful to see her, but to see her like this . . . he couldn't keep away the thin thread of shame.

Janani had taken the steel tumbler to the sink, washed it and placed it on the dish drainer. Now she was looking at him, still with that half-smile creasing her right cheek.

'What?' he asked.

'You've grown up, finally,' she said. 'I never thought you'd be taller than me.'

'I've been trying for years,' Sanjay replied, and despite himself, he smiled too.

'What was it about Bombay? Was it the food? The air?'

'Maybe. The bhel puri and the papdi chaat is delicious.'

She laughed as she reached for a plate from the cupboard.

'I'll take that,' he said.

Carrying the plate to the counter, he piled it with food as Janani collected the broom and pail, cleaning clothes draped over a shoulder and detergents nestled under her arm.

'What's this bhel puri?' she asked. 'Is it as good as sambar?'

'Almost,' he said, backing away to let her through the door into the dining room.

She dusted the cabinets as he sat at the table.

For a moment, there was lemon-scented silence, except for the sound of cloth on wood and the faint words drifting from the television in the next room.

Sanjay snatched at the fraying threads of his courage and spoke, pitching his voice low. 'Janani, should you have come back so soon? The baby . . .'

The cloth, blue with faint orange checks, continued to move, back and forth, over the mahogany. He shouldn't have asked. Maybe she'd hate him for asking. But he had to know.

'It's only been two weeks,' Sanjay said. He tried to keep his voice light. 'Shouldn't you get some more rest?'

Janani laughed, a short, sharp sound he wasn't used to. 'My

mamiyar doesn't believe in rest,' she said. 'But, really, I don't need it.'

'And the baby?' He rushed the words out without thinking about them. 'How is . . .' He let the words trail off as the cloth paused.

'It died.' She didn't look at him.

For a moment, he couldn't hear as the blood pounded in his head like waves smashing against rock. He just watched as the cloth began to move again against the counter.

'Janani.' His voice sounded muffled, as though he were speaking from behind a closed door on the other side of the house. 'How?'

She looked at him. Said nothing.

He read the answer in her face.

Amma had told him about the other baby. He'd still been in Madras then, clutching the hard shell of the phone to his ear and trying to understand Amma's words. The heavy sadness of them was not as bad as the lack of surprise, the resignation, the *it happens all the time, these villages, these villagers.*

Janani had moved over to the next cabinet, rubbing at it, her weight leaning into it. 'We don't talk about it.'

He could see the profile of her face. The sunlight picking its way through the window shutters refracted off a single trickle of water balanced at the top of her right cheek.

Sanjay had only seen Janani cry once when they were growing up. They had been petting the baby calf tethered in the carport when he had told her about the new high school he was going to be attending. She had wanted to come, had begged and pleaded with her mother. Geeta had seemed on the edge of tears herself as she shook her head and kept shaking it, trying to explain that there wasn't enough money, that girls couldn't go to secondary school, that there was another life for her. The tears had swollen

Janani's eyes, twisted her mouth, stained the neck of her dress. Sanjay had pressed himself against the car so hard the alarm went off.

Footsteps sounded on the wood in the hall. Janani ignored them. She was still rubbing against the same spot in the wood, all her weight leaning into it, as though trying to rub a hole big enough to disappear into.

Sanjay turned around.

Radhakrishan stood in the doorway.

'Finish eating and let her do her job, Sanjay,' his father said. 'And why were you home so late? Disturbing your amma?'

There had been a time when his father had made lemonade for him and Janani, had sat them down on the cool cement of the driveway and told them stories from *The Twilight Zone* and Enid Blyton books he'd read. Sanjay couldn't find a hint of that in the eyes of this man in front of him.

He took his empty plate to the kitchen, washed his hands, and left through the back door, the scent of citrus still in his nostrils.

Chapter Five

Sydney, 2019

My mother keeps her Indian clothes in a heavy wooden chest my dad bought for her in Singapore. It's a beautiful piece, a combination of dark and pale woods that swirl around each other to form arch-necked deer and fan-tailed birds under a canopy of trees, lacquered into a shine that turns the entirety into a dark mythical paradise. She rarely opens it, but today, she lifts the bronze latch, raises the lid and pulls out a pile of old salwar kameez.

'Here,' she says. 'They are very nice, but they haven't fit me for some time.' She smiles, shy and rueful, and pats her gently rounded stomach. 'Try them on.'

'Thanks,' I say, and smile back. It's the first time she's seemed relaxed talking about the trip.

They smell like the chest and dust and India, that distinct aroma of spice and wood and petrol fumes.

I can see, even folded as they are, that they're lovely. The salwar at the top of the pile has a tapering teardrop neckline, bordered in gold and sequins, the cloth itself a rich purple

'These are gorgeous, Amma.' I look at her. 'Did you make them?'

She ducks her head. 'You think they're nice?'

'Everything you make is nice.' It's true. I've inherited none of my mother's sewing talents. She has her own Indian clothing store and three staff. She teaches community college sewing lessons. Even she can't teach me to sew a button on a shirt properly.

'Ah, kutty.' She reaches out and squeezes my hand, then turns back to the chest.

I take them to my room, breathing them in. Shaking out the first, I see the colour's not faded at all, the rich purple vibrant from neck to a hem that will hang to mid-thigh, sleeves halfway down my upper arms, faux-pearl buttons sewn on the front between lines of gold. The trousers are marigold yellow.

The second set has a maroon top, embroidered with blue flowers that have improbable purple centres. Blue trousers that shouldn't match, but do, the same shade as the petals.

The next item isn't a salwar. I don't realise until I see the hooks holding the front together and that it's much shorter than I am expecting. It's a sari blouse. The deep red material is fading at the sleeves and neckline, but it still shimmers slightly in my bedroom light. The sari itself is missing.

I pick it up to put it out of the way and realise something is tucked inside it, card, or cardboard, that bends under my fingers.

I unfold the blouse and a couple of photos slip out.

That they're old is the first thing I notice. They look bleached, the colour seeped away. In the first, I see myself, standing beside Amma. The green skirt I'm wearing has faded to lime. I must be four or five. It looks as though it was taken at twilight, the sky a weak purple and my features shadowed but for my huge smile and the gap in my top front teeth. My hair is a cluster of play-swept curls. It was taken in India. There's a goat behind me, and on my right, an old woman with her sari gathered up, a basket of snake beans on her head.

I don't recognise her, or the man next to Amma. He's tall

and lean, and a moustache hides most of his upper lip. I don't remember this photo being taken. I don't remember the outfit, or the place. All I can do is wonder who these people are, how they are connected to me. An uncle and aunt, maybe?

I'm infuriated, and it surprises me. I've had a lifetime of this, of not knowing, not even remembering. There's a blackness drawn over my years in India, as though I only glimpsed that time through a stage curtain.

The other photo is of Amma alone, standing beside a woman about her age. They look so very young, younger than I am now. Maybe younger even than Rohan. Their cheeks are thin and their skin smooth over the sharp lines of their face. I know Amma's family were short on money. I've seen photos of her before, of my parents' wedding day, of her clasping my chubby toddler body, of Rohan as a featureless bundle of soft baby. And yet, it hits me again how thin she is, how huge her eyes in her face, how much laughter is in her eyes and her smile. She's got her arm linked through the other woman – girl's. A hessian bag of rice leans against her right leg.

Both photos seem to be taken on the same day – the same pale blue-walled hut is in the background, and in the dirt is drawn bright, beautiful coloured kolam designs, patterns of blue, white, green, red, yellow. It must be Pongal.

Both photos look cropped, as though there was something unpleasant in them that someone wanted to excise.

I must be there, somewhere, hidden outside of the frame of the second photo. That woman, she was someone, to me.

They remind me of pictures framed on the walls of Iphigenia's family home, of her cradled in her grandfather's arms in the hills of Thessaloniki. She knows, loves, the stories in those photographs.

I've looked at them for longer than I was intending when I

hear Amma's voice. Leaving the salwar kameez on my bed, I take the photos and the sari blouse and head back down the hall to her room.

Amma's waiting for me with yet another outfit in her hand. 'Ah,' she says, 'did they fit . . .' She stops. I'm holding the photos out to her.

'I found these,' I say. 'They were in this.' The sari blouse hangs from my hand like a pennant. 'Who are the other people in it? I don't recognise them.'

Amma stands with her mouth slightly ajar. She's looking at the blouse.

'That's where that was hiding,' she murmurs, but it's as though the words escaped of their own accord. Then she looks at the photos. Her eyes meet mine. 'Where did you find them?'

I raise my eyebrows and shake the blouse. 'In here. Strange, right?'

'Oh.' She shakes her head and reaches for them. 'Yes, very strange.'

I hold them turned towards her. 'Who are these people?'

'People from a long time ago,' she says. I recognise the edge of impatience in her voice. It's the first warning.

I push anyway. 'That doesn't matter. I still want to know.' It's an effort to keep my voice conversational, reasonable, but it seems to work.

'You didn't recognise me? I was young and slim then. And you.' She's staring at the photos, her hand still extended. 'How little you were.' She points. 'That is an old friend.' There's a pause, as though she's forgotten the woman's name. 'And that,' she indicates the other photo, 'that's just a cousin. Not close.' The other hand comes up to rub her cheek. 'We went to visit them for Pongal. You know what we drew these kolam with? Coloured rice flour. We'd buy it in the market.'

I turn the pictures to examine the man's features. He doesn't resemble Amma, but then, I look nothing like my cousins.

'Where's Acha? And Rohan?'

Tiny V-shaped wrinkles form as Amma frowns. 'I can't remember now. There must have been something else happening at that time. Other Pongal celebrations, I'm sure. Your acha's family is huge.'

I look closer at the pictures. It's amazing how faded they seem.

The last few years, Acha's convinced Amma to come out to see Pongal celebrated in Parramatta, in front of the pastel nineteenth-century town hall in Centenary Square. It was the usual food stalls and performances and colour, the square scented by sambar and masala dosa and, of course, pongal, the boiled rice and lentil dish that was the festival's namesake. Our little group was surrounded, every year, by big families of cousins, aunts and uncles, grandparents cooing over soft-cheeked toddlers in their prams. The sight of them always made me ache. Even with my parents and my brother, I was lonely in the crowd. Every year, except this one, when Iphigenia had come with us. We'd walked, arms linked, through the sea of excited Tamils, and I'd stolen my joy from her wide-eyed delight.

I'd like to see Pongal in Tamil Nadu. It irks me that I have, but there's not a single shred of memory of it. I wonder if we had been surrounded by family. If doting grandparents had grasped my toddler fingers.

'But you don't have any pictures of your mum? Your dad? Your sister?' I ask.

Amma sighs. It's high, like a whistling breeze. More warning that a storm's brewing. She looks around the bedroom and I notice her eyes fix on a picture of her and Acha on their wedding day, looking impossibly young, wearing thick flower garlands and shy slivers of smiles. There's almost nothing else from before that time. No jewellery from her mother, no books from her father. It's as though her life only started when she met Acha.

'There must be, somewhere,' she says. 'But if these photos were in a blouse, who knows where all the others are? Everything became a jumble when we left India.' One hand's still extended, and she clicks her fingers. 'Give them to me. I'll find an album to put them in properly.'

'A jumble?' I ask. 'Why?'

'Because we had to move quickly when your acha got his job here,' she says.

She doesn't sound relaxed anymore.

Silently I pass the pictures over. I watch as she shuffles them into alignment, pauses, and tucks them back into the chest.

'You know, Amma,' I say quietly, 'I wish you'd tell me.'

There's no annoyance on her face when she looks at me. Just a tired sadness I often see drag at her eyes when I ask about older times.

'I know, kutty,' she replies. 'But I've said before, some things are not important to tell. And even . . .' She hesitates. 'Some things that you shouldn't tell. The past is gone, no? And here, with you all, I am very happy. So I choose to focus on that, on the future. Now go and try the clothes.'

She closes the chest as I leave the bedroom, and the scent of burnished old wood follows me. I store her words in my mind, to take back to Rohan, to pry apart with him. It confirms, of course, what I already suspected – that all her family are dead, deaths she's never recovered from. Disease, maybe. Or the floods that so often submerged Madurai's districts. When Rohan was little, there'd been a news report of another railway accident in Tamil Nadu. I remember him asking Amma, his thick-fringed eyes wide, if her parents had been hit by a train. There are so many ways for the poor to die in India.

There's a captured moment of before we left India that very first time, framed, on the piano. I'm a toddler with kohl ringing my eyes, sitting on the bed beside the frail smiling body of my grandmother. Rohan's in her lap, a tiny, new-baked thing. She had died not long after that. And then we had left, as though her death had freed us. But it hasn't. Instead, I feel like I've been cast adrift, sent off on a journey with no sense of where I've come from.

'Nila?' Amma calls from the kitchen. 'Come get your dinner. *MasterChef* is starting!'

I have to smile. We can't miss *MasterChef*.

So I put the memories away, a little fresher than before- at least, the moth-holed memories that I have.

The next day, I leave the clinic, the smell of Deep Heat still lingering on my palms. I'm the last physio to leave, but the sports masseuse is still there, working on someone's ITB syndrome, bearing his weight down on the patient's leg. My own muscles twinge in sympathy.

Although the summer hours are beginning to fade, the sun's still visible above the horizon as I walk out onto Hunter Street with the beginnings of a headache. I make my way down across the ongoing construction that has disembowelled George Street, and to the harbour's edge. My breath's already starting to shorten, anxiety disturbing my stomach into flutters.

The sunset's beautiful, the water glistening and rippling like quicksilver as I walk along the wharf. Seagulls wheel lazily above the anchored boats. I keep moving, past the wildlife centre and the aquarium, past the oddity that is Sydney's Madame Tussaud's, and into Darling Harbour, my steps quickening the closer I get. Up, alongside a fountain filled with bronze statues of storks cavorting in the water, and finally, the café that has become our default meeting place, like any animal's watering hole.

My palms are slick, the heat still thick, when I see Iphigenia.

I'm suddenly reminded of how long it took me to learn how to pronounce her name after we first met; I the only brown girl in our kindergarten, Iphigenia shy and blue-eyed and able to turn cartwheels. We bonded over our names, so unusual for a Western Sydney school. Six years later, we won the same scholarship to the same private girls' high school. It was there we discovered where her name came from, performing Euripides' *Iphigenia at Aulus* in Ancient History, giggling in our makeshift chitons. It was a throwback, her mother told her, to her history, her culture.

Iphigenia's family have owned a Greek shop in Leichardt for thirty years but hold on to their heritage with all their strength. She speaks Greek better than I do either Malayalam or Tamil.

She sits waiting for me, lawyer's briefcase resting against her chair leg, sunglasses perched in her dark hair. Smiling. That smile, that reveals a shallow dimple above the right corner of her mouth, that shapes her blue eyes into flower petals. There was a brief time, right at the beginning of our friendship, when I was jealous of her blue eyes, jealous in the way only a child can be jealous, enough to bring tears to my eyes. We'd talked about it, years later, and she'd almost cried with laughter. There were months, she said, when she'd dreamed of having my curls, when she'd wrapped locks of her red-brown hair around her fingers and prayed that they would stay coiled.

We still chuckle about it.

*

64

The froth on my cappuccino shifts. It forms a swan-shaped cloud.

Iphigenia sits with her hands wrapped around her iced coffee. The call of seagulls that have drifted in from the harbour for scraps and crumbs fill the silence.

'I'm sorry,' she says.

'Thanks,' I say. 'I guess it's to be expected. He's ninety now. It's an impressive age.'

'It is.'

I don't have to tell her that I don't know my grandfather all that well, or that I'm not sure how I feel about him. She knows that. She knows everything.

'It'll be good to see the rest of your family, though,' she says. 'Spend some time with your parents. Be there for your dad. See India!'

There's a pause. I know we're both thinking about the trip we've planned for years, to see the Taj Mahal and go trekking in the foothills of the Himalayas and house-boating in Kerala, avoiding my dad's relatives, stuffing ourselves on three-foot-long masala dosas. I'll be as much a tourist as she is. Not someone who could belong, even just a little.

She says, looking down at the table, 'I don't want to bring this up now, but I know we'd talked about it happening this past weekend. Did you manage to speak to Uncle and Aunty?'

My breath releases like a deflating balloon. Of course the question was coming, of course it feels like a punch in the ribs. But I've forgotten how close she is to my parents. She's called them that, *Uncle, Aunty*, since we were five. It adds a knife-twist to the blow.

This conversation, this squirming, guilt-ridden, walking-on-coals conversation is one we've repeated, in myriad forms, for six months. We've brainstormed what I should say and how. We've compiled an Excel spreadsheet of everything Amma and Acha might say, and how I could . . . *should* . . . respond. I should have done it by now. And yet here I am, catching the shape of hope in the curve of her eyebrows, and all that comes to me is the burn in my chest that warns of monsoonal tears.

I glance around me as though inspiration will come from one of our hot-chocolate-sipping neighbours, the giggling high-school girls out too late, the elderly couple clasping hands across their table, the man staring at his laptop as though he's trying to melt it with his eyes.

Nothing comes.

I meet Iphigenia's gaze.

She nods. Her dark hair glows auburn in the sun, whereas mine, I know, is black as a crow's wing. 'You haven't,' she says.

My heart feels like it's moved much higher in my throat. I can't bring myself to mention Achacha. I've had months of excuses. Instead I say, 'I just . . . need to find the right time.'

'I know,' she replies. 'I was the same with my parents.' Her eyes on me are steady. In the fading light, they look darker, their colour bleeding into a steel-grey. All the noise around us has become a background buzz.

My face burns. I take a sip of my cappuccino. There are two sugars in it and it's too sweet. 'I'm sorry.'

'This is getting a bit much, hun.' She pushes her drink away, folds her hands on the steel tabletop. 'We shouldn't have to need to talk about this again,' she says.

A lead ball suddenly appears at the bottom of my gut. My legs twitch with the urge to run. Even with all our conversations, we've never spoken like this before. But I've seen it coming, like the niggles and twitches and stabs right before a tendon snaps.

'I know,' I say.

She reaches out and puts one cold hand on mine. 'I'll support you no matter what. You know that. But we're not kids anymore, skipping from day to day, just waiting for the future to sort itself out . . .'

'We've never been like that.'

'Damn right, we're not that stupid.'

My laugh sounds high through my tight throat, but she smiles when it escapes.

'Your relationship shouldn't be a secret in your life forever, Nila. You've found the person you love. It's . . .' She looks down. Takes a deep breath. 'It's just so very sad that you can't share it with your parents.'

I feel like I'm in a vacuum, struggling to breathe, and she's continuing before I can think of what to say.

'You need to deal with this. And you need to move on if it isn't going to work out. Soon. For everyone's sake.'

The lead ball seems to have split, a tiny piece of it lodging in my throat.

'You're right,' I manage to say.

She's done this, faced the battle with her parents. Faced the bemusement, disappointment, understanding, and then strategic planning to tackle the *yayas* and *pappouses*, those formidable, wonderful institutions who had seen her with a solid Greek man, stoutly Christian, preferably business-owning. All these years I've been half-thrilled, half-envious of my dearest friend's tribe of a family, who have fed me at family barbecues and taught me the Zorba. Who laughed, delighted, when at ten I told them I wanted to be a Greek Orthodox too, so I could worship the ancient Greek gods. What a relief it is that they've absorbed the news of her relationship with the barest of commotions. What a joy.

I could be jealous again. But I'm not. Not when I can feel the heat of her disappointment. Not when I know how much she aches for my sake.

Iphigenia is silent. She glances at the tables around us. Then she drains her iced chocolate.

'It's a gorgeous evening,' she says. 'Let's go for a walk.'

She stands and reaches for my hand. I push my chair back and rise too. Her fingers slip into mine across the table. We walk together down the stairs onto the warm red bricks of the harbourside. The sun has almost disappeared beneath the horizon, turning the sky to baby-blanket pink and lavender, the lights on Pyrmont Bridge now dropping glittering reflections onto the water.

'Where to?' I ask.

'Towards the quay?' she says. 'But via the gardens. The city will still be rammed with suits.'

I nod, and, hand in hand, we walk down the wharf.

We walk in silence up Market Street. Any conversation would be swallowed by the traffic, and we're too busy dodging pedestrians – harried-looking commuters, meandering tourists, oblivious groups of university students with their sights set on post-happy hour drinks. The windows of the office towers are beginning to gleam brighter against the slowly darkening sky. The stores on Pitt Street are still open, the glossy new Westfield gleaming in the almost-sunset. At its entrance, a woman puts her Louis Vuitton handbag on the floor, takes off her pencil heels and steps into a pair of ballet flats. Iphigenia sees her too.

'Not worth it,' she says. She's wearing elegant navy pumps that raise her heels an inch from the ground.

'No. I'd be working on your calves for years.' That draws a wry smile from her.

We cross into Hyde Park and sidestep the rush down the steps into St James Station. Ahead, the Archibald Fountain is blissfully free of tourists. On the central pedestal, the figure of Apollo stands with his arm outstretched, but Iphigenia and

I both gravitate towards our favourite part of the fountain – Artemis, crouching beside a deer, head turning, watchful, over her shoulder, a bow in one hand.

Without speaking, we turn, look around for pigeon shit to avoid, and sit on the rim of the fountain.

Iphigenia sighs, a long, soft breath.

'We made a decision, remember? No more secrets. We promised each other. It shouldn't be a big deal, to stop hiding who we love from our family.' The sun's reflecting off the grey-green fountain water, throwing out sharp shards of light. 'I can't deal with the fact that you might choose to do this for years, when we both know how painful it is. You should be able to shout about this.'

But can I? Amma has cut me off, withdrawn from me, for a whole month, for questions she hasn't liked me asking. What will she do when I tell her I'll never want, will never have, what she wants me to have? She's fragile, frangible. I could so easily break her.

My mind shifts to something else and I speak without thinking.

'A few nights ago, Amma sat me down and talked me through all the boys she'd shortlisted for me. She's managed to learn how to resize windows so she had two Indian matrimonial sites side by side. The best, of course – Shaadi.com, Bharatmatrimonial. We alternated between the two of them.'

I don't know why I'm telling her this. My mouth is moving of its own accord.

Iphigenia sits frozen. Then she throws her head back and laughs so hard she has to grab at her sunglasses to stop them falling into the fountain.

'It's not funny,' I say. 'She introduced each of them by their occupation. GP. Software engineer. Surgeon. Aeronautical

engineer. Lawyer. Some analyst at Macquarie Bank. Anaesthe-
tist. She was so bloody pleased with herself. I haven't seen her
that excited since I found her that restaurant with the virgin
Mojitos.'

'What kind of surgeon was he?' Iphigenia asks. Tears are
hanging off her lower lashes. 'Oh, wait! I can find you a lawyer!
I'm probably working with the perfect man!'

'It's not funny,' I say again, but I'm smiling too. And it is
funny, even though so many other things aren't, and I know
this is why I love her. Even in the worst of times, she always
moves to laughter, and brings me with her. I make a decision.
'Hey,' I say. 'This trip to India. I'll tell them by the end of the
trip.'

And the line's drawn.

Her laughter fades, and we're silent, promise and fear and
hope hanging thick in the air.

'If you can,' Iphigenia says quietly. 'Don't forget, you're there
because your grandfather's unwell. Priorities.'

I put a hand over hers, my chest too tight to speak.

Around us, there are snatches of conversation from passers-by,
mundane, effortless conversations about last night's episode of
MasterChef and AFL scores and kids' days at school. It annoys
me. I feel as though there should be some recognition from the
universe that something monumental has just shifted.

Without speaking, we stand and take each other's hands,
automatically, like we've done since we were pigtailed kids. We
continue down Macquarie Street, through the scent of grass
wafting from the Botanical Gardens until the gleaming sails of
the Opera House come into view, the harbour waters shifting
glass around it.

It's still warm and the city is beautiful in the soft lavender
twilight, but I can barely notice. I walk along and manage light,

automatic responses when she speaks, but all I can think about is a future without the person I love, and there's a painful leaden weight in the depths of my stomach that the summer sun can't seem to melt.

Chapter Six

Madurai, 1993

The first month

Now her mouth, lower jaw, blood cells and circulation develop.
She is the size of a grain of rice.

Somewhere, a rooster was crowing.

Janani's eyes opened to near-darkness. She lay listening to the early-morning stillness, breathing it in. Then, with a silent groan, she threw off the thin cotton sheet and rolled off the bed.

She sat for a moment as the world reappeared around her, looking down at her feet, her silver toe rings gleaming up at her.

Beside her, Darshan did not stir.

A wave of nausea swept through her, stomach to ribs. She clapped a hand over her mouth and stood. Hunched over, she hurried out to the bathroom, just in time to empty the contents of last night's meal into the dark hole of the squat toilet.

Leaning against the wall, she rubbed her stomach and let the sickness ebb away. The morning air was warm and thick. Sweat was beading at her temples.

She bathed quickly, splashing water over herself from the half-full bucket in the corner of the tiny bathroom. The water pail she used for cooking was close to dry too – it would be two trips she'd make to the pumps today.

Dressing in the darkness, her fingers pleated the folds of the sari she'd laid out the night before – emerald-green cotton. Leaning towards their one tiny mirror, balanced precariously on top of the chest of drawers her parents had sent as part of her marriage dowry, she drew on her maroon pottu. The half-light barely illuminated her face, casting shadows under the shelves of her cheekbones, glinting off her tiny, gold nose ring and the two gold earrings in each ear, slices of her dowry Vandhana hadn't been able to sell off. She imagined she could see lines now at the corner of her mouth, drooping downward, weighed by tiredness. With a sigh, Janani brushed her hair and plaited it into its usual waist-length rope.

She'd lit the tiny oil lamp at the altar off the side of the kitchen, whispered her prayers and was halfway through flipping the dosai for breakfast when Darshan emerged, rubbing the sleep from his eyes, his towel thrown over his shoulder.

'I'm taking a bath,' he muttered.

'Can you wake . . .' Janani started, but he was gone.

Leaving the sambar bubbling gently on the stove, a saucepan of milk simmering beside it, she hurried back into the bedroom.

Lavanika's body formed a mound under the sheet on her sleeping mat. She'd wriggled into the odd, uncomfortable-looking pose that she sometimes adopted, face down, her knees tucked up under her, the side of her cheek against her pillow.

Janani sat on the edge of the cot and watched her for a moment. Imagined, briefly, that there were two other little bodies beside this one, skin smooth as jasmine petals. Then she bent to kiss the sleep-flushed cheek.

'Lavanika?' she said. 'It's time to get up.'

A tiny snuffle was the only reply.

Outside, Janani could hear Darshan singing in the bathroom. It sounded more like someone wailing at a funeral, punctuated by the splash of water on the cement floor.

Janani slipped her arms under Lavanika's bony little body. 'Come, baby girl. Up, up. Before your appa finds out you're still sleeping like a lazy cat.'

Lavanika mumbled in protest as she was deposited on her feet, her curls a wild mane around her head. 'It's so early,' she murmured, as she did every morning. And it was early, barely six, the sun edged only halfway over the horizon.

Janani put a hand on one thin little shoulder and guided her daughter towards the bathroom. 'You don't want to be late for school,' she said. 'Remember what happened last time?'

Lavanika nodded, scowling and rubbing her hand where the marks from the cane had long since disappeared. It had been a shock – even Darshan could hardly bring himself to raise a hand against her, and Vandhana's open-palmed smacks made more noise than anything else.

Janani led her outside.

Darshan had emerged from his bath, bare-chested, rubbing at his hair with the meagre towel. His thin tallness made the slight swell of belly protruding over the top of his lunghi look absurd.

Janani shooed Lavanika into the bathroom.

'Idiot girl!' Her mother-in-law's voice sawed through the air behind her.

Turning, she ran back into the house, her stomach churning again at the sudden movement. Inside, Vandhana had emerged from her sleep, and was pointing at the steam drifting from the sambar. Darshan had already seated himself on the floor mat in the kitchen, a plate in front of him. Nothing seemed out of place.

'You go outside leaving these things here, boiling? What if they boiled over? What if the thatch caught on fire?'

Janani hurried forward, reaching to turn off the flame beneath the innocently simmering milk. 'Mamiyar, the sambar is off and I didn't leave . . .'

She brought her hand up in time to catch Vandhana's slap on her forearm, but then her mother-in-law grabbed as much flesh as she could between her thumb and forefinger and twisted. Burning pain shot through Janani's arm. She hissed and pulled her arm away.

'Stupid, useless girl,' Vandhana said. 'No brain in your head. Now hurry up and make the breakfast.' Turning away, she walked out the front door, lowering to sit on the step. She'd sit like that now all morning, waiting for Janani to serve the food, the coffee, waiting for her friends to walk past so she could hail them for a gossip.

Janani stood still for a moment, fingers twitching. Her arm throbbed just below the inside of her elbow where she'd been pinched. She took a breath, then turned back to her work, depositing two dosai and a ladle of creamy coconut chutney on Darshan's plate.

'Where are you going today?' Janani asked him. Somewhere far away, she hoped – Dindigul, Madras, or even chauffeuring some pilgrim wanting to go to Kanyakumari. She hoped this every morning, that he had found work outside his usual delivery of spoiled Madurai women from house to shop and back again, or taking their rude children to school. It was too much to hope that it would be even longer, that he would drive days, even a week, across the border to Bangalore or Cochin. Not for the extra money – Darshan would drink most of that on the trip, lounging around with other drivers in a heady mix of mutual boredom and freedom from wives and children.

No, it was the time away from him, when it was just her and Lavanika, while Vandhana slept or sat outside gossiping – that was precious.

Sometimes, when he came back from those longer trips with stories of what he had seen, the ocean stretching between India and Sri Lanka at Kanyakumari, the parks and skyscrapers and mad bustle of Madras, sometimes even movie stars and film sets, fighting through action sequences in the streets, Janani wished she could see them. She'd never been outside Madurai. But not with him; she didn't want to go with him.

An image flitted through her mind, of her standing in front of the Taj Mahal or Sabarimala or Marina Beach. With Lavanika. With Sanjay . . .

The thought shocked her like a dash of cold water in the face.

'The usual,' Darshan said around a mouthful of dosa and chutney, shaking Janani back to the present. 'The doctor's wife in Melamadai wants to do some shopping, visit some friends.'

'And do you need lunch today?'

'Yes. That old witch never gives me money for food, and she only pays afterwards.'

As the water boiled, Janani packed his lunch in a little steel container. Rice, carrot curry and fresh steaming sambar, the smell of coriander making her mouth water, even while a worm of nausea continued to writhe in her gut.

It was a familiar feeling.

She wanted to cry, but she wasn't sure why. The worm of fear was there, of course, but . . . perhaps the words she'd flung to Meenakshi Amman had been heard. Perhaps this was yet another chance.

She placed Darshan's lunch container and a tumbler of sweet, hot coffee by his feet. As she straightened, the flicker of the lamplight dancing before the altar caught her eye and she sent a silent prayer to Durga, that, if this was another baby, this time wouldn't be like the last.

She still remembered those months of drought when they'd skipped the midday meal, when she'd grown thin around her belly and Lavanika's cheeks had taken on a pinched hollow look, her eyes huge in her face. It hadn't stopped Darshan's long afternoons at the coffee shop, or the longer evenings in the dirty, dingy bar with the other men. Sometimes Janani thought he preferred the cheap beer and whisky to a proper meal. She thought of her own appa, of his hours of back-breaking work in the granite quarry, and her stomach turned again. If only Lavanika could have a father like that.

Lavanika emerged from the bathroom and slipped into the kitchen, curling up opposite her father. Darshan drained the last of his coffee, thumped the tumbler onto his plate and heaved himself to his feet with a groan. As he disappeared back into their room, Janani carried his breakfast things to the kitchen. Lavanika followed her and plates clattered as she pulled them from the splintering wooden cupboard beside the stove, ready for their own breakfast.

Darshan re-emerged dressed in a blue-checked collared shirt, wiping water off his moustache with the back of his hand.

Janani picked up the still-warm lunch container and followed him to the door.

'What time will you be home?' she asked, even though it was a useless question. He'd say sunset, and wander in an hour or so before midnight, singing with the cicadas.

He shrugged. 'For dinner, I suppose. When the old woman's finished gossiping.' He took the container, thrust his feet into his sandals and stepped outside.

'Will you play with me, Appa, when you come home?' Lavanika shouted from the kitchen.

Beneath his moustache, his lips lifted in a flicker of a smile. 'Of course, little bird,' he shouted back, as though he meant it.

Janani kept the disbelief from her face and wondered when her daughter would stop believing him.

The nausea had receded slightly when she finally stepped out of the house, her hand wrapped around Lavanika's.

'Janani!'

Janani turned to see Shubha walking towards her, her legs swinging in slight arcs around her huge belly. She was tugging her son Raman along by the hand, his short toddler's legs pumping in frantic strides to keep up with her, while his older sister trailed along behind them dressed in the same long maroon skirt and cream shirt that Lavanika wore.

Shubha stopped in front of her. Her eyes were just as lively as the day they'd met, although in the six years since then, her smooth cheeks had lost the last vestiges of teenage puppy fat. Her sari, a bright pink decorated with green vines, stretched over the roundness of a stomach nine months gone with child.

Lavanika jumped forward to wrap her arms around Shubha's thighs in a tight hug, her head, curls tamed into two ribbon-bound braids, barely reaching the swell of pregnant stomach. Shubha laughed, kissed her palm and transferred it to Lavanika's cheek.

'You're not working today, are you?' Janani asked, feeling her eyebrows rise. 'You're as big as Nagamalai.' She'd felt a pang at the sight of her friend's roundness. Perhaps even now there was a little life beginning to flicker within her own stomach.

Shubha looked in the general direction of the mountain. 'I feel bigger,' she said, knuckling the small of her back. 'But I'll try, just for one more week. We could use the money. And I'd rather be in the fields than at home.' She gave a tiny jerk of her head back to where her mother-in-law was untying the goats, mother and kid, at the front of their house, and winked conspiratorially.

Janani sighed. For years, she'd tried to coax Shubha into finding a cleaning job with a good family, or even several families. But Shubha's sunshine nature hid a shyness that made her shrink away from newness. She stayed working in the rice fields like her mother and grandmother had done. Janani thought she liked the company of the other women, too. She was a listener, a calm well for them to pour their wishes and troubles into. Their gossip would have driven Janani mad. 'Let's go, then, before we're late,' she said. 'And what are you reading so seriously, Nandita?'

The little girl looked up from the book hiding most of her face. She was barely a year older than Lavanika, but already she had the gravity of a much older child. '*Mahabharata*,' she said with a rare smile. She held it up and Janani caught a glimpse of a brightly coloured wrestling ring, one man holding another high above his head. 'Bhima's just beat up Jarasanda – ripped him into pieces.'

Janani shook her head, smiling. Ancient, sacred it might be, but she wasn't sure if a six-year-old should be learning a story about how a hero had torn another man in two and thrown the pieces away.

'Walk with me!' Lavanika took Nandita's hand and the two of them trotted ahead.

'How are you feeling?' Janani asked.

'Well,' Shubha said. 'Better even than with these two.'

'Good,' Janani said. 'And what will you do . . . after? Have you thought about it?'

Shubha gave her a sideways glance. 'It still scares me, Janani,' she replied. 'Narendran wants me to do it, and so does Mamiyar, of course. Look what happened here' – she pointed at her stomach. 'We shouldn't have had this one, let alone another.'

'That's not your fault,' Janani said. 'You didn't even have the choice of the operation last time. You were so ill.'

'Maybe I should just do it,' Shubha said. 'No more children. No more walking around the size of a cow. I feel like a cow too. I can't do anything but eat and work and piss at the moment.'

'What a life,' Janani remarked. She laughed, because, with Shubha, she could. She didn't say that she couldn't wait for the moment she could have the operation, when she could stop forever the ache of the fear, the hope, of carrying a child, the suffocating grief that had followed too many times.

The morning heat built as they walked through the streets, the houses petering out into rice fields and barren land as they neared the children's school. By the time the square, stocky brown buildings came into view, Lavanika and Nandita where already surrounded by friends, a huddle of identically dressed and groomed little girls.

Janani bent down as Lavanika raced back towards her in a shin-high cloud of dust to plant a kiss on her cheek, then skipped off to join the line of children standing to attention at the school door. They made a motley crew, boys and girls from five to twelve years old, first standard through to sixth, all crammed together in the square, mud-brick building.

At that age, she had been just as tiny, smiling, sun-darkened. But it wasn't school she had been thinking about. It was the weekends, at the Nambeesans', running barefoot through the garden with Sanjay. He'd been just as scrawny as she was. A bad eater, Radhakrishnan Aiyan had called him, and he was – Janani remembered him refusing to finish his dinner, sitting for an hour before his cooling rice and sambar before finally his father would let him go.

He was different now.

The thought made Janani smile even as it saddened her.

They were both different now.

The children were pouring into the school building. Janani waved as Lavanika disappeared through the door, then she and Shubha turned and walked past the towering neem tree at the front of the school building, its shadow reaching towards where the children's school bags hung, towards the crèche.

Until these buildings had been built, scattered throughout Usilampatti beside the fields and quarries, women worked with their babies on their backs as Shubha's mother had done, children who could walk getting in their way, sometimes drowning amidst the paddies. It had taken the taluk women a long time to get used to using the crèches, and even longer to beg their husbands' permission to use them.

Still, the building had always reminded Janani of the jail cells she'd seen on the television at the Nambeesans' house. It was little more than a concrete shell, glassless windows cut high in the walls, a rickety electric fan in the ceiling with brown, cobwebby arms that rotated slowly, moving the moist hot air in circles. In a way, it was a cell, a holding place for children too young to go to school, too in the way and underfoot for mothers who had to work to feed them.

When Janani had first left Lavanika, crying as she'd walked away, the room had been empty but for a mass of big-eyed anxious children and a weary-looking teacher. Now a pile of well-worn toys sat in one corner, dolls and toy cars, a red-wheeled tricycle with huge plastic tyres. Beside it, a rack of children's books lined the walls, all bright colours and huge loops of Tamil. Rope strung from the ceiling like a clothesline supported a chart of ABCs and a string of children's pictures, scrawls of paint that only the artist would be able to explain.

Children sat on the floor or ran in and out of the door, all of them toddling or walking, none older than five. Janani caught sight of a little girl of perhaps two, her hair bound up into a little fountain on the top of her head, and she was aware of an ache in her chest. Her second girl, Lavanika's first little sister, would be about the same age . . .

She tore her gaze away. *Stop it. Done is done.*

Raman clung to Shubha's sari, his eyes wide and moist, until another boy ran forward to take his hand.

'I hate leaving him here,' Shubha said as they walked out.

'I know,' Janani replied. 'But at least he has friends, at least they feed them, at least they've got playthings. They're not running away to play in the street instead, like the girls did.' She laughed. 'I used to tell Lavanika a demon would carry her away if she kept running off, and she said that would be more fun than staying here. When she was three!'

Shubha smiled. 'This place was barer than a cowshed then. I would have run too.' She stopped for a moment, kneading her lower back. Sweat was beginning to bead at her hairline.

Janani searched her face. 'Are you OK, ma?'

'Yes.' Shubha grimaced, gave her lower back one last rub, and began walking. 'The bigger I get, the hotter the sun feels. When will the rain come?'

Not until later in the afternoon, Janani thought, if it came at all. It was still only March. It would be a few weeks before the monsoon began to set in.

They paused on the road passing the school. From beyond the crossing, an old woman was walking unevenly towards them, a water jar tucked under one arm. The heat shimmered off the concrete, blurring her face.

'You aren't actually going to the field, are you?'

'I . . .'

Silence.

Janani turned to find Shubha staring at her wide-eyed, her hands pressed to her stomach.

For a moment, they gazed at each other, frozen.

Then something moved on the ground.

Janani looked down to see a dark stain spreading through the dust, leaving mud the colour of rust in its wake. As Janani watched, moisture began to pool at Shubha's feet, trickling slowly out from between her toes.

'Were you just waiting for me?' Janani said, fighting to keep her voice from trembling.

'It's not time yet!' Shubha said, her voice a pitch higher. She swayed.

Janani was at her side in two steps. 'It's time when the baby says it's time,' she replied. 'He's in charge now.' She kept her tone light, although Shubha was right. It wasn't time, not yet. Why was the baby trying to come into the world now, with only Janani here to help him? She tried to keep from her mind the idea of her trying to deliver a child right here, in the dirt, with autorickshaws and jeeps and bikes flying by.

Focus, you useless fool.

From the corner of her eye, she could see some of the other mothers looking at them, realisation leaking onto their faces.

One arm around Shubha, Janani waved in the general direction of the women, not caring who responded.

Shubha had a hand on Janani's shoulder, gripping so hard Janani could feel the stubs of her nails digging into her skin, knew there would be the shadow of a bruise around her forearm. She remembered the beginning of her own labour pains. They echoed in her as though they'd been there yesterday.

'What do we do?' Shubha said.

'It's OK.' Janani glared at the women glancing in their

direction. *Come here and help, you idiots.* 'You've done this before, you'll be fine.'

A few of the women were approaching now. Janani recognised Rani, who lived halfway between the school and her own street and who worked with Shubha in the fields. Not one of the gossips, thank any god who was listening.

'The baby's coming,' she said. 'Can you help get her home?'

'Of course,' Rani said. She pointed at the other two women. 'Come and help me. It's not far.'

An excellent lie, Janani thought, it was a twenty-minute walk at the best of times. But she had something else to do.

'I'm going to get the midwife,' she said.

'Janani,' Shubha gasped. 'It's going to be all right.'

'I know.'

Janani ran. People stared at her as she galloped past them, her sari hiked up in one hand, her sandals slapping the ground. Chickens flapped out of her path, squawking in concern, leaving a trail of feathers after her. For a while, a stray dog tried to keep pace, before it grew tired and stopped in the middle of the street, barking.

By the time she took the turn into Kamala's street, a stitch was pulling at her left side. Sweat dripped into her eyes, blurring her vision so much that she almost careened into the person hurrying towards her. She stopped, arms out in apology.

'Girl.'

Her vision cleared. 'Kamala Amma,' she said. 'I need you.'

'Women that far along should not even be thinking about work,' the old woman muttered. 'I told her, didn't I?' She hadn't stopped walking. Her bag was slung over her shoulder. It swiped across Janani's hip as Kamala passed her.

Janani spun around. 'Kamala Amma . . .'

84

'Hurry up, girl,' Kamala said. 'And if you want to be useful, take this.' The bag slid down her arm into her hand and she thrust it at Janani.

'Wait.' Janani found herself holding the bag and trotting to keep up. 'Where . . . How did you know?'

'It couldn't have been much else, with you thundering through the streets,' Kamala said. 'Stop asking useless questions and move.'

The villagers who'd stared at her as she'd run in one direction were still staring as they hurried in the other, but by the time they neared Shubha's house, something else seemed to have captured their attention.

Rani and the other two women were standing outside the small green-washed house. They turned as Janani and Kamala approached.

'She's inside,' Rani said. 'Narendran's mother and sister are there.'

'The husband?' Kamala asked

'Working,' Janani replied. Narendran was one of the richer Kallars – he'd inherited a small plot of farmland a few kilometres out of the town centre, towards Madurai. And still, Shubha wanted to work.

'Good,' Kamala said. She held out a hand, and Janani stared at it for a moment before handing her the bag. 'Go home, or to work, or wherever you're supposed to be, all of you. She's never had a problem with a birth before.'

Rani and her friends didn't need telling twice. They nodded, waved at Janani and walked off, murmuring to each other.

Now she was still, Janani could feel her heart's rhythm sending ripples up to her eardrums. Adrenaline was coursing through her; she was exhausted, but she felt like she could run forever. 'I can help,' she said, all in one breath.

Kamala put a hand on her cheek. 'You'll be in the way,' she replied. 'And she won't want you to see her like this. Go. I'll do everything I can here, and you take care of her afterwards.'

Janani nodded, even though there was something in those words that stirred something within her, almost an echo of the morning's nausea.

'Please let me know how it goes,' she said.

'I will,' Kamala said. 'And you – you take care, too. Especially now.'

Janani caught her gaze flicking down, so quickly she'd have missed it if she had looked away.

Kamala stepped inside and closed the door behind her.

Janani watched her disappear. Only then, finally, did she think about the bus to Gandhinagar. She would be late this morning.

Still she found herself standing there, looking at the closed door that hid Shubha from view, with one hand on her stomach.

Janani heard nothing for three days.

Work had kept her busy this week. Parvati Amma had been particularly ill, too weak to even cook sambar or rasam or the Keralan moru kutan she loved, and so Janani had taken over for her. After the long days, after Lavanika had come home from school and been bathed and fed, Janani had trudged the short distance to the top of the street. Every time, she had been met by Shubha's grim-faced father-in-law. No word. At least, none he was willing to share.

When the news came, Janani was preparing the evening meal at home, sitting cross-legged on the floor in the kitchen to start slicing potatoes. As she reached for the knife, her hand caught on the steel plate at the edge of the upturned bucket on which it sat. It fell, clattering like a temple bell, onto the floor. Janani jumped at the sound.

'What are you doing, you stupid girl?' Vandhana snapped. She was sitting in front of the tiny television Darshan had brought home the previous evening, a cast-off from some friend of his. It showed a woman wailing in grief and pulling at her hair, while Vandhana watched open-mouthed, at infrequent intervals shelling one of the pods of peas mounded in front of her.

Janani had to clamp down on an insult. Carefully, she added it to the mental pile of forbidden words she had for her mother-in-law. 'Sorry, Mamiyar,' she said. 'I was thinking about Shubha. I'm surprised there hasn't been any news.' She reached to pick up the plate, avoiding her mother-in-law's irritable glare.

Vandhana snorted. 'That's because they don't want to tell anyone she had a girl,' she said. 'And anyway, they've taken her to the hospital. For the operation.'

Janani froze, stretched forward over her crossed legs with one hand on the plate on the floor. It took her a moment to realise she wasn't breathing. Slowly, she let out her breath, unfolding her legs and stood, her eyes fixed on her mother-in-law.

Vandhana looked up at her. 'Kamala Amma came this morning, after you had left for the rich woman's house,' she said grudgingly. 'She told me.'

Kamala would have asked Vandhana to pass the news on, Janani knew, and she wanted so badly to fling the plate across the room at her mother-in-law's sullen, spiteful face that she had to grip it with both hands, so hard she could feel it cutting into her palms.

'When is the operation?' she asked.

'I don't know,' Vandhana said, returning to the television and the peas. 'Yesterday? Today? The delivery went well, so they'll do it as soon as they can.'

Janani wanted to run from the house, flag down the nearest autorickshaw. She imagined bursting into the operating room and holding her friend's hand as they cut into her, sliced through her delicate tubes, tied the ends into knots. Was that what it would be like?

'And the baby?' She didn't want to ask, but she had to.

Vandhana rolled her eyes, but scandal would always make her talk.

'They didn't do the honourable thing,' she said. 'I can't believe it. I've known Sujatha since we were girls, and she let her daughter-in-law walk all over her.'

A tide of relief approached Janani. 'Is the baby' – she couldn't say 'she' – 'at the hospital too?'

'No,' Vandhana said. She shelled another pea. 'They gave it away.'

Janani stared at her. 'Gave it away?' The words made no sense to her.

'They put it in one of those new cradles. Outside the health centre.' Vandhana shook her head, but she was enjoying this, practising her delivery for future performances. 'Can you imagine the shame? Not being able to decide the fate of your own child. Giving it up, just like that. They won't be able to hold their heads up. Now, are we ever going to have a meal, or will your endless questions continue?' Finished, she turned back to the television, the peas forgotten.

Janani picked up a potato. As she sliced into it, her hand was shaking.

Chapter Seven

Madurai, 1993

The second month

Now her heart has formed. Fingers and toes webbed like a frog's.
The sketch of features – eyes, ears, mouth, nose.
She is the size of a gooseberry.

By the time Sanjay got back from Madras on Friday, he was exhausted. The project for the new transformer was running into trouble again, and the incompetent ass he'd managed to acquire as his draughtsman felt like an anchor around his neck. He'd been in the office until close to midnight most days. It had been a joy to rush out for his plane. He'd lost consciousness as soon as he'd sat back in his seat, missing the tea and coffee vendor and the food service. The man beside him in the window seat had had to shake his shoulder when they landed at Madurai to jolt him into wakefulness.

He would have fallen asleep again on the way home, the air rushing in providing some relief from the stifling heat, were it not for the constant jolting of the rickshaw as it navigated through the traffic.

They came to a stop in front of the house. 'Thanks, brother,' Sanjay said as he clambered out of the rickshaw and handed over the fare.

The front door was unlocked. The smell of dahl and channa hit him and went straight to his stomach as he stepped inside. It was almost eight o'clock and he realised he was starving.

His father was sitting in the living room, browsing the *Times of India*. He looked up as Sanjay entered. 'Ah,' he said. 'How was your flight?'

'Fine thanks, Acha,' Sanjay replied. 'How was your week?'

'Good, good,' Radhakrishnan said. He paused for a moment, then set the newspaper aside and stood. 'Your amma,' he began, his voice lowered, 'she has had a hard couple of days. She had her treatment yesterday morning. She is feeling a bit better now, but she's tired.'

Sanjay felt as though his lungs had stopped working, his chest tightening with lack of breath. 'Is she OK?' he managed to say.

'She is fine,' his father answered. 'Just resting. Your Priya Ammayi is with her. She'll be fine.' He turned and returned to the sofa. 'Go and have something to eat,' he said, picking up the newspaper.

Sanjay stayed standing for a moment, letting his breathing return to normal, then kept walking. Radhakrishnan didn't look up as he left the room.

He found Priya emerging from his mother's room. When she saw him, she smiled, closing the door quietly behind her.

He was grateful she was here, his mysterious, odd aunt. Growing up, he'd worshipped her, so similar to his mother and yet so different. And she was different. She was fun in a way he'd sensed people thought she shouldn't be. Vaguely, he'd been aware that what she wasn't was a shining example of Indian womanhood. When she'd arrived a few months ago from years in the teeming mass of humanity that was Delhi, he realised why. She'd come back middle-aged, divorced, childless, alone.

She worked for a living, which for her generation of women was derisible, shameful, no matter how senior she was. Her thin body seemed to vibrate with energy under her mass of frizzy black hair, though she was at least a foot shorter than Sanjay and more than two decades older. With her red handbag, sunglasses, and the salwars she preferred over saris, she looked alien when they were out in Madurai together, but it hadn't stopped her stalking through the place as though she owned it.

'How are you, moné?' she asked. Moné. *Son.* She'd always been another mother to him.

'Fine. A bit tired. Hungry.'

She patted him on the arm. 'Go and have something to eat. I'm going to speak to your acha – he asked me to let him know how your amma is doing.'

'How is she doing?' Sanjay asked, and in the next breath, 'He should be in there himself.'

Priya smiled. 'She's OK now. The pain has lessened – she's sleeping.' She pursed her lips. 'Don't be too critical, Sanj. Your acha had a long day at work, and he has been with your amma from the time he came home until just a short while ago.' Her eyes stayed on him, steady. 'This is painful for him, too.'

She squeezed his hand, turned and walked out towards the drawing room. A few minutes later, Sanjay caught the murmur of voices, too soft for him to make out the words.

Painful for Acha, yes. But what was it like for Priya, watching her younger sister dwindle before her while her brother-in-law spent his days treating other people? It didn't matter that there was nothing, really, Acha could do. And he wasn't sure that Priya had ever really forgiven Acha for Amma stopping work when Sanjay had been born. Even though Amma had always said it had been her own choice, that she treasured the time watching him and Vijay grow.

He walked towards his parents' bedroom. Carefully, he turned the door handle and cracked it open.

The shutters had been drawn, but slivers of moonlight managed to slip through, just enough for him to make out Amma's still form, lying on her side, facing towards him. He couldn't help but inch the door open just enough for him to ease himself into the room. He tiptoed towards the bed and squatted down onto his haunches, so he could see his mother's breathing, the thin blanket rising and falling. Her face was calm, the lines of pain that now so often appeared over the kind, smiling creases around her mouth and eyes smoothed away in sleep. Her hair was mostly silver now, a glinting halo in the moonbeams.

Leaning forward, he placed a single, gentle kiss on her cheek, then left the room, leaving her in peaceful, painless slumber.

The dining table had been cleared, but there were sounds emerging from the kitchen, so Sanjay let his stomach lead him to it. Perhaps Vijay had come home already from the clinic.

The door was ajar. Pushing it open, he entered.

It hit something, rebounding to almost knock him in the face, and there was a gasp.

Sanjay caught the door, and inserted himself sideways through it far enough to squeeze his face around it.

Janani was standing behind it, her hand on her chest, eyes wide. She was holding a broom in one hand and a knife in the other. As his face came into view, she seemed to visibly deflate.

'I didn't mean to scare you,' he said.

'No, no,' she replied. 'You didn't know I was in your way.'

'Do you want to put that down, then?' he asked, gesturing with his head at the knife.

She looked at it, and gave a small bark of a laugh, one he hadn't heard in years. The knife went onto the counter, and she moved out of the way enough for him to ease into the kitchen.

'You're here very late,' he said.

'Yes.' She hesitated and looked up at him. 'Your amma hasn't been very well . . . did your appa or Priya Ma say . . .'

'Yes,' Sanjay replied. 'He said she's a little better now.'

'I've been helping Chitra with the cooking. Have you eaten? You must be just back from Madras.'

'I could eat everything in this kitchen,' he said and his stomach grumbled loudly in perfect accompaniment.

Janani laughed. 'Go and sit down, I'll bring you some food.'

'I can get it myself,' he said. 'It's late, you must need to be on your way home.'

'You'll make a mess,' she replied. 'Go on.' She turned and started uncovering pots. Sanjay obediently extracted himself.

In the few months since their first real conversation that week after Pongal, something had softened between them, continued to soften. More and more, Sanjay saw the character he'd known when he was a child. Their lives were completely different now, of course. Could they be any more different? And yet, she was interested, listened with her head cocked to one side as he talked about his engineering studies, the variety of his days in the office in Madras. He found himself explaining the basics of physics, of forces and levers. And then he glimpsed her world – the old gossips of the village, Lavanika having to be fished out of a canal she'd fallen into, Janani's husband Darshan's days and weeks away from home – Darshan already a man Sanjay was beginning to hate. But he craved it, craved knowing about her days, pressed her with more questions when she waved him away, saying she'd bore him, it was uninteresting, her life. As though his were anything but mundane.

Janani emerged, dragging him back to the present. 'Is this enough, do you think?'

She'd piled a plate full of rice and vegetable curries, a couple of chapattis folded to one side, and a bowl of heated dahl, the smell of turmeric and garlic rising with the steam.

'More than enough,' he said, taking a seat. 'Thank you. Have you eaten?'

'Oh,' she said, looking startled, 'yes.'

He began tearing at the chapatti. It was warm and soft under his fingers.

He was so content with the food in front of him that it took him a while to realise that Janani was standing off to the side of the table, watching him. There was an expression on her face that he couldn't quite decipher – she was looking at him as though he were a dog that just might turn unfriendly.

He stopped eating. 'What's the matter?'

'Oh.' She shook her head. 'Sorry. I was just thinking . . .'

She trailed off, dropped her head and frowned at the floor. When she looked up, her face had cleared.

'I wanted to ask you something.'

She had a friend, she said, a friend who had given birth to a baby girl. A girl she couldn't keep. And they'd placed the baby in a cradle.

'Do you know of those?' Janani asked.

'Yes,' Sanjay said, his teeth clenching. The announcement had come earlier this year, Jayalalitha's scheme to try to protect the baby girls of Tamil Nadu after the media frenzy around Dharmapuri and Salem and Usilampatti the year before. The stories had leaked out of India, and now they were everywhere, in America and Britain and Australia – tales of baby girls fed oleander sap and rice husks, left to froth and choke and die alone, unwanted.

The reports had faded, of course, but the government had decided something had to be done. The 'cradle baby scheme', they were calling it. There was a picture in the news report of the 'cradles'. Grim, stainless-steel cages, with only a few layers of blanket to shield soft baby skin from the cold, gridded base.

'She didn't want to,' Janani continued. 'They convinced her it was the only way, if they weren't going to . . .' She left the rest unsaid. A baby girl, suffocated, buried alive. 'Do you know what happens to them, those children? The children that are left?'

'They're sent to orphanages, I'm sure of it,' Sanjay said. That had been in the papers too. 'The government announced that they would fund their upbringing.'

'She doesn't want that,' Janani replied. 'She wants her baby back and she's sure, when he sees her again, her husband will feel the same. He will. He's a good man.'

Sanjay shook his head. It felt a world away, this place where people could not want their babies, could leave them on a dark night in a crib that was more like a prison. But it was just outside this house, and how could he be shocked, when the woman in front of him, a woman he'd known his whole life, had had her babies killed?

'It's very shameful,' Janani said. 'To give your child away like that.'

Sanjay stared at her, and she shook her head.

'People think it's worse to give your child away, your child who belongs to you. Admitting that you can't look after her, but that you don't have the courage to do what you should do.' Her face twisted, as though she'd bitten into a lime. 'If you have brought her into the world, you should send her back to Meenakshi.' She must have seen the look on his face, because the corner of her mouth twitched upward, into a bitter half-smile. 'That's what people say.'

There wasn't a hint of mockery in her eyes, but Sanjay wondered what she must be thinking of him. He pushed his imagination away and said, 'So your friend gave the baby up. You say people will think it's the wrong thing, but at least she's alive, and that's better.'

Janani rubbed a hand across her eyes and the hardness in them melted. 'She wants her back,' she explained. 'Do you think the baby could still be there?' In the silence that followed, she waved a hand at his plate. 'Eat,' she said.

He realised he'd forgotten about his food.

'If you sit down, we can talk properly.' He took another mouthful, barely tasting it, as Janani perched on the edge of a chair.

She had visited her friend yesterday, she told him, for the first time since her operation. From the way she flushed and looked down, Sanjay guessed she meant sterilisation.

'Shubha was crying. Her mother-in-law said she'd been crying for days.' Sanjay heard the bitterness in her voice. 'She just wants her back. She can't go to the centre, she's still mostly in bed. She begged me to go.'

Sanjay had lost his appetite. He pushed his plate away. 'So what are you going to do?'

'I'm going to go. I don't know how it will help. If it will help. But she asked me, and I have to go.' She bit her lip. Her hands wrung themselves unconsciously, slim fingers interlocking and pulling. 'Could you come with me? They'll talk to you, much more than they'll talk to me if I am on my own.'

'Of course,' Sanjay said, before he'd even considered it, and the way her shoulders relaxed and the lines arching up above her eyes faded warmed him even after he started to examine how this would work.

'Thank you,' she said. 'I hoped to go tomorrow, if you're still here.'

'I don't go back to Madras until Monday morning,' he replied. 'Tomorrow is fine.'

Janani nodded. 'Morning,' she said. 'Darshan, my husband, will be away for a job. My mother-in-law goes to see her friends in the morning. I usually go to the temple. I'll meet you there, eight o'clock.'

'Where?' Sanjay asked.

'The outside of Usilampatti.' She frowned in thought. 'Coming from the highway, you'll need to turn' – she gestured right – 'just past the Parameshwari Temple, just before Valandur Kanmai – you know it?'

He didn't know the temple, but he knew the lake and he nodded.

Janani stood.

'Thank you, sir,' she said.

'Don't call me—'

She laughed before he could finish. 'Annan,' she said, just as she used to do when they were children.

It seemed so familiar that he felt the same protective surge he'd felt then, to hear that pigtailed, gap-toothed little girl call him 'big brother'. And yet, she wasn't that little girl, not any-more. She was a young woman, who spoke to him, understood him. Saw him. And who knew more of some things than he ever would.

'That's not much better,' he said. 'Just Sanjay is good.'

'Eat,' she instructed, smiling and standing. A strand of midnight-dark hair had come free from her braid, floated down to settle at the corner of her mouth. 'I'm going to go home and feed everyone before I get in trouble. You can wash your plate, can't you?'

'I'll try,' he replied, smiling back at her, trying not to stare at that strand of hair. 'Can you get home now? It's late.'

'Auto,' she said.

He nodded, even though the idea of her alone in an autorick-shaw at this time of the night made him nervous, and refrained from asking her if she had enough money for the fare. Amma would have made sure of it.

'I'll see you tomorrow,' she said and disappeared back into the kitchen before he could reply.

He waited until the back door creaked closed before he pulled his plate back towards him and continued with his cooling dinner, his mind already one day ahead.

The sun streamed through his open window the following morning, waking him an hour too soon. Sanjay lay for a while, blinking in the light, unable to get back to sleep, then rolled out of bed and into the bathroom.

Showered and dressed, in a shirt and cream slacks he'd given a cursory iron, he made his way downstairs. The cook, Chitra, had already begun to make breakfast. Sanjay lingered over his idli and potato and coconut ishtu, washing them down with hot, sweet, strong coffee, feeling it warm his throat, his chest. He was starting to regret his decision last night. He knew nothing about how these primary health centres worked – even less about what they did with these babies.

He sat there, lost in thought, until his watch informed him it was seven-thirty and that he had to go.

As he made his way to the drawing room, the thud of footsteps sounded on the stairs, accompanied by the chiming of bells.

Vijay emerged, dressed in pressed slacks and shirt, his hair combed into submission.

'Oh, morning, Etta,' he said. 'You're up early.'

'So are you, Vijay,' Sanjay replied.

His younger brother sighed. 'I'm heading to the university library. A few of us are meeting to study together.'

'How is it going?'

'Good.' Vijay paused. 'It's just a lot of work, you know? It's life-consuming. It's not just about passing, it's about staying at the top somewhere.'

Sanjay whistled. 'You're at the top? Have you told Amma and Acha?'

'Of course. That was a mistake. I mean, Amma was overjoyed. Acha – well.'

They looked at each other, thinking what Sanjay knew was the same thought. Acha would have expected it.

Vijay stepped past him to open the front door, then turned back. 'Do you need the car, Etta?'

'No, you take it,' Sanjay said. 'I'll take an auto.'

'Thanks.' His brother looked at him curiously, as though seeing him for the first time. 'Where are you going this early? You should be in bed for another two hours at least.'

'Ha,' Sanjay said. 'I'll tell you later. Go on, you'll be late.'

They walked out the front door together.

Sanjay managed to get an autorickshaw without too much trouble. The morning had retained some of its freshness and cool air whipped by him as they sped down the highway. It seemed to lift him, somehow. The reluctance of earlier had faded. Perhaps it was the newness of this that was exciting, the chance to do something other than relax in the comfortable company of old school friends in a life that seemed shallow as a drought-stricken Vaigai.

Up ahead, the quicksilver gleam of sun on still water heralded the lake. 'Here,' Sanjay said hurriedly, but the auto driver had already begun to turn. Sanjay leaned against the frame of the auto and scanned his surroundings, glad the man knew where he was going.

They passed by two tiny villages less than a kilometre away from each other, separated by sparse fields in a patchwork of green and brown, and a few minutes later were pulling up in front of the primary health centre.

Janani was already there.

Sanjay jumped out of the auto and paid the man, his eyes on Janani. She was in a light blue sari today – it didn't look new, but the pale colour stood out like rain-washed sky against her skin. She'd pulled the pallu over her head. When she saw him, she smiled, but he noticed that she shrank back into the shadows of the health centre building and looked nervously around her.

'Have you been waiting long?' Sanjay asked.

'No, no,' she said. 'Just a few minutes. Thank you for coming.' She smiled at him, then her eyes narrowed. 'I thought I'd ironed that shirt.'

He looked down and ran a hand over his stomach before he could help himself. 'The rickshaw driver was a maniac . . .'

Her soft chuckle reached his ears.

'Come,' she said.

She let him lead the way.

The reception area was crowded, primarily with the old and the young. An elderly woman in the corner doubled over with a hacking cough. Beside her, a mother sat back in half slumber, a limp child of about five dozing in her lap. By the door, an older man sat with a rag wrapped around his wiry, muscled leg, just above the knee. Drying blood was obscuring the majority of the dirt on the cloth.

Sanjay and Janani made their way past the waiting area towards the reception desk. It was empty.

'Let's just wait here,' Sanjay said, just as a harassed-looking woman perhaps a few years older than him emerged from around a corner on the other side of the desk.

'Eniyan!' she called.

The older man with the dirty rag looked up and raised a hand. His face was a grimace of discomfort that drove the lines of age and hard work deeper into the walnut-coloured skin.

Someone else joined the woman at reception. He was dressed in the same crisp white that she was, blue latex gloves over his hands. She pointed at Eniyan, and he hurried over to help the man stand. Together, they staggered back into the depths of the centre.

The woman at reception was now flipping through a file at the reception desk, frowning. Her name tag read *Thanmila*.

'Excuse me,' Sanjay said.

The woman looked up from under the white cap that failed to conceal thick, wiry black hair.

'Vanakkam,' he said.

She returned the greeting without seeming to realise she'd done so. There was no change in her expression.

'I'm Sanjay,' he said. He felt Janani look at him and realised that he hadn't thought to invent a name. He managed to avoid blurting out his family name. A Nambeesan out here, a clearly Malayali name, would be memorable.

The woman stared at him. 'Can I help you?' she asked. 'I'm a nurse here. If you need medical help, unfortunately there's a wait.' She gave a vague wave to indicate the waiting room. Then she seemed to see Janani. 'Or is your wife pregnant? You can make appointments for scans . . .'

'No,' Sanjay said, aware of Janani exclaiming the same thing. 'No, we just have a question to ask.'

The nurse raised her eyebrows.

Sanjay resisted the urge to turn his head and look at Janani, who was hovering half a step behind him, lurking in his non-existent shadow. He cleared his throat.

'We're enquiring about a baby girl who was left here about . . .' he looked at Janani. 'One week?'

She nodded. She was gripping the edge of the reception desk, her fingers sharp angles.

'One week ago. In the cradle.' He gestured in the general direction of where the cradle in question stood attached to the outside wall of the building, a steel-and-mesh cage lined with cotton blankets. Just about suitable for a few puppies, perhaps, or a baby goat.

'Why?' the nurse asked.

He looked at Janani.

She took a breath and stepped forward.

'The family – they're happy to take her home,' she said. 'It was a difficult choice, at the time.'

'And who are you?' the nurse asked, her eyes narrowing. The air seemed thicker around them.

'We're here for the family,' Janani replied.

Thanmila hesitated, her eyes moving past them to the mass of people filling the room. Sanjay heard the door open, and voices calling out in greeting as someone else entered.

'Please,' he urged. 'We just need a quick answer for now – is the baby safe?'

She sighed. 'I wasn't working here last week, I'll have to ask,' she said reluctantly.

'Thank you,' Sanjay said, holding the woman's gaze.

After a moment's pause, Thanmila turned and hurried out through the door behind the counter. It swung shut behind her.

Sanjay felt a touch on his sleeve and turned to see Janani gesture at him. He leaned down to hear her whisper. 'Do you think they'll tell us?'

'I'm sure they'll tell us something,' Sanjay said, much more confidently than he felt.

It seemed an eternity before the nurse reappeared. She wasn't alone; a grizzled-looking man was with her, the collar of his white shirt wilting slightly. He strode forward to reach them first, one arm cradling a folder with a sheaf of loose papers.

'Vanakkam,' he said, and it sounded more like a threat. 'Doctor Ragunandan.' Despite his height – the top of his balding pate barely rose above Janani's head – there was a steely strength in his voice. 'You're asking about a baby left in the cradle? Are you the child's family?'

Sanjay found himself shaking his head automatically.

'I'm a friend of the family,' Janani said into the silence.

The man's gaze, intense even through his glasses, shifted to her. His face stayed expressionless, helped by the thick moustache obscuring his upper lip, but his eyes were measuring, judging.

'When was the child left here?'

'Last Wednesday evening,' Janani said.

Sanjay almost jumped when he felt something clutching at his forearm, just above his wrist. He recognised the slim, strong fingers as Janani's. He was surprised at the strength of her grip.

For a moment, they stared at each other, frozen in a silent scene of push-and-pull. The doctor glanced down at the papers in his hand.

'Wednesday, February seventh. She was left during the night?'

A squeeze of her fingers, urgent and hard, was Janani's reply. 'Yes,' Sanjay answered for her.

The man looked up. 'Yes, a baby girl was picked up on Thursday morning.'

'Can we see her?' Janani asked.

The spectacled gaze transferred across to her. Sanjay watched as understanding softened the man's expression, smoothing the lines on his forehead, bringing a twist to the corner of his mouth.

'No,' he said simply. 'The child is no longer here.'

Beside him, the nurse fidgeted, shifting her weight from one foot to the other.

Sanjay looked at Janani. Her eyes had widened.

'Where is she?' he asked, turning back. He kept his voice calm.

The man cleared his throat, looking down at his papers. How many babies did they find, Sanjay wondered, that he needed a reminder about what happened to each one?

'Babies left here are sent to orphanages – the Madurai Central Orphanage, if it has space,' he explained. 'They're cared for there, until they're adopted out.'

Something about his words, the set of his shoulders, made Sanjay look at him a little harder. It was difficult to read his expression behind the glasses shielding his eyes, but he was uncomfortable

Janani looked from the doctor to Sanjay. 'Can we go there? To whichever orphanage she was sent?'

'Why?'

It was the nurse who spoke, sharp and clear, her words too loud for the hushed level of their conversation. When they all looked at her in surprise, she crossed her arms over her chest and dropped her voice.

'Would you . . . Would the family . . . take her back?'

'Yes,' Janani said, sounding a little less sure than she had.

The nurse pushed on more confidently. 'At least the orphanage can care for the children, and give them a family happy to bring them up.'

Sanjay didn't turn his head, but he felt Janani's hand tense on his arm.

The doctor took over, his voice firm. 'I think it's best if you tell the family the baby will be taken care of. It's done. They should move on.'

Sanjay opened his mouth. He wasn't sure of what to say, but certain there was something more to be said. An uncomfortable itch at the back of his mind urged him that they weren't being told everything.

'What if the family want her back?' he asked. 'What then? Which orphanage should we go to? Who should we ask for?'

The doctor shook his head, but it seemed to Sanjay like a reaction, rather than an answer. The man glanced at Janani.

'Perhaps madam should wait outside,' he said.

'I need to know,' Janani said, keeping her voice low. 'Please.'

Another shake of the head, different this time, weary. His shoulders slumped.

'I'm sorry,' he said quietly. 'The infant did not survive. She passed away early the next morning.' There was real regret in his eyes.

The nurse looked away, biting her lip.

Sanjay felt a lead ball form in the pit of his stomach. He saw rather than heard Janani's gasp, saw her sway slightly like a tree in the monsoon. Her hand covered her mouth, moved slowly up to cover her eyes. The fingers on his arm dug hard.

'Was she sick?' he asked.

The doctor spread his hands, palms up. 'She was certainly not strong. Underweight. It rained hard that night. It was likely just too cold and damp for her.'

Sanjay turned to Janani. She was looking at him, face solemn, as though she hadn't realised her eyes were bright and heavy with tears. They stood like that, a quiet pocket of stillness in the chaos of that small, overrun waiting room.

Janani glanced back at the doctor. 'Where is she?'

The doctor looked down. 'The body has been buried.'

Beside Sanjay, Janani seemed to shrink into herself, wither like a fallen leaf. It was time to go. 'Thank you,' he said.

'I'm sorry,' the doctor said again.

Sanjay could feel their eyes on his back as they went. He wondered what they were thinking, what they imagined that baby meant to him, to Janani. He wondered if they'd held the child, been with her as she died, buried her tiny body.

He didn't know Shubha, knew nothing of her, but he grieved now for her child.

Curious glances followed them as they made their way through the waiting room, which seemed to have become even fuller. Janani had let go of his arm and was walking a step or two behind him, her head down and her pallu shielding her face. She stayed that way as they emerged into the hot glare of the sun, and the welcome smell of the bougainvillea planted along the outside of the centre. It wasn't until they passed through the car park and were nearing the highway that she lengthened her steps to walk beside him, and let her pallu fall back over her shoulder.

'I'm sorry,' Sanjay said, hating that it was the only thing he could think to say.

Janani nodded. 'I feel sick.'

'Here.' He handed her the small water flask he'd brought with him.

She accepted, flashing him a sideways glance. The sun picked out her wet cheeks.

'Will you tell her?' Sanjay asked as she tilted the flask to let water trickle past her lips.

For the first time, her face crumpled. She shook her head. 'It would just be cruel,' she said. 'I'll tell her what they told us at first. That her daughter will find a family who can afford to raise her and educate her and give her a comfortable life.'

'It's a terrible thing.' He couldn't shake the image of a baby girl, squirming and crying, alone in a wet night.

Janani had turned away, as though something had caught her attention. He followed her gaze. By the side of the building, a large gridded metal crate had been attached. It was uncovered, and the bottom had been lined with blankets. A sign above it read, in both Tamil and English, CRADLE BABY SCHEME. There was more below it, but Sanjay couldn't make it out from this distance.

'It is terrible.' Janani's voice was so quiet, Sanjay could barely here her. 'But is it more terrible than . . .' She shook her head. 'This life is full of terrible choices, and who can say which is the right one? Only Iraivan.'

He wasn't sure if even God – any of them – would make themselves known, but he couldn't answer. He didn't deserve to, did he? What were his choices, compared to hers?

They had come to the highway. Sanjay began scanning for autos.

'I'll take you home,' he said.

'No,' Janani said even before he'd finished the sentence.

Sanjay was surprised at the stab of hurt and humiliation that brought, even though he'd realised as soon as the words had come out of his mouth that it was a ridiculous suggestion.

He glanced at Janani. Her eyes had widened, lashes almost reaching her eyebrows.

'No, I mean . . . it wouldn't be good if people see us together.' She managed a smile, a shaking, effortful thing.

'Of course.' He shook his head. 'It was a stupid thing to say.'

An autorickshaw was rattling towards them. Sanjay waved at it, and it slowed, angling slightly to drift off the highway towards them.

'Thank you,' Janani said. As the auto pulled up on the side of the road, she turned towards him. 'Can I tell you something? I need to tell someone. I couldn't speak to Shubha, not now.'

'Yes of course,' Sanjay said.

'I'm pregnant.'

He didn't know what to say. Involuntarily, he glanced back at the health centre. From the corner of his eye, he saw Janani's head turn to follow his gaze.

They looked at each other. Her face was calm, and so it was almost eerie that tears continued to slide down her cheeks.

I can help you, he wanted to say. *I will help you.*

Instead, he said, 'Best wishes. Stay healthy.'

'Thank you.' Janani pursed her lips into a tight smile and climbed into the auto. Sanjay couldn't help himself reaching out as though to put a hand on her back, as though she might tumble out. She glanced at him from under thick, wet eyelashes as she sat down. 'I'll see you on Monday.'

Sanjay watched the auto disappear down the highway towards Usilampatti and imagined her looking back through the plastic rear window.

Chapter Eight

Madurai, 2019

We touch down at sunset.

It seems like I've just dozed off before the landing announcement sounds over the PA system. My head has fallen into an awkward angle and sharp pain shoots through my neck as I manoeuvre it back into place, circling my shoulders to relieve the tension. Hair sticks haphazardly to my cheek and forehead. As the grog of sleep clears, nerves begin tap-dancing in my gut, the usual nausea that anxiety forces on me in a new arena. Time's turned this place and the people I'm about to meet into strangers. My mind flicks through a thousand anticipatory images, awkward hugs, forced small-talk, hushed, sombre conversation. I hope I don't have to use the airport bathroom.

The plane's wheels hit tarmac and the cabin judders. I remember reading once that the first three minutes and the last eight minutes of a plane's flight are the most dangerous. My eyes closed, I listen as the ear-piercing screech of the landing tapers off and our momentum slows, halts.

The lights come on.

People are standing well before the seat belt sign switches off, ignoring the air stewards' half-hearted attempts to slow them down. That annoys me. I stay stubbornly in my seat.

'Come, Nila,' Amma says from beside me. She's tense, as she

has been all flight, her shoulders halfway to her ears, one hand gripping the armrest. It's unnerving – she's not a nervous flier.

I point at the seat belt sign just as it blinks to darkness.

We shuffle off the plane. On this stretch, the three hours between Singapore and Madurai, the flight has been almost entirely Indian, an eclectic mix of men in business suits, young families with fussing children, older women wearing saris and trainers.

India. Even in the air bridge, even as late in the night as it is, the essence of it seems to seep through, a wall of humid heat, the smell of earth and moisture.

Madurai airport is atypically small, compact, efficient. We ease through immigration to find the two rattling baggage carousels. Beyond them, through the glass barrier of Customs, I can see a sparsely furnished, white-tiled arrivals area and clear glass doors leading out into a car park dotted with coconut palms and sporadically flickering fluorescent light.

Our suitcases appear on one of the carousels with surprising speed and Acha hauls all three of them off, even though he knows I'm more than capable of lifting them myself. I let him, then take mine and Amma's immediately, wiggling the handles out of his fingers. He smiles.

'Where do we go now?' I ask as we emerge into the arrivals hall. It's packed with waiting families, hire-car chauffeurs with bored, blank eyes holding aloft signs, and opportunistic taxi drivers.

'Your uncle will be coming,' Acha says, looking distracted.

I feel a touch on my elbow and turn to see Amma beside me, also scanning the hall. She's reached up to wrap her hand around my arm. It's been years since I've grown to the point where her head just reaches the top of my shoulders, but now I realise, or remember, just how small she is. There's a tilt to her eyebrows that makes her look lost and worried. I want to smooth them back into place.

'You OK, Amma?' I ask.

She looks at me. 'Do you want some water?' she says. 'We should buy a bottle. Remember, don't drink the tap water.'

'I know,' I reply. 'I won't.' I bend slightly to kiss her cheek. Her skin is smooth as a baby's.

'Etta,' someone calls, and we look up.

I recognise the man striding towards us more from Facebook photos than actual memories. My uncle – my kochachan – is shorter than I remember, and stocky, with a mop of dark hair that rivals my dad's. He claps my father on the back and embraces my mother in one smooth movement. The next moment, he's turned and enveloped me in a hug. I immediately recognise the smell of him, too much Tom Ford aftershave, and I remember that I like this man.

'So good to see you,' he says, as though I've returned after an absence of a few months, rather than more than a decade.

'How's Acha?' my father asks in Malayalam.

Kochachan pauses. 'Come,' he says. 'Let's talk outside.'

Before I can react, he's taken both suitcases from me and is heading to the exit.

Acha smiles at us and hurries after him. Amma and I trail behind the men.

'He's a nice man, your kochachan,' Amma says. 'Very kind. Generous.'

She sounds like she's speaking mostly to herself.

The car turns out of the airport. The three of us sit in the back, Amma sandwiched in the middle. Kochachan, sitting beside the driver, waits until we're on the road before he speaks. He twists his torso around so that he's facing Acha. His smile's faded.

I notice how much more lined his face is than in my memories.

'Acha is not doing very well, Etta,' he says. 'These past few days, he's been worse. I'm very glad you could come.' His eyes move to Amma, to me. 'All of you. Even if Rohan could not.'

There's silence. It feels as though time's frozen in the interior of this car, as though the world outside it is a completely different one. It's a long moment before I can turn my head to see my father's face. In the mix of moon and street light that flickers through the window, his face looks coated in ash, like a Tantra practitioner.

My uncle runs a hand through his hair. 'He'll be happy to see you.' The hand drops. Night and light flicker across his face.

Another silence. Only Amma moves. One hand takes mine, the other floats to rest on my father's thigh.

Acha clears his throat again. 'OK. Then tell me. How are Manju and the kids doing?'

The tension in the car relaxes, like a muscle released by an acupuncture needle.

My uncle turns back, sitting slightly straighter, and begins to talk.

I'm relieved not to have to make conversation. My head throbs with tiredness. Outside, I'm just able to see the arid landscape beyond the road, which, soon enough, gives way to perfectly divided squares of rice fields and pitch-dark bodies of water.

We turn left, and suddenly we've joined a stream of traffic, cars and lorries and autorickshaws that look like they've been patched together since the 1960s, all jostling for position. Horns sound like war bugles.

Kochachan turns in his seat, looking back at me. He points back through the windscreen. 'Do you remember this place?'

He sounds different, louder, a forced edge to his cheeriness.

'No, Kochachan.' I can barely see it in the darkness. Lights of a thousand different hues and intensities are accumulating in the distance. We pass restaurants, and I make out a solitary English name. *Amma's Kitchen*. Petrol stations and grocery shops, sari stores shuttered for the evening and flat-roofed houses flick past us.

'This is Thiruparankundram,' he says. He gestures to the left, where we are passing by a hill which seems to be formed out of a single huge, smooth stone. 'There are ancient temples here, cut into the rock. And then, on this side,' he opens the window and cranes his neck out, 'just there, is the famous Murugan temple. It's rock-cut, also. It's the second famous temple in Madurai, after Meenakshi Amman. All of Madurai is a shrine. They call it the City of Temples.' He manages a smile. 'The people are not any more holy, though.'

I look through the window past my parents and catch a glimpse of a tiered structure and the glimmer of lamplight. I can almost smell the ghee and jasmine flowers.

'How old is it?' I ask.

'Oh, that sort of thing I'm not so good at,' Kochachan says. 'Your father was the one who was good at history – hundreds and hundreds of years old, yes, Etta?'

'Over a thousand,' Acha says. He's looking off into the distance. 'The rock temples – some images date from before Christ.'

That thought seems to settle in the car, and we drive the rest of the way in silence. I've never heard of this place and it shocks me. What did it look like, I wonder, two thousand years ago, when, on the other side of the world, the Romans hadn't even dreamed of the Colosseum? I wish Iphigenia could see this. She would love it.

It's not long before we're pulling up towards a large, arching metal gate. The driver hasn't even jumped out to open it before a dog starts barking, breaking the night with a chesty, even percussion. It gets louder as the gate opens, creaking in woeful accompaniment.

Kochachan says something to the driver, but it's in Tamil and all I can make out is the man's name, Mahesh. He clambers back in and drives through the gate, coming to a stop under a pergola. There's a second car beside us on one side and, on the other, sweeping steps that lead to a veranda and double doors in dark wood.

I follow Acha's lead, open the door and step out into the thick, warm night. I breathe in the scent of jasmine and see the trellis attached to the side wall of the house, the white flowers gleaming in the car's headlights. Turning back to the car, I see Mahesh is already extricating our suitcases from the boot.

The source of the barking becomes clear.

Around one of the pergola's supporting posts is a chain, and to the chain is attached a black Labrador. It's still barking, but its tail is moving so vigorously its entire hindquarters are shaking, as though it's trying to sweep the floor. We have to walk past it to get to the steps of the house. I can already see Amma veering to the left to avoid it. Fair enough, given a childhood avoiding street dogs who, at best, had fleas, at worst, rabies, and were perpetually hungry.

Kochachan notices. 'Don't worry, he is very friendly,' he says, just as the dog jumps up, plants his paws on my chest and aims at my face with his tongue. 'Down, Hercules!' my uncle commands.

The dog drops and nuzzles my knees, his body shaking with the vibrations from his tail. His black ears are silky beneath my fingers.

'He's only a year old,' Kochachan says. 'Still a teenage puppy.'

He doesn't look like a Hercules and I love it. I give the dog one last pat.

Amma has taken advantage of the distraction to stride towards the steps leading up onto the veranda.

Kochachan opens the door. It's quiet inside until we bring in our suitcases, their wheels rumbling along the tiles. I remember this drawing room. It seems much smaller than it did when I was last here, a child who was swallowed up by the leather armchairs and marvelled at the swirl of grey and snow-white marble, inlaid with carved slices of glistening stone and abalone shell.

Now we're inside, I can hear the faint sound of the TV coming from further along in the house.

'Come,' Kochachan says. 'Manju is waiting for you.'

A door in the far wall, dark mahogany carved with floral designs, leads into the living room. I remember this too, the maze-like layout of the house, door after door, to keep the rooms dark and cool in the year-round heat.

'Ah, look who has come!'

My aunt is a rounded, cheerful-looking woman despite the swollen skin beneath her eyes that speaks of tears. She pushes herself out of the sofa and comes to us.

Manju Ammayi has always been kind to me; her arms around me are strong and warm even though I can see the additional lines in her face, the silver hair threading her braid. She smells like sandalwood soap.

'Goodness, how this girl has grown!' she says in Malayalam. 'What a beautiful woman she has become!' She turns to give Acha a hug. 'I'm so sorry, Etta,' she says, holding him at arm's-length and looking up at him. She has the kind of face that would have you happily telling her your darkest secrets and crying into her shoulder.

My father gives her the ear-to-shoulder South Indian nod that can mean anything, and squeezes her hands. He doesn't thank her. That's not the done thing.

'What's the news with you, Manju?' he says, also in Malayalam.

She smiles, a tired, sad smile. 'The last few weeks have not been easy, but we are doing well.' Turning, she folds Amma into an equally crushing embrace. 'You all must be hungry, after the flight.'

'Speak in English,' my uncle says, looking at me.

Manju Ammayi's forehead wrinkles. 'Doesn't the child understand Malayalam?' she asks the room at large, still in Malayalam.

'Of course she does,' Acha replies. He shakes his head at his brother.

'Very good.' Kochachan holds his hands up.

'But I only speak a little,' I say with my awful accent and Manju Ammayi beams at me.

'Your Malayalam is excellent,' she says.

'Is Acha sleeping?' Kochachan asks. He nods at a closed door off the side of the living room.

'He's resting,' Manju Ammayi replies. She looks at Acha. 'You should all go and see him. He's been asking for you. I'll make you something to eat.' She leaves the room.

I am intensely aware of Amma beside me, rigid as a board. My chest is tight.

'Come,' Kochachan says.

He walks to the door, knocks gently, opens it. The darkness on the other side swallows his head.

'Acha? Etta has come. He's here.'

Silence.

My uncle steps back, a slight smile on his face, pulls the door wider, and gestures to us.

I wait. Acha moves forward, and after a second, so does Amma.

Still I wait. I don't want to go in there. I'm not good with sick people. I don't know what to say. And I've never known what to say to my grandfather. Not when I can see the . . . dissatisfaction . . . in his face, when he looks at me.

At the door, Acha turns and looks at me.

'Come, molé.'

I can't say no to the sadness in his eyes.

We leave the light off. The faintest beam of moonlight trickles through the windows, shuttered now against the mosquitoes. Shadows drape over the chest of drawers, the wardrobe, the dressing table that probably hasn't been touched since my grand-mother died.

And the bed.

We walk in single file, Acha, Amma, me, like supplicants approaching a king.

My grandfather turns slightly and the moonlight catches the whites of his eyes. A sheet covers him up to his Adam's apple, but his arms emerge, and the sight of them shocks me. He has always been thin, but now he's just skin papered over bone. His cheeks are pools of black shadow. But his eyes are fixed on us, tired, alert.

'Acha,' my acha says. He walks to the bed and he kneels down by it.

They look at each other, father and son.

One delicate, blue-veined hand reaches out. It shakes slightly as it navigates its way to Acha's shoulder. My grandfather's lips move.

'Moné,' I hear, barely more than a whisper.

Acha rests his own hand atop his father's. I've never seen them touch like this, tentative, gentle. My throat is tight, achy.

'See who else has come,' Acha says. He angles his body away, leaning back, exposing us. Achacha's gaze moves to my face. To Amma's.

For a moment, everything is frozen. The sounds of Manju Ammayi clattering in the kitchen filter into the room, and I'm grateful for the distraction.

We wait, Acha, Amma and I. There's a sense of something, something profound, something I don't understand.

Achacha's other hand moves. Slowly, it rises from the bed, and reaches towards Amma and me.

I hear Amma let out her breath. It sighs into the darkness. Then her fingers wrap around mine and she steps forward – not towards the head of the bed, but the foot. Bending down, she touches the sheet that drapes over my grandfather's feet, then touches the same hand to her head. Her eyes move to me, and I read the instruction in her eyes as she lets go of my hand.

Trying to quash my awkwardness, I do the same.

My grandfather's arm is still stretched towards us. Amma walks to stand beside Acha and, very gently, she takes his hand, as gently as she would a newborn's. I see my grandfather's eyes move to me, and the tenderness in them is strange. Unfamiliar. My face is burning with the threat of tears.

I reach out, scoop my fingers in beside Amma's to rest on Achacha's soft, papery skin.

We stay there, just holding him.

Acha wakes me the following morning. I open my eyes, in a fog of jet lag, and find him sitting on the bed beside me.

'Your achacha is gone, molé.'

Acha and Kochachan wash their father's body and lay him out in a front bedroom. There are phone calls and more phone calls, and a priest arrives mid-morning to sprinkle holy water over the body, to start the funeral rites. The house smells of incense.

Nobody seems to need me. My cousins have already left the

house, for school, for university, before I'd even woken. I'm glad. Now, alone, I finally get a chance to switch my phone out of flight mode. There's a new message glimmering on the screen.

Take care of yourself over there. Love you. Miss you already.

I sit out on the veranda with Hercules, and try to figure out how I feel, how I'm supposed to react. What I'm supposed to do next.

There's no grief. Sadness, maybe, at what might have been. Of the relationship with my achacha that I never had. My memories of my grandfather are of a towering, willowy, grim-faced giant who ignored me most of the time. Even his shadow felt imposing. He'd scared me.

I shouldn't feel relief. But I do. In the last few weeks, my imagination has sketched out a hundred scenes of my grandfather finding out about me, and they've stained my nightmares.

Inside, Acha and Kochachan talk about the funeral. Snatches of it drift through the window to me. The cremation. The priest who'll conduct the last rites that Acha will perform in thirteen days' time.

Thirteen days later. Two days before we fly back.

My phone tells me it's six p.m. in Australia. I could call. We could talk about it, about how fragile my grandfather's hand felt in mine, how he'd never find out, how I'd never speak to him again.

I don't call.

Miss you too.

'Nila?'

I'm sprawled on the bed, trying to read, trying not to fall asleep. Looking up, I see Amma peering around the corner of the door.

'Come for dinner.'

Downstairs, everyone's clustering in the dining room. As I walk in, my aunt is saying, 'I'll ask Radhika to come down.' Her voice lowers, 'The poor thing has been quite upset. Arjun . . .' She throws a wary look at her husband and Kochachan makes a sound like an irritated horse and shakes his head. 'Arjun will be here in the morning.'

As we take our seats at the massive glass-topped table of dark wood that dominates the dining room, the door opens. The girl who appears had been a chubby, curly-haired toddler when I'd seen her last. Now she's a slightly plump teenager, her long curls tamed in a braid that reaches to the middle of her back. She's already in her pyjamas. I can see the redness in her eyes. More tears.

My parents get up to give her a hug. I follow them, slightly nervous, but her smile is welcoming.

'I have to say the silly thing,' I comment. 'My God, you've grown.'

Her face lightens, and she laughs. 'I'm sorry I didn't see you when you came last night, Nila Chechi. Was your flight OK?'

Chechi. It's strange to hear that word being used by someone who isn't Rohan.

'It was, thanks,' I say. 'How are you?'

Stupid. She lost her grandfather today.

Her smile dims. 'I'm good. Last year of school, you know? So studying hard. Always studying. Achacha's always . . .' She stops. 'I'd love to come and see Australia. It looks so beautiful. So clean.'

'It's pretty nice.' I like this girl, I decide, this cousin I don't even know.

'Should I put the food out?' Manju Ammayi asks my uncle, low-voiced.

'Yes,' Kochachan says. 'If he can't trouble himself to be here, he shouldn't eat with us.'

My aunt lets out a breath and turns back to the kitchen.

Amma looks up. 'Can I help, Manju?'

My aunt looks back at my mother. 'Oh, it's not much work, Janani. Our maid Girija has prepared everything . . .' An odd look passes over her face, as though she's seen something, thought of something. 'But it would be nice to talk. Please come.'

Amma stands up and walks around the table to join my aunt. She seems smaller than usual beside Manju Ammayi's robust form.

Radhika is scrolling through her phone. 'Nila Chechi, have you seen *Ek Ladki Ko Dekha Toh Aisa Laga*?' she says.

I'm still watching the door to the kitchen. 'I haven't seen a Bollywood movie in ages. They're a bit intense for me.' And so long they need an intermission.

She looks up at me. 'No way. I have to take you. You just haven't seen the right film.'

Her young face is so friendly, so bright with excitement despite those tear-reddened eyes, that I can't help but smile. I sit beside her at the table and let her talk, about school, friends, music, TV, listening through a fog of jet lag. She's launching into questions for me when Manju Ammayi reappears in the kitchen doorway.

'OK,' she says. 'Let's eat.'

Amma rarely makes dosa at home, it's so time-consuming, but when she does, it's crisp and delicious and one of the best meals in the world. Manju Ammayi's cooking is just as good. The sambar is piping hot, the chutney oozing with the flavour of fresh coconut.

I have no problem with conversation. Radhika keeps up a stream of chatter. I can almost forget the still, silent inhabitant of the front bedroom, if it weren't for the tightness in Acha's face, and the way Kochachan rubs his hand through his hair, again and again, until it's twisted into a dishevelled mop head.

On the other side of the table, Manju Ammayi is peppering Amma with questions about her job. Amma looks more animated than she has done since we landed. She loves talking about her sewing and her teaching. She still remembers most of her students' names, even those she taught for short six-week courses. Growing up, I'd gone through a moody phase of intense jealousy of those students, who spent all day being taught by my mother, being taught something I seemed unable to learn. I was the sun and my mother was the Earth and how dare anybody else tug at her orbit?

There's a lull in the conversation just as Kochachan broaches the topic no one's mentioned. 'All the Madurai family will be there tomorrow. The others, from Trivandrum and Bangalore and Mumbai, will come for the last day.'

The others. All the relatives. My mind is distracted from that terrifying thought when Kochachan glances across the table at Amma. His lips are tight. Acha's looking at her too.

My mother clears her throat. 'Etta,' she says, 'I don't have to come. I can stay here.'

Acha makes a strange, muffled sound.

My uncle says something in Tamil. My Tamil's significantly worse than my Malayalam. I understand my mother's name, and the word 'sister'.

Amma looks down at the floor. I find myself exchanging a glance with Radhika. It makes me feel better to know I'm not the only one who doesn't know what's going on. Better as though I'm not lost in the woods alone.

Manju Ammayi takes my mother's hand. 'Do you and Nila both have a sari to wear?'

'I do, Chechi,' Amma says. 'Nila has only salwars.'

I've worn a sari twice in my life – once for some play about Rama and Sita for my parents' Hindu Society when I was eight years old and once for a wedding. I remember I was the evil demoness Shurpanakha in that play. My teacher had forced heavy gold earrings into my ears. They'd drawn blood.

'Come then, Nila kutty. Hopefully we can find you a blouse that fits.'

As we leave the room, I see Acha put a hand on Amma's arm, and squeeze.

Chapter Nine

Madurai, 1993

The third month

Now her tail has disappeared. Her fingers and toes have lost their webbing and gained their nails. She is plum-sized.

'Come on, girl, we'll be late.'

Janani double-checked the stove, put a plate over the pot of still-steaming rasam and hurried to the door. The quick movements made her aware of the nausea rippling through her stomach. She ignored it. It was better at least than it had been for some time. It had been like this with the others, the sickness fading after the third month. Hopefully she'd soon be able to stop drinking the gooseberry juice Vandhana was forcing on her every morning.

Her mother-in-law was waiting impatiently outside, her hemp bag over one shoulder. 'If the centre is crowded, I'm not sitting for hours,' she muttered as Janani reached her.

Janani said nothing. She couldn't understand why the woman had insisted on coming. She hadn't come the last time, so this new interest was strange. Janani wished she had Shubha walking beside her instead. But Shubha was still a listless, blurred shadow of herself, and how unfair would it be to ask her to come on the start of this particular journey?

She followed a step behind Vandhana, trying to avoid conversation. Fortunately, she didn't have to. Vandhana kept up a steady stream of monologue, complaining about the walk to the hospital, about the motorbikes swerving gracefully around goats and chickens, the rumble of laden timber trucks as they reached Usilampatti Main Road, the drunk curled at the corner of a house under a palm tree, a bottle of Tasmac whisky still a quarter full beside him.

Before she knew it, Janani had begun to pick up the pace, until she could see the cream and blue buildings of the hospital, bright as the sky above them.

'Wait, girl!' Vandhana's shout followed her.

Janani stopped and waited for her mother-in-law to reach her.

'Sorry, Ma,' she said.

'Fool,' Vandhana snapped.

It was still early; Janani could see doctors locking the doors of their cars in the parking lot, and only one autorickshaw stood parked by the bus stop.

Still, 'See? I told you so,' Vandhana said, and Janani followed her pointing finger to where four or five people sat on the metal seats outside the hospital door. Another few were approaching. An old woman, bent nearly double, her maroon sari pallu drawn over an iron-grey bun, was hobbling heavily on the arm of a girl who could not have been more than fifth standard – eleven years old at most. Behind her, a young woman bounced a crying toddler wearing a blue singlet and dishevelled cloth nappy on her hip. None were here for a pregnancy scan, but that seemed not to make a difference to Vandhana's sour mood.

The last time she had been here, it had been busier, Janani thought before she could help herself. Pushing aside those memories – the hope, the anticipation – she followed Vandhana into the hospital.

The morning heat had already settled into the building. Ceiling fans hummed as their arms swirled through the warm air. Janani wiped away the sweat beading on her upper lip. From the corner of her eye, she was aware of the young girl leading her grandmother carefully after one of the doctors.

She had been here before, but still Janani had to ask a passing nurse in fresh, strictly starched white cap and tunic the way to the obstetrics department. To her surprise, Vandhana took a hold of her, one scarred hand clutching Janani's arm above her bangles, and began to lead her in the right direction. They walked together through the fluorescent halls, followed by the smell of antiseptic and an unthinkable number of other substances. Janani kept her eyes straight ahead and tried to imagine that the hand on her arm was Amma's. How she wished her mother were here.

At Obstetrics, Janani gave her name to another nurse, who pointed them in the direction of the ultrasound unit. A handful of chairs were lined up against the wall opposite the door. They took a seat beside a young woman with a toddler who was mid-cry, his face contorted, his bulging nappy dwarfing the tiny legs that emerged from it. Janani caught his eye and made a face, puffing out her cheeks and crossing her eyes. The baby stopped, confused and then mesmerised, watching Janani tilt her head one way, then the other. The mother smiled, the lines of stress on her forehead fading. She looked so young, her big eyes round with anxiety, the fan stirring the petals of the marigold blossom tucked into her braid, but she could only be a couple of years younger than Janani herself. At least she had had a boy.

The door of the clinic opened and a nurse's head emerged, the crisp white cap balanced upon it.

'Mathumai?'

The young woman started to her feet, swinging the little boy onto her hip, her sari pallu crumpling beneath him. He began grumbling again. Janani gave him a final smile as they disappeared inside.

They waited.

Vandhana was drifting into snatches of sleep, her head drooping and then jerking in cycles. Janani listened to the sounds of the hospital, snippets of conversation from the staff, brisk shoes tapping on the worn linoleum floors.

It felt like hours, but in reality the clock showed only twenty minutes had passed when the young woman re-emerged and the nurse called her name. Vandhana jolted back into wakefulness beside her.

'Ma, you can stay here,' Janani said, as she stood.

Vandhana grimaced and pushed herself to her feet.

The ultrasound room was almost exactly as she remembered it. The table's cold steel was covered in a green sheet. On one wall were posters in English – Janani recognised a letter or two – and Tamil, explaining how important it was to wash your hands, to use disinfectant, labelling the parts of a man and a woman's body, explaining how a baby grew inside a womb.

Her hand drifted unconsciously to her stomach. She turned her head away and dropped her gaze to the sink at one corner of the room, the long-necked tap flecked with brown rust.

'Vanakkam.'

Janani looked up to see a man, tall and thin, walking back from a desk that stood at one side of the room. His head was bowed so that most of what Janani could see was the shining bald pate ringed in black-grey hair. Then he looked up, smiled and introduced himself as Doctor Rajiv. His eyes fell on Vandhana.

'Is this . . .'

'Her mother-in-law,' Vandhana said.

He nodded. 'Can I ask you to lie down?' he said to Janani. As the nurse helped her onto the table, he asked, 'How far along are you?'

Was it three months? She couldn't remember when her last period had come, and she could only guess based on the ebb and flow of the sickness in her stomach 'I . . . I'm not sure,' she replied.

'That's all right. Let's see how everything is going.'

He turned to Vandhana, whose grip on Janani's wrist had not loosened.

'You don't have to stay, madam. You can wait outside.'

'I can stay,' Vandhana replied. She took a step towards the table.

'There's no need,' the doctor said. 'It's better if you make yourself comfortable. It will take some time.' His voice was kind, but there was iron in it.

Vandhana gave Janani an inscrutable look, then turned and walked out of the little room. Janani watched the peeling door close behind her, feeling as though a cloud had moved from over the sun.

'Is it OK that I do the scan?' the doctor asked. 'The nurse will stay the whole time.'

Janani nodded. She liked this old man. He looked kind, healthy, caring. She could imagine him at home, doting on toddling grandchildren.

The nurse helped Janani rearrange her sari. As the cool metal, slippery with gel, moved over her skin, she watched the image of the baby flickering on the screen. It was the perfect reflection of the baby itself – barely real, still just half a dream, a ghostly presence. She tried to make out eyes, fingers, nose, toes. She tried not to think, *please, Devi, a boy*, but the harder she tried, the harder the thought forced itself into her mind. She listened to the barely audible murmur of the doctor and the nurse's voices, speaking words she didn't quite understand, and let them lull her into thoughtlessness. It was almost relaxing – but for the thought of Vandhana, sitting, tense and waiting, outside the door.

Janani felt the sudden tearing urge for Amma. For her mother's arms around her, the smell of rasam on her skin, the whisper of her voice on Janani's hair. It had been months since she had seen Amma and Acha, that weekend of Pongal, one of the rare times Vandhana allowed her to go back to Chellampatti. The village had been bright with Pongal colours, kolam drawn at every house, the women wearing their brightest, newest saris. She thought of Amma, standing outside the front door at the top of the road, wrapped in luminous green cloth, her face glowing in the light of her smile, and swallowed hard through the lump beginning to form in her throat.

The table was beginning to press uncomfortably hard against her shoulder blades by the time the doctor finished. He turned away, towards the screen, manoeuvring buttons and keys, as the nurse wiped the gel from Janani's skin and adjusted her sari.

'Is the baby healthy, Doctor?'

'Yes, everything is normal.' He looked back at her and smiled. 'Your baby is about thirteen weeks now.'

The fluorescent light, dimmed by the sunshine leaking through the window, reflected off his glasses, half-hiding his eyes. Still, Janani could feel an unanswered question and an unquestioned answer hanging in the air between them.

'You need to eat more,' the doctor said. 'More rice, more vegetables, more lentils, OK? Fish and chicken also. You need to stay strong, so your baby can grow.'

Vandhana had always insisted warm rice and yoghurt was the only thing an expectant mother should eat. It was what she'd had for all her own pregnancies, and it had worked for her, she said.

'I'll try,' Janani replied.

'Do you work?'

'Yes. I'm a cleaner.'

He nodded. 'Take care. Don't push yourself.'

He was kind, but it was a blank, distant, tired kindness, Janani felt, like a wilted flower, like cloth fading in the sun.

The nurse, who had stayed virtually silent, helped her off the table. As she stood up, Janani could feel the weight of the un-spoken question – and its answer – hovering in the room, like thundercloud about to burst.

She didn't want to know.

Her skin still sensing the metal, Janani walked back the way she had come.

Vandhana was rising faster than Janani had ever seen her as the door opened.

'Well?' she said, stepping forward until she was an arm's-length from Janani's face.

'Everything is fine,' Janani said quickly. 'We can go, Ma.'

Vandhana didn't move, and as she was planted directly in her path, Janani didn't either.

'And,' Vandhana said, 'what is it?'

Janani noticed muted roaring in her ears. Her face felt very hot.

'He didn't say, Ma,' she replied.

Footsteps sounded behind her and she turned her head to see the nurse coming to collect the next woman. Janani inched forward, trying to move out of her way.

For a moment, Vandhana looked as though she would pro-test, then she drew her lips together into the shape of a dissat-isfied prune. Movement further down the hall distracted her

– a couple, coming towards them. The woman was older than Janani, and significantly more pregnant; her stomach bulged beneath her flame lily-pink sari and she had begun to waddle, her legs passing around the outside of her body rather than under it. Janani found herself staring at the way the husband's arm settled on his wife's arching lower back, at how his body leaned towards her, and his eyes rested on her more than anywhere else. She imagined Darshan walking that way, here, in this hospital corridor, and almost laughed out loud. But then, her mind slipped, transformed Darshan into Sanjay. For a moment, she could almost feel the warmth of his fingers against her spine, the softness in his dark eyes. And then she pushed that impossible image away.

There was a squeeze on her arm. 'Let's go, then,' Vandhana said. She jerked her head for Janani to lead the way.

The couple had passed Janani in the hall before she realised she couldn't hear Vandhana's steps behind her. Stopping, she turned back.

Vandhana was just moving away from the nurse. She shuffled past the pregnant woman and her husband and made her way slowly forward. As the man took a seat and his wife disappeared into the clinic, Janani saw the nurse gazing after her, a lingering glance that lasted until the closing door hid it from view.

Janani spun away, a tremble welling up inside her, as though moths had taken flight in different directions in her gut. She kept walking, the people around her faceless, lifeless, meaningless. She let her feet take her through the car park onto the side of the road. There, she stood and watched the traffic rumble down Usilampatti Main Road until she sensed Vandhana appear at her elbow. Together, they crossed the road in slow steps, hands held up in surrender to the cars and buses and lorries. Together, they made their way back into the tangle of streets and alleys, small enough and quiet enough for the stray dogs to roam and goats to be tethered outside their masters' houses. They walked in silence.

It wasn't until they reached the neem tree at the beginning of their own street that Janani chanced a look at her mother-in-law's face.

It told her everything.

'. . . get rid of it.'

Janani had just seated herself cross-legged on the floor in front of her rice and lentils, her stomach aching with hunger. Night had fallen, the monotonous chirp of cicadas now the loudest of sounds. Lavanika had long since gone to bed. Vandhana and Darshan sat in front of the television, speaking in low voices over the tinny music of some serial.

She had barely caught Vandhana's last words, but they turned the mouthful Janani had just taken into quarry dust.

There was nothing from Darshan for a long moment, and then, 'Are you sure?'

A sharp nod from Vandhana.

Janani's appetite was gone, even as her stomach growled. She ate methodically, slowly, for the chance to sit forgotten and listen.

Another long pause. It was a wonder that Vandhana could sit so close to Darshan, with the smell of liquor rolling from him.

'We can't afford . . .' Darshan's voice was lost amidst a screech of grief from the television.

Vandhana put up a placating palm, and though her words were smothered, her head shake spoke of solutions, answers, a way out.

The food on Janani's plate was gone, although she didn't remember eating it. Unfolding her legs, she stood and stepped out through the back door, where the pail of water sat, still almost full. She washed the dishes mechanically, one after the other. The steel wool rubbing against the metal dishes filled her ears.

Drying her hands on her sari pallu, she went back inside. They were still talking. It seemed to be about whatever was on the television now – a cremation, everyone dressed in white mundus, the women wailing from a distance.

The only chair spare was the one with the crack in the right front leg, that made it lurch like a kneeling elephant any time one of them sat on it.

She hated them.

And for the first time she realised that under the fear, the hope, she loved this almost-baby within her. Meenakshi Amman had given it to her. It was hers.

'I'm keeping this child,' she said.

Their heads whipped towards her. The slack surprise on their faces almost made Janani laugh. She felt a recklessness burn through her. Her fingers itched to pick up the pail of water outside and throw it over them, over the television.

But there would not be enough water to make Lavanika breakfast in the morning.

Vandhana recovered first. 'What are you talking about?'

'I heard you,' Janani said. She looked at Darshan. He held her gaze for a moment, then he shook his head and turned back to the television. Turned away. He'd never crept out from between his mother's sari pleats. Shouldn't he care? This was his child too. But then, so were the two who lay cold under the coconut palm. She couldn't think of Sanjay ever allowing that. Sanjay, with his kind heart. Sanjay would have fought for them, even the seven-year-old Sanjay she'd known, who had cried angry tears when the temple calf was ill, clutching Janani's hand as they sat beside it in the straw.

'If you bring another girl under this roof, you can go,'

Vandhana said. 'You're out of the house. You can crawl back to your parents. They can feed you and your little cows. They can break their backs for the dowries.'

Janani kept her face still, but dread filled her, as it always did at this threat. It would ruin them, Amma and Appa. They would never be able to lift their heads in the village again.

And for the first time, the thought flitted into her mind – perhaps it would just be easier to do as Vandhana said? It would be done and gone and maybe next time it would be a boy and everything would be better . . .

Janani remembered the prayer she'd whispered to Meenakshi Amma with Lavanika pressed tightly against her legs. There was a sudden weight against her arms, warm and soft, the ghost of newborn skin. Shame, hot and bitter as bile, rose in her chest.

'Ma, that's enough,' Darshan said and Janani's mouth fell open in surprise. 'We'll talk about it later.' He had barely turned away from the flickering television, but his voice carried a hint of irritation that silenced Vandhana in a way Janani could never do.

Her mother-in-law's lips pursed so tightly they disappeared into a wrinkled dark gash across her face. She turned her back firmly on Janani.

The following morning, Janani woke beside Darshan's sprawled, snoring body to the sound of Vandhana clattering pans. She pulled a clean sari from the cupboard and slipped out of the room, careful not to wake Lavanika.

In the kitchen, Vandhana was at the stove top. The scent of boiling tea and milk infused the air. She didn't look up as Janani emerged from the bedroom, and Janani took advantage of her turned back to ease the front door open and make her way unseen to the bathroom.

After she'd bathed, she strung her washed nightdress out

on the thick rope between the house and the biggest coconut palm. She tried, but it was impossible not to throw the customary, throat-tightening glance at the ground beneath the young coconut palm. Green shoots were beginning to emerge from the earth.

She turned away before her eyes could begin to burn.

When she re-entered the house, there was another, unfamiliar smell in the air, its edge acrid, bitter. Vandhana had taken the tea from the stove, but there was a second pot occupying the hob, steam rising above it.

'Can I help, Ma?' Janani said.

'Cook the idli,' Vandhana said without looking at her.

Janani inched past her to reach down for the dimpled idli plates and the batter that she had ground the day before. The smell, as she removed the steel cover, brought on a wave of nausea. She bit down on the inside of her lip and scooped batter into the four round shallow depressions in the first plate. It oozed and expanded to fill each circular hole like wet white mud. The first one done, she placed it into the heavy steel pot she used to steam them, then filled the second plate.

Beside her, Vandhana added a teaspoon of sugar and a squeeze of lemon to whatever she was stirring on the stove.

'What's that, Ma?' Janani asked.

'Something to help your stomach,' Vandhana replied, not looking up. She turned off the gas.

There was a grunt from within the bedroom door and Darshan emerged, rubbing his hand over his face. 'Tea,' he said, before lumbering outside to the bathroom.

Janani grasped the hot steel lip of the pot, shielding her hand with her sari pallu. She poured steaming tea into a tumbler, then began to cool it, letting it flow into a second cup and then back again in a sweet, milky waterfall. Vandhana stayed hunched over the stove, her body hiding the contents, shifting only to let Janani put the idli onto the gas to steam.

It wasn't until Darshan returned and Janani had handed him his tea that Vandhana turned off the gas and began to pour the contents of the second pot into another tumbler.

'Here, drink this,' she said as Janani returned to the kitchen.

A glimpse showed Janani the cup was full, steam rising from what looked like some sort of plant tea. It smelled of lemon and of something else half-familiar, as though it had wafted past her in the street. 'What is it?' she asked.

'A herbal remedy Radha told me of,' Vandhana said.

Sliding her fingers around the empty top half, Janani brought the cup to her nose and sniffed. She took a tentative sip. The hot liquid was sour on her tongue, sweetened slightly by honey. Familiar and not familiar. She took another sip and looked up. 'Which plant?'

There was a pause. The slurping noise of Darshan drinking his tea.

'Mayurkonrai leaves,' Vandhana said, checking the idli on the stove.

Mayurkonrai. Janani thought of the plant, its beautiful red and yellow flowers flaring like a peacock's tail. She tried to put the name together with the half-remembered smell drifting up from the cup in her hand. Mayurkonrai.

She froze.

Mayurkonrai.

She was a child again, bouncing an old ball against the wall of her parents' house, the sun just beginning to withdraw its rays beneath the horizon. A flash of movement caught her eye and Janani turned to see Girija, her favourite aunt, limping up the street towards them. She was crying. Her sari was a dishevelled mess, her hair pulled out of her braid. Janani yelled for her mother, ran to Girija, stopped short at the sight of blood streaming from her nose and a bruise purpling her cheek. For the next few hours, she had peered around the door of her parents' tiny bedroom, trying to make out the hushed conversation in the main room. Her mother, grandmother and Girija clung to each other, weeping. Her grandfather had paced around the room, looking angrier than she had ever seen him.

The cuts and rips and bruises faded, but Girija was changed after that. She never laughed as easily. The stories she used to tell, about gods and goddesses, rakshasas and heroes, dried up like a summer well. And a few months later, there was a whole week when the house smelt of mayurkonrai leaves, steeped in hot water. Janani remembered her grandmother thanking Mother Devi when, at the end of the week, Girija curled up in pain and began to bleed, heavily and suddenly.

'I'm not drinking this,' Janani said. 'I know what you're doing.'

Vandhana stared at her. For a moment, she looked as though she were struggling with what to say, her lips parting and closing a few times. Janani could see the thought of lying flickering in her expression.

'Isn't this easier?' she snapped finally. 'Better now than after you've had the cursed girl-baby, you stupid donkey.'

Janani looked at Darshan. He was watching them warily, but there was no surprise on his face. Vandhana had obviously slipped the word to him.

'Girls and more girls!' Vandhana said, dropping her voice to a hiss. 'Is that all you can bring to this house? Are you trying to ruin us?' She jabbed her finger at the cup in Janani's hand. 'I should have been there for the last ones. Checked with the doctor. Rid us of them before they came. Now drink it!'

Janani looked down at the tea. It would be so much easier. The life inside her was just a maybe, a half-formed promise whose soul still sat with the gods. She could let it go, and try again. What a miserable life it would have. What misery it would bring.

An image pieced itself together in her mind, a dreamy flickering black-and-white spectre of a ghost-child on a screen. She remembered watching that screen the last time she had lain in the consulting room, and the time before that . . .

She hurried to the back door, pushed it open and poured the contents of the tumbler onto the earth.

'Janani,' Vandhana said. She was so close that Janani almost jumped. When she turned around, she was almost nose-to-nose with her mother-in-law. 'Do you know how many girls I sent back to Meenakshi Amman? If I had not, we would be living in the street, eating dust. Heaven is the help of the helpless.'

Janani stared. For once, Vandhana's voice didn't hold the sharp, hard contempt it usually did. This close, Janani could see the lines in the older woman's face. Not the lines of Parvati Ma's, that sloped up and hinted of smiles, but harsh straight lines that spoke of years of straining effort. What had life done to her, to shape her this way?

'No,' Janani said, much more calmly than she felt. 'No. It will be OK, Mamiyar. I'll work hard. I'll care for her. But I'm not doing this.'

Vandhana's face was darkening to the shade of a blackberry. She was gripping the ladle she was holding as though she were going to bend it with one hand. 'Drink it, you stupid bitch! You can't do anything right, the least you can do is fix your mistakes! Drink it!' Her arm rose above her head and Janani felt her own hands rise to her face.

'Just leave it for now, Amma,' Darshan said.

Surprise stopped them both, and they turned to him as one. He wasn't looking at them and Janani saw why immediately. Lavanika was standing at the bedroom door, straight and still as a broomstick, looking between them all with eyes so wide they seemed to take up half her face.

For a moment, the only movement in the room was a fly, buzzing aimlessly, confusedly around. Then Vandhana turned away, muttering under her breath, to pour a cup of tea, her scarred hands shaking. The milky smell of it did nothing but turn Janani's stomach.

She crossed the room to Lavanika, dropped to her knees and held her. Lavanika's arms snaked their way around her neck. Janani could feel her little girl's heartbeat, thumping, thumping against her ribcage

'Come, let's go and have your bath,' she said quietly. 'Can you take your towel and your school dress, and get the water ready?'

Lavanika nodded against Janani's shoulder. They disentangled themselves, and Lavanika slipped back into the bedroom. A few seconds later, she was shuffling out with her towel clutched to her chest, and then she was out the door.

Janani went to where the rest of the mayurkonrai infusion sat, steam still spiralling above it. Lifting the pot, she went to the back door and poured the rest of the disgusting liquid into the dirt, ignoring the worm of fear in her mind. She watched Vandhana from the corner of her eye. Her mother-in-law did not look up once, but the clenched muscles in her jaw, the stiff hunch of her shoulders, told Janani louder than any scream that she was beyond fury.

She should have expected it, but Vandhana could still move fast enough to surprise her. As Janani turned to place the empty pot on the kitchen counter, Vandhana's hand came swinging towards her face. It caught her high on the cheek and in the eye. Janani's eyes watered immediately and she stepped back, hands coming up to her face in time to block Vandhana's second slap.

They were in the wrong place to stop the blow to her stomach.

It was an older woman's blow, a strange, ungainly wheel of an arm, the side of a bony fist connecting with her belly button, but it was propelled by fury and it doubled Janani over.

She staggered back a step, and let herself keep going, away from Vandhana, towards the door. She had to get out of here.

'I'll knock that thing out of you!' Vandhana said, but she looked drained, as though her anger had sapped her strength.

Darshan was watching them, but to Janani's relief, he didn't stop her as she kept moving, as quickly as she could, out of the door. She closed it behind her, hiding the two of them from sight.

Lavanika was entering their tiny concrete bathroom, teetering under the weight of a full bucket of water. Janani forced herself to run and take it from her before it fell.

'Good girl,' she said. Her breath was still short, from the blow or the shock she wasn't sure. Her left eye stung.

She bathed Lavanika quickly and pulled her green school dress over her head.

'You haven't brushed my hair, Amma,' Lavanika said.

'Run and get your comb,' Janani said, 'and put your chappals on. We're going for a walk before school.'

Even if it was a forty-five-minute freedom, she had to get away from here. And she had to see Shubha.

They turned left and walked up the street, Janani's feet moving without thinking. The village had woken up. Old Murugan sat on the steps of his house, milking the goat his son had recently bought him. He grinned at Janani as she walked past, giving her a friendly view of his few mottled, yellow-brown teeth. Lavanika waved at him.

'Are we going to see Nandita?' Lavanika asked and Janani realised that they were nearing Shubha's house.

'I don't know, Lavi.' It had been two weeks, now, since their visit to the health centre. She had seen Shubha once since then, that same strange day when she had revealed her pregnancy to Sanjay. That strange, mad day when she had knelt by Shubha's bed and whispered kind lies to her, of her daughter's new life, a life of food and school and a good marriage. Shubha had turned to face the mud-brick ceiling and said nothing, just squeezed Janani's hand while tears left tracks like snails down her cheeks and towards her ears. Since then, her mother had met Janani at the door every time she came to visit. Shubha was recovering. She wanted to see no one.

There was movement outside Shubha's house now.

'Amma, slow down!'

Janani hadn't realised that her steps had quickened; looking back, she saw Lavanika trotting to keep pace.

'Sorry, little one,' she said. 'Look, can you see who is at Aunty Shubha's house?'

'Isn't it old Kamala Amma?' Lavanika said.

Janani watched the movement coalesce into familiar forms, postures, gestures. It was the old midwife standing outside the front door, and just inside, Shubha herself.

She wasn't prepared for the sense of relief that soaked into her, through her chest and her stomach and then down into her legs, weakening them. The worry that had hid itself from her drained away with it. Shubha was well, well enough to stand, at least. Shubha would recover.

But by the time Janani was within shouting distance, the door had closed.

Kamala was coming towards her, squinting in the sun, her gait just ever so slightly uneven. A jute bag was slung over one shoulder. Janani imagined she could smell the soaked leaves of mayurkonrai, see the blazing red of its flower through the rough, furred fibre of the bag. She would have turned and walked away, if it hadn't been Shubha the woman was coming from.

'Lavanika,' Janani said, turning. 'Why don't you run and see if Nandita is at home. If she can walk to school with us. Can you do that?'

She was answered by a whoop, and off Lavanika ran, her sandals kicking up dust, her school bag smacking unheeded against her hip, braids flying, arms flailing. Janani followed, until she had reached Kamala.

'How does someone so small have so much energy?' the old woman said.

'I don't know,' Janani replied, and she had to smile. They were still in the back of her mind, those days, when her body felt weightless, or even more, like a coiled spring.

'I remember delivering her. The shoots of that hair already a thick, soft mess, and those eyes, so big and alert, taking in this new world.'

Janani remembered that night too, her fear and her pain just one big seething mass so that she didn't know where one ended and the other started, the smell of her blood and her bladder and her bowels, Kamala's gentle voice and gentle hands keeping Vandhana at bay, and finally, that warm tiny body laid against her chest. The love she had felt that moment had burned away the pain like a flame in pre-dawn darkness.

But with that memory came the pain of the two after it. When the ache in her body had been drowned in the ache in her heart.

'And how are you now?' Kamala asked. 'Are you well?'

'I'm well.' She hesitated. 'Shubha. Did she speak to you?'

'She did.' Kamala's face settled into seriousness. The lines of age disappeared into the smooth darkness of her skin. 'She is almost healthy, in her body. In her mind . . .' She paused. 'It will take some time. You should talk to her. Her family don't understand, but if she can't heal, here,' Kamala pressed the fingers of one hand against her chest, then her head, 'it is a very sad thing.'

'She won't talk to me,' Janani said.

'She won't want to, but you must,' Kamala pressed. Then her eyes narrowed and she leaned forward. Janani caught the smell of sandalwood and cardamom. 'What is that mark on your head? Is that blood?'

Janani put a hand to where Vandhana's palm had caught her. Her fingers found a raised welt, still tender. Her touch dislodged dried flakes – when she brought her hand down, her fingertips were dotted with specks the colour of rust. One of Vandhana's silver rings must have sliced her skin.

'Kamala Ma,' she said. 'I'm pregnant.'

Kamala nodded. There was no surprise in her face.

'It's a girl.' Her throat rebelled at the words, squeezing in temper, forcing her to push past it.

Every line in the old woman's face seemed to spring forth at once, to sag in unison towards the ground. She looked old, older than Janani had seen her.

'Do you know of mayurkonrai?' Janani asked.

A bony hand, stronger than she could have expected, shot out like a monkey snatching food out of a child's grasp, and wrapped itself around her wrist. 'Don't dare. Think of your little Lavanika. Think of your amma with her arms around you. What will happen to this world, when there are none of us left?'

They stood there, Janani frozen in shock, Kamala's grip burning on her skin.

'No,' Kamala said. 'You didn't.'

She dropped Janani's arm.

Janani felt her chest expand outward as she let her breath escape. And then, suddenly, she was crying. She was furious with herself, that she couldn't stop herself weeping in the open. A young man passing on a bicycle, standing up on the pedals, stared so hard he almost veered into a yelping street dog.

Kamala's arms were around her, and that sandalwood scent grew stronger. The morning was early enough that the heat of her body was not yet too much. Janani let herself be held.

'I want my child to live. I don't care if it's a girl.' The words came out onto the old woman's shoulder, as though they might be trapped there, long enough for her to take them back.

'Then get out.' Was it anger that made the old woman's words so flat?

Janani drew back and wiped her eyes on her pallu.

Kamala's hold shifted to her upper arms, as though she were keeping Janani standing. 'Get out, girl. Is a life like mine, alone, independent, such a price to pay? It's a hard life, but it's mine.'

'Amma! Amma!'

Lavanika's voice cut through the air like an aruval through a coconut, and just as jarring. Kamala's hands fell away and they both turned. Lavanika was running towards them and, just behind her, her usual shyness shattered by a smile of pure, guileless delight, Nandita was running too.

Janani felt Kamala's gaze on her. By the time she turned, Kamala was walking away, that tiny hitch in her step making the jute bag swing, sandalwood and spices in her wake.

Chapter Ten

Madurai, 2019

I'm wearing a yellow skirt and a pink blouse. A pattu pavada. My hair is shorter than I can ever remember it – I can feel the curls brushing my shoulders. The scent of jasmine surrounds me and I know, somehow, that it's coming from the string of flowers in my hair.

Around me, people are dancing and singing, their sandalled feet raising dust that tickles my nose.

'Nila?'

I look up and see Amma, younger than I've ever seen her, younger than me, her eyes gleaming with joy. Beside her, a slim dark man standing head and shoulders above her. They're both too tall, and I realise it's because I'm too short. Bangles chime at my wrist – looking down, I see that my arms are small and chubby and there's chipped pink polish on my nails.

'Nila?'

I turn, and Iphigenia is beside me. Her fingers, strong and callused, grasp mine, our palms pressed together. It's night now, and her face, pale and luminescent in the moonlight, is serene as a marble sphinx.

We're standing in a room, *this* room. My eyes are drawn to a stack of photographs on the desk. They're familiar, and not. Amma and Acha are there, laughing, smiling, in front of the

Opera House, by the manic grin of the entrance to Luna Park. I'm there too, almost as bright-faced. I'm holding a child, a child whose head is turned against my shoulder. Beside me is a man, or the outline of one – his features are blurred, his build nondescript. I can't make out anything about him, but nothing about him is familiar. In every photo, his arm is around me, melding me to him, until my outline blends with his.

Iphigenia looks at me, and though she's smiling, a chill sadness has turned her eyes to blue glass.

I stare back at her, aware of my heart's tempo increasing, and for a moment we're frozen in mute silence. Then she glances away.

I follow her gaze to the mirrored door of the wardrobe. We stand side by side, reflected into each other's eyes.

Almost.

I have no face.

'Nila kutty.'

I wake, sweat-damp and breathing hard. My eyes open to a darkness just beginning to fade into the purple-grey of dawn. Inhaling the just-washed fragrance of the cotton pillowcase, I wait for the thumping of my heart to subside as I make out Amma hovering above me.

'It's time to get up.'

My head pounds with dehydration and curtailed sleep. Getting into bed and dozing off in the muggy heat are two different things. I'd spent at least an hour tossing and turning, before I'd fallen into restless dreams. I think I remember hearing my parents' voices filtering through the wall.

The bedroom is my father's old one. It still has a thousand traces of him – the old photo on the desk of an impossibly young Acha standing serious-faced in a school uniform with a badge on the jacket, the thick electrical engineering textbooks.

I stand in the centre of the room as Amma helps me into my borrowed sari. It's lovely and soft, thin cotton in a kaleidoscope of reds and greens and blues.

My head is still full of dream matter. The thought of the grief on Iphigenia's face makes my skin prickle, but it's the tatters of the other dream that tangle in my mind. They must be memory. There must be others.

My mother mutters and hands me folded pleats to hold as she inserts various safety pins. Every now and again, she stands beside me, facing the mirror, and frowns at herself as she mimes putting the sari on.

'I'm not used to doing this for other people,' she says.

Finally, we make our way downstairs. The house is bathed in the featureless grey of very early morning. I try to shake the feeling that every step is another chance for my sari to unravel.

'Malini and Varun have come with their families,' I hear Kochachan say, 'and Vasudev has brought Bindu Veliamma with him and the family. Everyone else will come for the twenty-seventh.'

'The pujari is a good one,' says a voice that nudges me to recall it. 'We've known him for years.'

In the drawing room, we find Acha and my uncle standing beside an older woman. It takes me a moment to recognise her, and it comes to me just as she says, 'Do you remember me, molé?'

It's as though my grandmother's features have been stamped on another woman. 'Veliamma,' I say.

She holds out her arms and I walk obediently into them. The scent of rose and Nivea moisturiser engulfs me. Veliamma. 'Big mother', I'd translated for myself when I first met her, at age eight. My father's aunt, who'd spoken to me in English and never laughed at my Malayalam.

'How pretty you look,' she says.

Veliamma must be in her seventies now, but face cream, melanin and the trendy, short cut of her salwar make her look twenty years younger. Her posture's excellent, my clinical brain notices.

'Look who else is here, Ammayi,' Acha says. There's a deep warmth to his tone that reminds me of the times he'd catch Rohan and me to him as we went running to him on his return from work.

My great-aunt turns to Amma, and her face breaks into a smile that reveals dozens of lines of rich life. 'Janani,' she says. 'How long it's been.'

Amma disappears into her embrace. They hold each other for a long moment. I sense a closeness I know nothing about. Resentment creeps up into my chest. I've been robbed of that. What could my relationship with Veliamma have been if I'd come here, year after year?

It's then that Arjun emerges.

My first glimpse of Arjun shows me someone as unrecognisable as Radhika is – no longer the fun, chubby-cheeked seven-year-old who had been my friend when last I was here. He's wearing Coldplay pyjamas. His hair's long and brushed off to one side. The first waft of what must be last night's cologne reaches me as he's almost down the stairs. Eyes sunken and hooded, he looks haggard.

'What time do you call this, Arjun?' Kochachan says. I've never heard my uncle so serious.

'Just in time?' Arjun says.

I let out an involuntary snort.

Arjun glances at me and the expression on his face – as though he's been kept awake for days – melts into a grins. 'Sorry, Acha. I got caught up with Deepak and the others last night.' His Indian accent is long and languorous.

'On the day your achacha . . .'

I'm amazed how quickly Arjun's expression changes, re-forming into mutinous anger. It's enough to stop Kochachan mid-sentence.

My uncle shakes his head. 'We're having breakfast, and we are leaving in two hours. I don't care if you eat or not, but you need to be bathed and in your mundu. It's your grandfather's funeral.' His words hang in the air. Radhika's appears behind her brother; the lightness has drained from her face.

'Fine.' Arjun rubs a hand over his face. 'Hi, Ammama, Ammayi. Nice to see you again, Nila. Hey, Veliamma. Be back in a minute.'

Without another word, he turns and walks back up the stairs.

There are few words spoken at breakfast. It's a waiting time, a reflecting time. Afterwards, we file back through the house to pay our respects to Achacha. It's harder than I was expecting to walk into the room where his body lies, stretched out on a white-sheeted bed. Now, in the light, I'm confronted by a with-ered, shrunken version of the man I'd first met almost twenty years ago. He looks like a sleeping ascetic, with his white, gold-hemmed lunghi and his sacred thread over his shoulder, but for the ice under the body. In death, he seems a lot more forgiving, the sternness of his features relaxed.

The room's full of the smell of incense and the fresh fragrance of the flowers. After last night, it's easier to feel regret, but what's stronger is the jab of grief for Acha, who stands over his father with barely a flicker of emotion. Amma's standing tight by his side.

A cluster of family – those who could make it in time – appear throughout the morning. They greet Acha and Kochachan with folded hands, then, one by one, they say their goodbyes to their patriarch. Then it's my turn. I'm passed from aunt to cousin to uncle, and try to burn their names and faces into my brain.

*

We head across the city in Veliamma's car. Her driver looks as though he's over a century old, slightly hunched, wrinkled as a walnut shell, face split in a perpetual grin that shows off his missing teeth. He winds an erratic way through the traffic, following the hearse that carries Achacha's body.

I sit sandwiched between my mother and my aunt and stare out the window into the semi-darkness, watching the horizon continue to lighten into lavender that bleeds into blue. The packed landscape of the city whizzes past me – petrol stations and bakeries, restaurants and temples all interspersed between rows of houses in a chaotic, lively sprawl.

The road takes us beside the train tracks. A train races us to the impressive Madurai Junction station. Another one pulls out as it arrives, tugging slowly in the opposite direction. I watch the people entering through the grand main entrance, with its pillared colonnade.

'Victorian, that train station,' Acha says. 'That's one positive legacy of the British. A world-class rail system.' It's the most he's spoken all morning.

'I'm not sure it was worth it, Acha,' I say.

'Neither am I.'

'Look there,' Amma says, suddenly.

I look at where she points, out through her window on the right. Outlined against the sky, I see the tapering towers of a temple. They are covered in sculpture, painted in bright, festive shades of a world of colour. I think I have spotted them all until the car moves and more towers come into view from where they were hidden behind their siblings.

'Beautiful,' I say. It's spectacular, a soaring song in sculpture, a stone cry to the heavens.

'Meenakshi Amman temple.' Amma's voice is almost a

whisper. She hasn't stopped staring through the window, as though she's seen a celebrity, or a car crash.

'That's not Victorian,' Veliamma comments. 'It's a little older.' She gives me a crooked little smile, then looks at my mother. Says something in Tamil I can't quite catch.

Amma is still staring, her head protruding from the window, craned so far I can only see her shining black hair. As the temple fades from view, she turns. Her eyes are very wide under her filled-in eyebrows.

'I'm well,' she says, also in Tamil, and smiles. She rarely speaks Tamil, even though it's her mother tongue, even though she spoke it for the first twenty-two years of her life, until she and Acha married. It's as though the melody of Malayalam has been the only one she's wanted to live her life to since then.

I jump when I feel her hand on my wrist. Her fingers snake their way down to interlace with mine, and she squeezes, hard. If only her thoughts would flow through her palm and into me. I store that squeeze into the back of my mind, one more of a thousand questions I'm thinking might never be answered.

The pujari – priest – is waiting for us at the crematorium on the far side of the city by the banks of the Vaigai river. It's a big flat area of land, desolate, with rows of sheds dotted over it, and beyond them, a sea of graves. It's so grim that I shiver, even though it's already warm enough to sweat. Radhika has run to join us, and I'm glad she's here. Her sweet face feels like some sort of talisman against the dead.

'The Vaigai is one of the sacred rivers,' Veliamma tells me as we follow the priest to what will be my grandfather's funeral pyre. 'Its story is quite like the Ganga's. It's known as the kriti-mala, sacred garland, because of the way it loops around the city, and around Meenakshi Amman.'

'It's not looking great right now,' Radhika says apologetically.

'No,' Veliamma says. 'It is not, is it? In summer, the river dries up. Some of the cow and goatherd families live there, for the grazing and the closeness to the water. Then they move for the rainy season. Then, the river can flood.'

I see women bathing themselves in the partly parched river, their sari underskirts hitched and knotted above their knees. Beside them on the raised humps of grassy riverbed sit piles of laundry that they soak and soap and thrash against rocks.

'We stop here,' Veliamma says, holding out a hand. Both Radhika and I stumble to a halt. Beside me, Amma's face is tight, sombre. She's been very quiet.

Acha and the other men carry on, following the priest all the way to the pyre.

We stay where we are as Achacha is lifted onto the pyre. The funeral happens at a distance for us, the women.

My great-aunt tells me that, these days, women do attend funerals. But my grandfather was a stickler for tradition, so we stand fifty metres away as my father, directed by the priest, sprinkles water and leaves on my grandfather's body – 'Ganga water, tulsi leaves,' Veliamma whispers – and the men circle the pyre three times. A traditional pyre – no electricity for my grandfather. I can't help but hold my breath as Acha slowly lowers a torch to the wood. Kochachan stands beside my father, and behind them, Arjun, his head bowed. I wonder how hungover he is. If the smell in the air – old smoke, new smouldering flames – is making him nauseous.

I stand beside Amma, the two of us pressed together in a circle of women and girls neither of us really know. I'm thankful for Manju Ammayi and Veliamma and Radhika, standing on either side of us.

There are others here, other cremations happening, other

mourners gathered around, but this feels the most spaced out of any place that I've yet seen in India. A wind's picked up. It howls, although there's nothing for it to howl around. It shifts the heat-dried dust. It speaks of thousands of corpses whose ashes it has carried away.

Amma takes my arm, making me jump. 'Let's go,' she says.

That's when I notice that the men have turned away and are walking back towards us. The funeral fire makes dark outlines of their bodies.

'We don't watch the pyre burn,' Amma says.

And so we all turn and walk away, leaving the flames to leap into the sky, leaving Achacha's body to catch alight with only strangers to see his soul drift into the cloudless sky.

Chapter Eleven

Madurai, 1993

The fourth month

*Now her face moves, smiles, frowns. She hears the sound
of her mother's heartbeat.*

The phone rang just as Sanjay opened the door.

'Hello?' he heard Vijay say as he took his shoes off and placed them in the rack. He walked through the drawing room in mindless fatigue.

'Sanjay.' He jumped at the unexpected voice and turned to see Amma sitting in the drawing room. Priya was with her, sitting close, turned towards her sister with one arm stretched along the back of the sofa behind her head.

Seeing them like this, the two of them together, was like looking at his mother reflected in a horribly warped mirror. Priya was vibrant, alive, although she was two years older. He knew, every time he saw his aunt, that Amma was getting sicker. It was hard to tell now, day by day, how Amma's condition was deteriorating. The changes were so subtle, so gradual. But to see Priya beside her was a punch in Sanjay's gut, a sharp-nailed blow that pierced the skin and strangled his intestines. He thanked God that his aunt had not wanted to stay with them when she came back from Madras. A constant reminder would have been unbearable.

It spiderwebbed down his spine again, the tingling, chilling fear.

His mother was dying.

Sanjay wondered, despite how much Radhakrishnan forbade them to mention it, whether Amma knew.

'You're home early today, kutty,' Amma said, smiling. The skin around her lips, so pale and drawn, creased into a smile.

'Yes,' Sanjay said. 'I started work two hours earlier to get home at a decent time. You're always asleep otherwise.'

'Etta!' Vijay called. Sanjay looked over to see him cradling the phone against his chest. 'Call for you.'

'One minute, Amma.'

He set his suitcase to one side and walked over.

'Gone shopping?' Vijay asked, grinning, pointing at the plastic bag he still clutched in his left hand. The *Madras Silks* logo was emblazoned on the side of the bag.

'Yes,' Sanjay said. 'Not for you, though.' He took the phone from his brother. 'Hello?'

'Mr Sanjay Nambeesan?' The voice was deep. Sanjay could imagine it coming from a man solid as a banyan trunk.

'Yes, sir.' He slapped a hand at Vijay and his brother scooted past him towards the drawing room.

'My name is Mr Ram Shankar.' Confident English, with a Marathi twang to the accent. 'I am calling from Intel, in Bangalore. I am sorry for the late call, but it was a long day of work, you know?'

Sanjay murmured some nonsense, his mind blanking.

'You applied for a power engineer position with us some days ago.'

His heart made itself known immediately, like a puppy straining at a lead.

'Yes, that's right, sir.' He sounded calmer than he felt.

'Could we arrange an initial interview?' Mr Ram Shankar said. 'On the phone?'

'Oh . . .' Sanjay felt himself twist away from the drawing room, as if he could draw all the sound into his body. 'Of course, sir,' he said.

'Excellent.' There was a pause, and Sanjay heard the rustle of paper. 'Tuesday. Tuesday, five p.m. Is that suitable?'

He had no idea if it was suitable, but he'd make it suitable. 'Of course, sir.'

'Good. I will speak to you then.'

Sanjay replaced the phone and turned. From the corridor, he could see Vijay had gone to sit on the other side of their mother. He was reading the latest copy of *Time* magazine, but he sat very close, Amma's hand on his knee.

'Who was that, kutty?' Amma called.

'No one important, Amma, just someone from the bank.' His hand was sweaty around the handle of the plastic bag. Forcing a smile on his face, he walked back into the drawing room.

'What's this?'

Priya helped his mother open the bag and pull out a carefully packaged, folded square of blue silk and silver embroidery.

Amma looked up at him. 'What is this you have brought me?'

'It's a sari, Ma, how bad are your eyes now?' Vijay said.

'Rude boy.' Her smile had grown, reached her eyes. It was bigger than Sanjay had seen it in weeks.

'You were complaining the other day about how you hadn't had a new sari in years, that you didn't know what to wear to Malini's wedding. Now you do.'

'It's beautiful, Parvati,' his aunt said, running the tips of her fingers over the silk. 'Your son's inherited your taste, thankfully.'

The tinkle of tiny bells, like birdsong. There was a clatter in the hallway, a splash of water, the slap of wet cloth on tiles, and

Janani emerged, walking backwards, bent over and mopping the floor. Her anklets chimed with each step she took. She turned as she approached the front door, washed the last two tiles and stood. She brushed away a piece of hair that had escaped the tight bun her hair had been captured in, looked up, and noticed them.

'Hi,' Sanjay said. 'How are you?' It sounded awkward to his own ears.

She smiled.

'Janani,' his mother said. 'Are we in your way?'

'No, Parvati Amma,' she replied. 'Don't pay attention to me.'

'You're well, Janani?' Priya asked.

'Yes, ma,' Janani said, nodding. She looked at Sanjay again. 'You just got home? Have you eaten? Do you want some coffee?'

'Janani's made the most delicious avial,' Vijay said. 'Almost as good as Amma's.'

Sanjay smiled. 'I'll eat in a minute.' He realised then that his stomach was growling.

'He brought me this,' Amma said, holding the sari up for Janani to see. 'Come and see. Isn't he a good boy?'

Sanjay rolled his eyes and so did his brother.

Janani took a step forward. 'It's beautiful,' she remarked.

'You'll need to get the blouse stitched,' Priya said. 'Are you still going to Sendil? He was good, from what I remember.'

'Ah. I haven't had anything stitched in months,' Amma replied. 'I'll have to go there, though. My blouses don't fit me anymore, I've lost . . . But I don't know if he'll have time, before the wedding.'

Sanjay cursed himself. He hadn't thought of that, the fuss of having the blouse material cut from the main length of the sari, of measuring, designing, stitching. He hadn't thought of how much weight Amma had lost, how loose her blouses now sat on her. The wedding was on Sunday. Damn.

'I can stitch it for you,' Janani said.

They looked at her.

'I can measure you now. Or, or in the morning. I have a sewing machine, at home. It's old, but it works. My periamma taught me to stitch, before my wedding. I stitch my little one's clothing, my clothing. Sometimes the women in the village bring me some work, too.' The rush of words cut off suddenly. Her eyes flickered between them. Embarrassment was colouring her face. 'But, Parvati Amma, you should go to the proper tailor. I'm not that good.' She looked away, her eyes dropping to the floor, searching the room for something to fix on. Her shoulders lifted in a shy shrug and she blinked, rapidly, eyelashes beating like butterfly wings.

Sanjay managed to wrench his gaze away to his mother. She was smiling, and it was her usual smile, the wonderful, bright smile free from any notice of her pain.

'Will you do that for me?' she said. 'That would be very special.'

'Ha,' Priya said, in English. 'What an excellent surprise.'

Janani looked incredulous. Her gaze moved to Sanjay, and she let out a laugh, then clapped the back of her hand to her mouth. He wondered what his face was saying.

'Close your mouth, moné,' Priya said and he realised he was gawping like a frog.

'OK. Good. I'll leave you all to the clothes talk,' he said. He picked his suitcase up, cradling it in his arms, aware of the glistening, soap-scented tiles.

As he tiptoed down the corridor, he heard his mother ask Janani what clothes she liked to stitch best, and he felt a smile leaking onto his face.

*

He woke early the following morning. Amma was already up, bathed and ready for him to help her out onto the veranda, to sit in the tender morning sun and sip some tea. It was Vijay's role during the week. Sanjay ordered him away on the weekend. It was rare he got time alone with her.

'Bring the newspaper, kutty,' Amma said. 'Tell me what is happening in the world.'

Acha, who had risen even earlier, had deposited the newspaper on the drawing-room table before he left for the surgery. Sanjay brought it out, pulled his chair closer to his mother's, and wrestled it open. Wrestled. That's what it had felt like, for the last couple of months. A struggle with the news. The ink of the stories had leaked from the pages and into his life.

Amma mentioned it first.

'Still they have not caught the bombers?' she said, quiet.

'Not yet. They're blaming the Muslims, of course.'

'Of course. They will not blame themselves, for the VHP pulling down the mosque, for everything afterwards.' She was cradling her tea, and he could feel her eyes on him.

He knew exactly what she was thinking. Suez had offered him a position with them, in Bombay. He could have been there, when Babri Masjid fell, when the Hindus had ripped down the stones of the mosque and reclaimed their holy Ayodhya. And so he might have lived through the weeks following, walked by Jogeshwari, Dadar, Dongri, as the riots ripped through buildings and bodies, blood painting the streets, fire leaping like prayers into the night sky.

And he could have been there, two months later, in a Bombay ripped apart by bombs. The Muslims, the journalists said, had struck back. The news had shaken him, hard enough to surprise him. He had friends in Bombay. Distant family. During the riots, it had been the poor who had suffered, Muslim families running from Hindus as behind them their homes were torn apart. The bombs, wreaking their wrath on the Stock Exchange, on hotels, in the airport, at markets, took aim at everyone else. Sprayed shrapnel into their limbs and eyes, Muslims and Hindus alike.

He could have been there. Should have been there.

He hadn't, and still Amma had spent evenings crying at the thought that he could have been there.

'They'll find them, Amma,' he said. 'They already have suspects. Bombay is full of crime gangs who'll use religion to get their own way.'

She frowned, and he could have kicked himself. He was supposed to be reassuring her, not worrying her even more. Painting a picture for her of him as an eighteen-year-old university student arriving wide-eyed to live seven years in a Bombay with criminal gangs behind every corner.

'It is such a terrible thing,' she said instead. 'Religion should be a great unifier. Are we not all one before Bhagavan? Whether you call him Bhagavan or Bhagavati, Krishna or Shiva, Allah or Jesus or Buddha. Such hard lives people live, Sanju, that they turn the beauty of God into evil.'

If only it had been Amma at the head of the crowd in Ayodhya last December. They'd have gone home, all a hundred and fifty thousand of them, and hugged their Muslim neighbours.

Sanjay put an arm around his mother's thin shoulders, careful not to settle its full weight.

'Anyway.' Amma reached out and squeezed his knee. 'You are here. I am so glad, kutty, that you have come home. It is good for your acha too, you know. We are both getting older.'

'You're not that old, Amma,' he said. 'Even Achacha lived until ninety-four. You both have a long time.' He smiled through the sudden stab of grief in his chest. A future grief, for a future loss that he couldn't unsee.

'Yes, yes,' Amma said. 'Come, read me something else. Something happier.

Sanjay turned to the sports pages. The test matches were over, but the journalists were still fixated on England's dehydrated performance during their tour of India. There was a picture of Kambli, holding his bat aloft. He showed Amma, as he explained to her the cricket test series.

His mind kept drifting.

Yes, his friends in Bombay were fine. They were not in the Stock Exchange or the hotels, or by the parked cars that had exploded as suddenly and shockingly as a firecracker held too close. He'd asked about Diya, in a roundabout, casual, friendly way. She was fine, too. More than fine – she was engaged. He thought of her in a marriage sari, red and gold and front-pinned, a Gujarati bride. Her face, he was surprised to notice, had almost faded from memory.

'Cricket.'

He jumped hard enough to rip the paper. Looking up, he saw Janani standing by Amma's chair. She held one hand up in apology as his eyes met hers, her lips twitching. Not even her anklets had broken through his thoughts to announce her arrival.

She gestured at the paper. 'Some of the boys in our village street were playing yesterday morning. They hit a scooter driver in the head with the ball. Luckily he wasn't going very fast. And the boys aren't much bigger than Lavanika.' She chuckled.

Sanjay shook his head as the frantic race of his heart slowed. 'Sounds a bit like us at that age. Making trouble. Doesn't it, Amma?'

'It does.' She was smiling up at Janani.

'We were worse, Parvati Ma,' Janani said.

They were all silent for a moment, thinking perhaps of the

same things – a cracked window after a game of throwing fallen figs at each other, the knee scraped to the bone by a sliding fall across the concrete driveway, the jaggery stolen by the handful from the kitchen, stuffed into their mouths until they felt sick.

'You're here early,' Sanjay said.

'Yes,' Janani replied. 'I thought I would take Parvati Amma's measurements now.' She turned to his mother. 'Are you ready, Ma?'

'Yes, of course.' Amma turned to look at him, one hand raised, and he stood and took her arm, helping her out of the chair.

'Thank you,' he said to Janani. 'I didn't know you sewed.'

'My periamma taught me,' she said, again. 'One of the ladies she cleaned for taught her.'

Thank God for useful aunts, he thought. 'I can't even sew a button on a shirt.'

Janani rolled her eyes. 'You're a man. You can't do anything useful.'

Amma laughed and Sanjay glowered at her, though he couldn't keep the smile from his lips.

They walked slowly back into the house, the newspaper rolled into a tight tube in Sanjay's hand. When they got to the living room, Amma called out, 'Etta? Janani is taking my measurements. Can we come into the bedroom?'

Sanjay saw Janani freeze, and edge towards the right, out of line of sight of the door. He pursed his lips, but then, his father inspired this reaction in most people.

His parents' bedroom door opened and Radhakrishnan emerged, dressed in cream trousers and a pale blue collared shirt so pressed it could have stood without a body to prop it up.

'Measurements? Why is she taking measurements?'

Amma made a *tch*-ing sound. 'The sari, Krishnan Etta, that Sanjay-kutty brought. Janani is stitching the blouse.'

Sanjay couldn't help sneaking a glance at Janani. He still remembered the Hindi lesson at school in which he'd learned that kutty, 'child' in Malayalam and in Tamil, sounded very similar to 'dog' in Hindi. He'd told Janani as soon as he'd come home. It had reduced her to tears of laughter and they'd spent the whole afternoon calling each other 'kutty' and collapsing in stomach-cramping giggles. He could see the slight curve in her lips now.

His father was still stuck on the measurements. Switching to English, he said, 'She's stitching the sari? Janani? You don't want to go to the tailor? She can take the measurements, but we can take the sari to him.'

Amma flapped a hand at him. 'Go and do your doctoring, you're no good at this. Janani, come.'

Acha's lips pursed. 'Give me the paper,' he said to Sanjay. 'I still have a bit of time before I need to leave.' Sanjay held it out. Taking it, Acha walked out to the drawing room, the smell of his aftershave wafting past them.

Sanjay loved his mother then so fiercely that it felt as though all the water in his body was boiling, as though it would froth from his mouth and steam from his ears. As Janani and Amma disappeared into the bedroom, Sanjay ran up the staircase, taking the second half two steps at a time.

'What's with the banging, Etta?' Vijay yelled from behind his closed door. 'You elephant!'

Sanjay ignored him, thumped into his own room next door. On the desk were the pile of papers, the job ads and immigration forms for countries that were a world, and a fantasy in his mind, away from Amma. He scooped them up, slid the recalcitrant ones across the faux-wood into his hands. An edge caught the side of his thumb, slicing a fine line through it in indignation at the rough handling. He barely noticed. He'd need to call Intel back. He'd need to tell them, sorry, but at this point in time he couldn't relocate to Bangalore.

He couldn't leave. Not now. Not yet.

The front door opened just as he had clattered back down the stairs. Panicking, he grabbed the nearest thing he could see – a copy of Acha's Indian Medical Association journal – and slapped it in front of the papers he held against his hip.

Sunshine silhouetted the figure who had just entered, but it was a familiar figure.

'Come and help with this thing, boy,' Priya yelled.

He scuttled down the hall towards her, past Acha, who was looking up from the newspaper in his lap. His aunt's arms were wrapped tightly around a bulky, boxy burden that curved in at strange angles, a large space in the middle of it. It glistened black as ink, floral patterns etched into it in gold.

'Don't look at it like that,' she said, thrusting it at him. 'It's a sewing machine, not a teleporter.'

'A sewing machine?' he asked. It was heavier than he was expecting, and awkward, crunching the papers he still held, its arm digging into his collarbone. 'Why?'

'Why?' she asked him. 'Because that girl has a witch of a mother-in-law and barely enough to feed her drunken husband and her little child, and her sewing machine is probably older than me.' She stroked the thing like it was a pet. 'This Singer is only a decade old, at most. I've used it about twice.'

'For which girl?' Acha said. He had stood and was walking towards Priya, arms stretched out as though to help, but Priya waved him away with a shake of the head.

'Janani, of course,' Priya said, rolling her kohl-lined eyes. 'What other girl do we have here?'

'What is this?' Radhakrishnan said. 'This is a good-value

Singer. You could sell it, Priya. What will the girl do with it? She might sell it herself.'

'And if she does,' Priya replied, 'she has more use of the money than me, Etta.'

She readjusted her dupatta and walked past them towards the living room. Acha mumbled unintelligibly and sank back into his chair, concealing himself behind the newspaper.

'All of these people I didn't know had sewing talents,' Sanjay muttered, following his aunt, trying not to look back at his father.

'No, no talent,' Priya said. 'Or patience. That's why I've only used this thing twice.'

Sanjay was examining the tapestry of Krishna above her head, feeling like he was seeing it for the first time. It was a blend of pale greens and dark blues, Krishna dancing with the village girls under the night sky, the scene picked out in glistening threads.

'Was that made on a sewing machine?' he asked.

Priya followed his gaze and snorted. 'Thank Bhagavan you're not a tailor or an artist. Put it over there.' She was pointing at a clear spot on the tiled floor beside the main couch.

He walked around the table.

'On the rug,' she said, 'not the tiles.'

He placed it as he'd been ordered and in the process dropped a sheaf of paper. Priya's eyes burned a hole into the back of his neck as he struggled to collect them.

'What are those?' she asked.

He shook his head, seized the last errant page, tucked the lot of them into the fold of the newspaper and stood up. 'Nothing,' he said.

His aunt was staring at the mess of forms, and it was clear she'd made out enough titles, headings, scrawled handwriting to understand. Acha had turned the CD player on, and they were alone, but still she lowered her voice as she asked, 'Your applications? What are you doing, moné?'

If there was anyone he could tell, it was her. 'Staying here is the right thing, Ammayi,' he said. 'Thinking about . . .' The words stuck somewhere between his chest and his throat. Instead, he gestured at the closed bedroom door.

There was sympathy on Priya's face. It wrenched at Sanjay's gut to see how much she looked like Amma. 'I know,' she said. 'And if it's the right thing for you, stay in Madurai. But, kutty, you can't stop living your life. Your amma doesn't want that.'

'Amma doesn't know everything,' Sanjay said.

'She knows enough.' Priya smiled. She turned her head away. Her black-and-silver braid brushed against the green cotton of her salwar. 'She knows enough.'

Sanjay found himself unable to think of anything to say. It struck him, every time he saw his mother, how frail she was. But how much harder must it be for her sister?

A sharp sound, half-gasp, half-cry, came from behind the closed door of his parents' bedroom. Then a domino clatter, and a thud.

'Help!' came a voice – Janani's. 'Someone come!'

Sanjay had already dropped the papers on the table and was halfway to the door. He wrenched it open to find his mother almost on her knees in front of Janani. Janani's arms were under Amma's shoulders. She was leaning back, pulling his mother towards her, trying to support her with her own body. His mother's head lolled back, eyelids flickering.

Sanjay leapt forward. 'Acha!' he yelled, but, of course, Radhakrishnan no longer had a young man's hearing. He put his shoulder under his mother's body and wrapped his arms around her, easing the weight from Janani. 'Get Acha,' he said over his shoulder to Priya Ammayi, but she had already gone and a second later he could hear her calling.

'I don't know what happened,' Janani said.

He gently detangled her arms and picked Amma up. She was light as a child. Her bones felt like twigs against his fingers. Carefully, he lowered her to the bed.

'It's OK,' he said. 'She's a bit weak. That's all.'

Footsteps sounded at the door. 'What happened?' his father said.

Sanjay stepped backwards to the foot of the bed, clearing the approach. He leaned against the carved mahogany bedpost, breathing in the scent of old wood.

'Janani was taking her measurements. She fainted.'

Janani nodded, understanding the Malayalam. Her smooth face was twisted, her bottom lip caught between her teeth.

The look Acha shot at Janani was inscrutable. Not friendly, not hostile. To Sanjay, he said, 'Bring my medical bag – it is in the front room, by the brown sofa. Then you can go. Give Amma some space.'

'I will stay,' Priya said.

Acha looked at her and said nothing.

Sanjay and Janani left the room, just as Vijay came thundering down the steps. He took one look at them and darted into their parents' bedroom. Sanjay strode to the drawing room and picked up his father's faux-leather medical bag. When he returned to the bedroom, Radhakrishnan had one of his wife's hands in his and was smoothing back a tendril of silver hair. Priya sat on the side of the bed, two fingers on her wrist. It looked like a frozen scene from a Malayalam drama.

Sanjay set the bag down on the floor beside his father, waited for the nod of acknowledgement, and left silently, towing Vijay along behind him.

He hated himself then. He should have done medicine. He could have helped.

Outside his parents' bedroom, he noticed how much brighter the house had become, the morning sun hanging well over the horizon and flooding through the windows. It glinted off the frame of the huge family photo on the front wall of the living room. The yellow light, the deep red of the rug, the shimmering lapis lazuli and jade and mother-of-pearl in the marble table all seemed too cheerful for his mood. Janani was lingering by the marble table, waiting for them.

'We'll leave them for a while,' Sanjay said. 'He doesn't seem too worried.' He forced a smile. 'He knows what he's doing.'

'I'll go and make breakfast,' Janani said, quietly. 'You two come and eat.' She left, tinkling bell notes trailing behind her.

A quarter of an hour that felt like an eternity passed before his father and aunt emerged. Sanjay and Vijay sat together on the couch. They hadn't spoken – Sanjay was glad his brother was feeling as uncommunicative as he was.

'Low blood pressure,' Radhakrishnan said. 'It's normal enough with the treatment, the medication.' He sat, elbows on knees, and put his head in his hands as though he himself felt faint.

'But she's OK?' Sanjay and Vijay said in chorus.

Their father looked up. 'Yes, yes. She regained consciousness. No, don't,' he said as Sanjay stood so quickly he felt something click in his lower back. 'She's sleeping. Leave her for a little while. Let her rest.'

They sat in silence. From the kitchen came the sound of fresh batter sizzling on the dosa pan and the smell of warming sambar.

Radhakrishnan huffed a short sigh and levered himself to his feet.

'I'll go and call her doctor and let him know what happened.'

He disappeared down the hall. They listened to him pick up the receiver, then to his murmured, inaudible words to the breast cancer specialist at Government Rajaji Hospital.

'Come, boys,' Priya said. 'Let's go and have some breakfast. Poor Janani is cooking there all alone.'

'Will he tell her, do you think?' Sanjay asked. 'Ever? I hate this lying. I hate it.'

'I know,' Priya said. 'But what good would it do, for her to know?' She was frowning, but it was not an irate frown. It was worried, uncertain. 'Your acha thinks the knowledge might make her worse. Let's trust him.' She shook her head and stood. 'Come. Let's eat.'

Vijay took his food back up to his bedroom. Priya and Sanjay sat at the table and thanked Janani as she brought them steaming fresh dosa and more coffee. Silence reigned, Sanjay lost in his own thoughts. If his aunt spoke, he didn't notice.

Radhakrishnan appeared ten minutes later.

'It's as I said,' he told them. 'This is to be expected.' To Janani, he said, 'I'll eat in the room.'

He took the plate of dosa, chutney and sambar from her and disappeared without another word.

Sanjay barely noticed when Priya drew his empty plate away from him. 'Go and wash your hands,' she said. 'Let's tell this girl about her new sewing machine.' She jerked her head in the direction of the kitchen. 'You're going to have to help her take it home. I don't want her carrying it in an auto, it's too heavy.'

They had been driving for five full minutes. A. R. Rahman's soothing voice was straining from the radio, for which Sanjay was thankful, because otherwise there would have been silence. Janani hadn't said more than a few words since Priya had showed her the old Singer. She had knelt on the ground beside it, run her fingers over it, stroked the handle. When Priya had told her it was hers, she'd looked up as if she hadn't understood the words.

Now, Sanjay chanced a quick glance in her direction. Between them sat the Madras Silks bag, the peacock blue of the sari silk just visible through the yellow plastic. Janani held the sewing machine on her lap. She was examining it, tracing the golden lotus pattern in the black wood.

'Is it OK?' he asked. A sudden thought struck him – what if her own machine was better than this one? He imagined Janani's disappointment, embarrassment – anger even – at being given this piece of rubbish.

'It's perfect,' she said.

From the corner of his eye, he saw her head move, and he looked at her fully, properly, just for a second, long enough to see her smile. The dimple he remembered was sunk deep into one cheek, her white teeth gleaming. He turned away.

'I'm glad. I know nothing about sewing machines.'

'I can't keep it at home, Sanjay Annan,' she said. She must have read something into his silence, because she added, 'I love it, I'll treasure it. But there's no room at home. If Mamiyar sees it, she'll wonder where it came from. She might forbid me from sewing. At home, she wants me to focus on chores. On Darshan. She can be . . . demanding, that way.'

Demanding, Sanjay thought. She wasn't demanding. She was an evil bitch of a woman, scarred and twisted. And Darshan. The husband. A portrait of him was sketching itself out in Sanjay's mind from the little Janani had said – a lazy waste of a man, probably middle-aged and hairy, overweight, with half-missing yellow teeth. But it made him feel worse, to think of Janani living with that.

'Where, then?' he asked. 'I mean, you could keep it at our house, do your sewing there . . .'

'No,' she said. 'I wouldn't have enough time, with everything else. And I can't stay longer. It would be more time away from Lavanika.' Her head was down, she was frowning at the machine. 'I have a friend. The one who . . . The one I spoke to you about.' She glanced at him then away. 'I'll leave it with her.'

There was more silence as they slipped onto the highway and rattled down it, windows closed against the dust and the roar of the granite lorries and petroleum tankers passing them.

'Tell Priya Amma thank you, again,' she said. 'I'll have the blouse finished for tomorrow.'

'Amma doesn't need it until next week,' Sanjay said. 'You'll need to work very hard to finish it by tomorrow, won't you? And you've already worked so hard today.'

Janani laughed.

'Just a couple of hours,' she said. 'I enjoy it. And I want to make sure there's time if I need to make any adjustments. Parvati Amma gave me fifty rupees.' There was wonder in her voice. 'Fifty! I told her it was too much, but she insisted. That it was as much as she'd pay Sendil Annan, the tailor.'

'Good,' Sanjay said. 'You deserve it.'

'I've never sewn anything for her before,' Janani said. She sounded hesitant. 'I'll do my best, but if it's not very good, I'll give her back the money.'

'Don't say that,' Sanjay said. 'It will be excellent.' He felt like he was encouraging the junior draughtsman he'd been asked to mentor at work.

From the corner of his eye, he saw her flash a smile at him. Her fingers, he noticed, were threading and unthreading themselves in her lap.

A.R. Rahman turned into Sujatha Mohan in the silence that followed, the singer's sweet, pure voice drawing attention to it.

'And you?' Janani said finally. 'What will you do today?'

Sanjay was surprised, and pleased, that she'd asked. 'I'll try to see some friends,' he answered. 'And . . . well. There are some job applications I am looking at.'

'Job applications,' she said slowly. 'You're looking for a new job?' When he nodded, she asked, 'Is there something wrong with your job?'

'No, no,' he replied. 'I'm just looking at what else might be there. Something more challenging, interesting.' He hesitated. 'In other places.'

'Other places?' Janani said. 'Not Madras?'

'No,' he said. 'Bangalore, or Delhi. Maybe Bombay. Maybe somewhere else.'

She was quiet. 'You're leaving again?'

'No,' he replied, wishing he hadn't said anything. The music had become mournful and he was starting to feel tight and uncomfortable. 'I'm just looking. Nothing is settled.'

'Your amma is very sick, I think,' Janani said. 'She would be sad if you left. But then,' he saw from the corner of his eye that she'd turned to look out the window, gazing up at the sky as though it would provide her with an answer, 'Radhakrishnan Aiyan is a doctor, and Vijay Annan will be one soon, too.'

'I know.' He looked at her, then back at the road. It curved away before them into the dusty distance. There was a lorry coming towards them. A sign at the front read: *Caution! Inflammable*. 'I'm looking in Madurai, too.'

He saw her head jerk towards him. Then she said, 'Here. Left here.'

As he turned off the highway, Janani lifted the pallu of her sari and draped it over her head.

'It would be easier if they don't see me with you,' she said. 'There will be a lot of questions. That's my house, there,' she added, turning away from the window, gesturing discreetly.

He glanced at it, saw the pale blue-washed building, saw the clothes flapping on the line. The coconut palms.

'Keep going,' she said.

He stayed in the middle of the road. The traffic was mainly scooters and bicycles that navigated around them – only once did he have to tuck into the side of the street, startling a sleek black crow and a stray, pale-furred dog with a chunk of flesh and hair taken out of one leg.

'Just up there,' she said, pointing out a house larger than her own, on the right side of the street. It stood at a fork where the road split into two, doubling the rows of houses.

Sanjay cut across the street and pulled up beside the house, leaving the engine rumbling and the air conditioning blasting into their faces.

'Let me come with you, I can carry it for you,' he said.

When there was no response, he looked over at Janani. She was staring directly ahead. There was no sign she'd heard him.

Sanjay followed her gaze.

The road sloped upward, lined by tightly packed houses, unbroken by greenery. It seemed to then drop off. A group of men were clustered around a house at the top of the slight hill. They were shouting. Fists were being thrust into the air, fingers pointed, all the anger directed at a frail figure standing by the side of the door. He was shocked to see it seemed to be an old woman, the sun glinting off her grey hair. She was standing still, her face calm.

'What's going on?' he asked. 'What are they doing?'

Janani shook her head and looked over at him as though she'd just remembered he was there.

'You should go,' she said. 'Those men shouldn't see you.'

She opened the door. As soon as it cracked ajar, the sound of raised voices filtered through. *Witch,* Sanjay heard, and *thief, lying thief.* Ahead, he could make out a couple of men emerging from the tiny house, pushing past the old woman, and hurling items into the street. They looked like clay jars and small bags. Some of the men jumped backwards. The jars had broken, their contents spilling onto the ground.

'Are you sure you should get out now?' he asked, wary, worried. 'There seems to be a lot of trouble up there.'

Janani shook her head. 'It's poor Kamala Amma,' she said. 'The midwife. Sometimes this happens, if something goes wrong with the birth. Or when . . . when she refuses to take care of something. When a girl child comes.'

Sanjay looked at Janani, aware his mouth was hanging open.

She swung her legs out of the car, the sari bag hanging from the crook of one elbow, her arms wrapped around the sewing machine. 'They're leaving her,' she said. 'I'll get Shubha, we'll go and help her. She'll be OK.'

Sure enough, the men appeared to be backing slightly away, still shouting and gesturing. Slowly they began to turn.

There was a tinkle – Janani had hopped from the car, unbalanced slightly by the weight of the machine. 'Go quickly, Sanjay Annan,' she said, eyes wide, intent, and he heard the note of urgency in her voice. 'They'll come this way. Go. And thank you.' The door slammed closed.

He lost sight of her as she rounded the back of the car. A moment later, she was at the door of the house, knocking. Sanjay lifted the handbrake and began to edge forward, away from the kerb, eyes still on Janani. The door opened, and a delighted smile lit her face. As she stepped inside, she turned back to him and that smile fell on him. She made a quick shooing motion with her hand. He watched until the door closed behind her.

As he turned the car back the way he'd come, he glanced back up the road. The men were walking towards him, but their attention was glued to each other, hands on each other's shoulders, lips moving furiously.

Behind them, the old woman was moving amongst her possessions, scattered in the dust. She straightened slowly, and Sanjay's eyes brushed hers just as he completed the turn. She was older than his mother. Much older.

The engine thrummed as he stepped on the accelerator and left the scene in the dust, taking his anger and shame and relief with him.

Chapter Twelve

Madurai, 1993

The end of the fourth month

There are nails on her tiny fingers and toes. Her teeth and bones are strengthening. She is the size of a mango.

'I told Devika and Geetha about your sewing,' Shubha said. She was grating coconut, the sound almost as loud as the *click-click-click* of the sewing machine. 'They'll come to you too.'

Janani looked up. She was finishing a pattu pavadai blouse, in bright pink cotton, the sleeves edged in gold, for a girl one class above Lavanika. The sewing machine sat quiet. This was a job for her fingers, the needle threading its way through the hooks that would hold the blouse closed at the back.

'Thank you,' she said. She already had three pieces of work this week. Parvati Amma, delighted with her sari blouse, had begun to tell her neighbours about Janani's tailoring. Already she had added a sizeable amount to the little bag nestled into her oldest saris. The hours she spent here, sewing and keeping Shubha's company, she told Vandhana were longer hours scrubbing floors and cooking for the Nambeesans. She handed over a small portion of additional money, and Vandhana kept her mouth quiet.

Shubha smiled, or at least, her lips flickered briefly. The grating sound became sharper. She inspected the inside of the coconut, adjusted it on the blade, and continued scraping.

Silence fell again. They had the house to themselves – Narendran was still working, Shubha's father-in-law was smoking and drinking coffee with his friends, and her mother-in-law was dozing in the shade of the fig tree outside, where Lavanika, Nandita and little Raman were playing. It was like this most days, when Janani slipped into Shubha's house after a day at the Nambeesans' and retrieved the sewing machine from where it sat, snug and out of the way, in a corner of the room beneath a wall calendar that showed a peaceful Saraswati sitting on a lotus blossom.

They were halfway through Vaikaasi – at the end of June. It had felt like a long month. The next days promised more heat, heat that wrapped itself around everything it touched, clung tight like a separate body, inescapable.

'How are you feeling, Shubha?' Janani asked.

'Well,' Shubha said. 'I'm well.'

Screech, screech, screech of the coconut on the blade. Then silence, broken by a barely audible, shaky breath.

Janani looked up to see the coconut dropped onto the white mound of shaven flakes and Shubha's head in her hands. Her shoulders were shaking.

Abandoning the blouse, Janani scrambled to her feet and took the few steps across the room. She knelt by Shubha's stool and wrapped her arms around the trembling body, squeezing her as the sobs came harder.

'Don't cry,' she said. 'Don't cry. Your tears will land in the coconut and then your thengai sadam will be too salty.'

A watery laugh emerged from the cavern Shubha had created with her hunched body. After a moment, she raised her head. Droplets dripped from her chin, darkening the rice-blade green of her sari.

'What kind of mother am I,' she said quietly, 'to give my baby away?'

'Oh, Shubha,' Janani said. Reaching up, she wiped her friend's tears away. It wrenched at her, to see this rounded, happy face so sad, the long dark lashes glued together with tears. And those words. If she was a mother that gave her baby away, what was Janani, a mother who let her babies be killed? 'It was for the best. Think, she can have a happy life, with people who have the money to send her to school, maybe even to college, and find her a happy marriage.' Guilt, grief, burned through her, but she ignored it, focused all her energy on the lies.

'I know what they say about me in the street,' Shubha said. 'She was mine. My burden. And I passed that on to others.'

Janani shifted her hands to Shubha's shoulders and shook her, once, gently. 'To hell with them,' she said. Those stupid, big-mouthed, small-brained gossips in the street, acting as if their knowledge was divine. 'It was your responsibility to give her a chance of a life. What life would she have here? Our life? Could you give her more than that?' And even though she believed it, part of her screamed that that life was enough, that they would have found the specks of happiness, like scattered gold dust, in their lives, Shubha and her baby, she and her girls. Her poor, perfect girls.

Shubha gazed around her, eyes wide, as if searching for an answer on the low, hard sleeping cot, in the cracks in the ceiling, the pink-painted mud-brick walls, the rattling fan. Then her face crumpled, and Janani felt like a murderer. She shuffled forward on her knees and curled her arms around Shubha's back. Her friend's head nestled on her shoulder. Fresh tears soaked into Janani's sari blouse.

'You did your best, my love,' she said quietly, stroking Shubha's hair. 'It will feel a little better every morning.' *Better* didn't mean *healed*. But the pain would ease enough to breathe through.

'Maybe,' Shubha said. Her fingers gripped Janani's left arm like it was a rope thrown to save her from the bottom of a well. 'If God wills it. Maybe.'

The next day, Janani jumped from the bus at Usilampatti, her hands sore from kneading chapatti dough. The Nambeesans were hosting a puja at their nearby Ayappa temple, and they were feeding the priests. She had assisted Priya Amma and the few other chefs-for-hire to prepare a vat of sambar, mounds of rice, more chapattis than she could count, heaps of delicious-smelling thayir sadam. Parvati Amma had tried to help, but after she'd staggered into a pile of steel plates, sending them crashing to the tiles, Priya Amma had pulled a chair from the dining table, positioned it at the entrance to the kitchen and steered her sister into it.

'Direct from there,' she'd said.

Just as Janani had washed her hands and collected her fraying bag to leave, Priya, that wonderful woman, had stopped her. By that time, Radhakrishnan Aiyan had returned home, earlier than usual, to prepare for the puja. Janani had been achingly aware of his glare on them as Priya scooped food into containers, stacked them together inside a Bharati Stores bag and handed them to her to take home.

'You're giving away the sadhya?' Radhakrishnan had said. 'Do we have enough?'

'Stop it, Krishnan Etta,' Priya Ma had replied. 'Those pujaris all eat too much anyway.'

It was the end of a day that could only have been better if Sanjay had been there, but he was at work in Madras, wouldn't return until late this evening. More and more she couldn't help but think, as she washed and swept and cooked, about Sanjay going about his other life in Madras. Did he have friends? she wondered. Was there a woman in Madras that he might one day marry? The thought grabbed at her chest, clutched at her breath. It was a new pain.

She pushed it from her exhausted mind. She didn't have time to consider it. There was still work to be done – she'd promised Tharani she would have her sari blouse for her in the morning, and she was almost finished with it. Rather than walking, she took an auto to the school.

The remaining children were playing under the neem tree outside the school building. It seemed a game with a logic all its own, a dancing, shouting, dodging game. A few of the older children stood more sedately in a huddle in a corner, the girls' plaits still neat and tidy. Lavanika's hair, when Janani spotted her, looked as though an egret had been walking over her head, turning her curls into a chaotic nest.

'Amma!' Lavanika shouted, sprinting towards her. Her school bag was nowhere to be seen and there was a rip in the hem of her school tunic.

'Hello, little apple,' Janani said, and stumbled backwards as the dusty, warm little body ploughed into her. 'Ready to go? We just need to go to Shubha Attai's house for a little while. You can play with Nandita there.'

'Nandita's here!' Lavanika said, pointing. 'Raman, too.'

Janani looked past her. Nandita was easy to spot – she'd broken off from the group and was waving at them. Raman was a little distance away, sitting on the ground, rolling a little car back and forth across the dirt.

'Hasn't Shubha Attai come to collect them?' Janani asked. Of course not, she thought, she would have taken Lavanika too.

'No, Amma,' Lavanika said.

Janani stroked her daughter's wild hair. 'Go and get your

school bag. And where's your pottu?' she asked as she gestured for Nandita and Raman. She'd take them back to their home, and hopefully find Shubha on the way.

Shubha had said nothing about not collecting her children. She was carrying Raman now as well as her bag, each of them dragging at a shoulder. The streets were busy, children returned from school playing ball and cricket and anchangal, men sipping coffee and gossiping, women grinding rice and shouting gossip at each other from doorstep to doorstep. Twice, Janani had to stop to put Raman down. The second time, the girls came skipping back and took Raman's hands, toddling him between them.

When they reached Shubha's house, the sun was beginning to fade and the dusk hummed with the sound of mosquitos. The house itself looked lifeless, the door closed, the windows already shuttered.

'Tatti and Tatta have gone to Maamaa's house for a few days,' Nandita told her when Janani asked. 'Appa's probably still at work.' She picked Raman up and joggled him up and down on her non-existent hip.

So where was Shubha?

As they were nearing the front door, Janani was aware of someone else approaching from the other direction. She looked up to see Kamala coming towards her. Concern stabbed through her, and dread at the thought of another attack. The memory of the poor old woman's house, ripped apart by Rani's angry husband because she wouldn't get rid of their new daughter, was something Janani thought she would never forget. It had taken her and Shubha a couple of hours to set it to rights. Rani had come past at the end, and cried with remorse.

'Is everything all right, Kamala Amma?' Janani asked now.

The old woman was surprisingly empty-handed, no sign of her midwife's bag, no rice from the government store, no herbs or rags or coconut leaves.

'With me, everything's fine,' she said. 'I came to see Shubhangi. Something felt . . .' she looked at the children. 'Strange,' she finished.

Janani stared at her, then looked at the house. She put her bag down on the ground. 'Can you watch the children, ma?' Without waiting for an answer, she said to the girls, 'Stay here with Kamala Amma, all of you.'

Janani left the door open to let the last of the day's sun into the house. The light of the single electric bulb in the main room buzzed and flickered as she switched it on. It revealed neat, quiet emptiness. The kitchen was clean, as though it had been untouched since morning.

'Shubha?' she called.

No answer, just the spitting sound of poorly flowing electricity.

Perhaps she wasn't feeling well. A headache, or the stomach cramps she sometimes suffered, forcing her to lie down for a while, to sleep. Perhaps she had gone out, and was on her way now for the children, taking some new path, passing by a friend.

Janani made her way towards the partly ajar bedroom door and pushed it open.

She was aware of the black, shapeless mass before she saw it. Perhaps she was even aware of what it was because she ran towards it before her mind could form words.

Up close, Shubha's face was turning purple above the thick rope cutting into her neck. Her head rested at a strange angle from her body, as though she had fallen asleep on the noose.

Sounds were coming out of Janani's mouth. They didn't make sense to her. Her legs moved before she could think, grasping at Shubha's legs, her arms tangled and sliding in Shubha's sari. It was the purple sari, the one with pink flowers dotted through it. Janani had always loved it. It made Shubha's dark skin glow.

She lifted with all her might, trying to slacken the rope. Her legs bashed against the edge of the low bed frame and, cursing herself for an idiot, she forced herself up on it, just as Shubha must have done in the minutes before she stepped off to suspend herself from the ceiling beam.

It felt like hours, that she stood there, crying, babbling, her heart pounding through her chest against Shubha's back, but it could only have been seconds before she caught a flash of Kamala's face at the door, drawn with horror, and then others, men Janani barely recognised through the salty liquid blinding her, through eyes screwed up as she wailed, burst in. They were on the bed too, Shubha's weight was taken from her, and knives sewed at the thick coir rope.

Janani fell to her knees on the thin mattress. She watched droplets fall from her face onto the mattress until she heard Kamala's voice calling her, from far away. It was something to do next, somewhere to go, so she crawled off the bed and stumbled out of the room, leaving the smell of the incense burning at Vishnu's feet on the old chest of drawers in the corner.

Kamala met her in the doorway. Almost before Janani could register her, her spindly arms were around her.

'The children are outside,' Kamala whispered. 'I've called an auto, it's waiting. We need to get her to the hospital, child.'

The hospital? Beside the dark, heavy mass clouding Janani's mind, something else flickered.

'Wipe your face, quickly,' Kamala said, and to suit her words, she pulled away, took her pallu and mopped at Janani's cheeks and eyes as though she were a muck-faced child. 'Go and hold the children until Kannan and Prabhu have carried her out, and then the three of you go to the hospital.'

Kannan and Prabhu – that was who was inside. Of course. But they were neighbours, not family. Where was Shubha's family?

'Narendran,' Janani managed to gasp.

'I'll tell him,' Kamala said. 'I'll take the children to your home. Now go.'

It was still light enough to sting Janani's salt-burned eyes as she staggered outside. The girls were playing some clapping game, Raman standing by them and clapping his own hands at random, a huge, almost-toothless grin on his plump little face. Janani bit her tongue so hard she tasted blood, rubbing furiously at her eyes. Bending, she felt inside her bag for the still-warm containers of food. The smell made her nauseous. 'Come here, children,' she called.

They turned and she knew her face was saying too much because their smiles faded almost immediately.

Lavanika ran to her first. 'What's wrong, Amma?' she asked. 'We heard noises . . .'

'Come this way, all of you,' she said, as Nandita walked towards them, Raman back on her hip. She led them around the corner of the house and squatted down, pulling them all close, her arms wrapped around three pairs of tiny-boned shoulders. 'Your amma has had an accident,' she told Nandita. The little girl's eyes widened. 'We are going to take her to the hospital.'

Sounds came from the front of the house, footsteps and lowered voices. As Nandita turned to look, Janani put a hand to her cheek and gently forced her head back around.

'Listen to me,' she said. 'I'm going with Amma to the hospital. Kamala Amma will take you all to our house. Lavanika's patti will look after you for a while, until your appa comes home, OK?'

'What happened to Amma?' Nandita asked. She was clinging to Raman as though he were her favourite doll, crushing him into her chest. The tranquil little boy seemed happy enough, playing with the string bracelet tied around his sister's wrist.

'Just an accident, my love,' Janani said.

A figure loomed behind the children and Janani had to suppress a cry, but it was Kamala, just Kamala.

'They're ready,' the old midwife said. 'Go.'

'Amma!' Lavanika said, clutching at Janani's hands. 'I want to go with you!' The beginning of tears glittered in her eyes, and Nandita looked as upset – they could feel it, Janani knew, the tension of fear and horror that emanated from her, from Kamala, that drifted out of Shubha's front door like a black cloud. Raman had sensed it too. He was beginning to squirm in Nandita's arms, his features scrunching together.

'I need you to go with Kamala Amma. Take this,' she handed Lavanika the bag of food containers, 'and take Nandita and Raman home, OK? I'll be back soon.'

Without waiting for an answer, she kissed the two girls, patted Raman's bobbing head, and left them.

Hours later, Janani was exhausted now. The chair she sat on in the Intensive Care Unit was uncomfortably hard and wobbled every time she shifted. And yet, she might have slept, but for the flickering fluorescent lights against the windows framing the night sky that pried open her eyelids. Her head was starting to pound. Her stomach had ached with hunger some time ago, but that had faded to an emptiness beneath her ribs.

The world felt like a bleak, bright nightmare. It had done from the moment she had seen that dark hanging mass. It had continued through the jolting, tense auto ride, Shubha's body lying across her lap and Kannan's, her legs trailing on the floor, the rickshaw driver's hands bloodless on the steering wheel. It had swelled as they reached the emergency room and doctors and nurses flooded around them, pulling Shubha from their arms. Janani had followed them, refusing to leave, waving a brusque farewell to Kannan and Prabhu. Now she sat on her own, a plastic cup of water warming in one hand. She wished Sanjay was here. She wished it so badly she ached, so badly that she didn't question why.

'Janani.'

Sanjay.

Her head jerked up. Her sight resolved itself as she blinked in the harsh light.

Not Sanjay. It was Narendran. His drawn, tired face looked down at her.

She burst into tears.

She cried as though her body were trying to expel some poison.

She didn't see Narendran squat down before her but felt his hands on her shoulders. His face swam in and out of focus through her tears.

'It's OK,' he said, although of course it was not OK. 'She will be OK,' he soothed, although how could she be? And yet still Janani clung to his words, her hands gripping his forearms.

They stayed together like that, leaning into each other in a way that was very improper, grasping each other like logs in the flooding Vaigai, like the monsoon rains were washing them away. Finally Janani ran dry of tears. She rubbed her hot, puffed face with her pallu. Her eyes stung, her temples throbbing.

'Go home, ma,' Narendran said. 'Amma and Appa have come home. They are with Nandita and Raman. Go home to your Lavi. Here,' he fumbled in the pocket of his trousers, creased and crumpled from a too-long day. Rupee coins shone dully in the white light. 'Come. I'll find you an auto. It's very late.'

She stood without realising it, and followed him blindly down the corridor. Her feet trudged after his. Everything seemed too bright, too loud – doctors rapping out instructions to nurses, worried relatives barking at anyone in a uniform, children crying. It felt like she was looking into the inside of her own mind.

Then they were outside, thank Bhagavan, and the light was no longer piercing through her skull. The night was thick with heat, but it smelled of dirt and trees and fumes, washing away the sharp stench of antiseptic. Narendran had left her on the side of the road. She looked around, suddenly terrified, and saw him flagging down an auto.

'Come, Janani,' he said. He barked directions to the auto driver, who gave Janani a curious look and waved his head in acknowledgement.

Janani hesitated. She was afraid to get in, dreading the sight of a darkened mass lying across the seat. Holding her breath, gritting her teeth so hard her jaw hurt, she climbed in. There was nothing, just the warm plastic of the seat, traces of the scent of vadai. Her stomach growled, surprising her.

Narendran handed over a few coins. 'She will be OK, ma,' he said. 'Thank you for staying with her.'

He stepped away, and the auto rattled off into the night.

The journey home was too short, and too long. The glow of warm yellow light leaking through the shutters told Janani not everyone was asleep. The thought of facing Vandhana made her stomach twist. Everything felt dry as straw – her skin, her tongue, her eyes.

'Just here, Annan,' she said as the auto drew closer to the house.

The driver pulled to a trembling stop by the door. Janani eased herself out, muscles tight now from sitting in the hard plastic hospital chair.

The front door was unlocked.

She eased it open, and it creaked its usual, discontent song.

Vandhana started up from the pallet in the corner. Her movements woke Lavanika, curled up beside her.

Both of them stared at her. She gazed back.

'Amma!' Lavanika cried. She struggled up, stepped on the hem of her nightdress and almost tripped. She ran to throw her arms around Janani's waist, burrowing her head into her sari.

Janani bent, rested her cheek on the soft little head, and breathed in the dusty sandalwood scent of Lavanika's hair.

Vandhana was sitting up, squinting, bleary-eyed.

'Finally you have come back,' she said. 'See, Lavanika? Now go back to your own bed, child. Don't wake Appa.'

'Amma, will you come?' Lavanika asked, pulling away to look at her, and Janani kissed her cheeks and then her forehead.

'I'll come in a minute, Lavi,' she said.

Her eyes already drooping, Lavanika shuffled towards the bedroom door.

Janani looked at Vandhana. Her mother-in-law regarded her, expressionless.

'How is she?' Vandhana asked.

Silence. Janani's throat felt too tight to speak.

'Alive,' she said. 'For now.' Her eyes tried to weep, but the well was dry now.

Vandhana nodded. 'A bad time,' she said. 'Have a shower, and some food.' She pointed to where a plate sat, another covering it. 'I heated it when Narendran came to take the children home. Then turn off the light and go to sleep. You have work in the morning.'

She lay back down with a muffled groan.

Janani stood still, as though her body had forgotten how to move, feeling as though she were dreaming. She looked at the plates. Stepping quietly forward, she lifted the upturned one.

The steel rim framed thayir sadham and vegetables and sambar and pappadum. She didn't have any more tears, but the simple, unexpected, impossible kindness tried to wring some from her anyway. Her stomach writhed. She replaced the cover.

Quietly, she crept into her bedroom and retrieved her night-dress, her towel and the lamp.

Outside, she poured the rest of the water into the bucket. Slowly, she undressed, leaving her sari, her petticoat, her blouse in an untidy pile on the bathroom floor. She had enough saris to never wear this one again.

She scooped the water onto her head. It trickled down her body, from hair to feet, and she felt it rinse away the dust, the tears, the touch of dying flesh.

At dawn, Janani slipped from the house, Darshan's snores covering any sound she might make.

She took the water jugs, but when she stepped onto the road, she found her feet taking her in the other direction, away from the water pumps, up the street, past Shubha's quiet house and further.

Kamala was sitting outside, on her front step, grinding something in a small stone mortar on the ground between her legs, her brilliant green sari rucked up out of the way. As Janani drew closer, she smelled the fragrance of crushed cardamom.

'Why did she do it?' she asked, of herself, of Kamala, of the spirits in the air. Why did she do it, as though Janani didn't know, as though she hadn't thought of it herself, some days.

Kamala was quiet for a moment longer.

'Sometimes the pain becomes too much to bear,' she said eventually. 'And some people feel it much more strongly than others. The burdens of their lives feel heavier.'

'I should have done more,' Janani said. It was the first time she'd spoken the words out loud, and now that they were hanging in the air, she realised how so much of what had been sitting on her shoulders, heavy as a calf, was that thought. She should have noticed, listened, seen, understood, *known*. She should have done more. She should have stopped it.

But almost before she had spoken, Kamala was shaking her head. 'How could you have done more?' she said. 'You are not her. It was her fight, not yours. You were friend and sister enough to be there.'

Another moment of silence as a gang of boys came tearing down the street, shouting with laughter. Janani recognised a few of them – kabaddi players, heading to the courts for an early practice, she suspected.

'My sister died,' Kamala said, and the boys vanished from Janani's mind. 'When I was a girl. She had already had her first child, a strong little boy. But her husband beat her, very badly, even after his son came. Every day. Her dowry was not enough, he said, and that our father had promised him more. When he broke her arm, our father gave him another five hundred rupees, which he had been saving for my dowry. But the beatings continued. I know that Ramani knew they would always continue, that he would keep asking for money and beat her anyway. He was an evil, drunken monster. So my sister walked into the river one day, during the rains.'

Janani watched Kamala, barely breathing. The old woman's pale, beautiful eyes stared into the distance, looking at something a long time ago.

'I feel like I always knew,' Kamala continued. 'I could sense it on her, a sadness – or maybe it was my sadness, that I wouldn't have as much time with her as either of us would have wanted.'

We never do, with our sisters, Janani thought, they get married and then they're gone. But this was different. Final. She wanted to reach out, lay a hand on Kamala's shoulder, but it didn't seem enough.

The old woman looked up from the cardamom, the dust of which was rising in unseen particles, flavouring the air. She laughed, a short bark of a laugh. 'I swore then that I would never marry. I ignored my amma and appa. I worked hard, for myself, for them. Not living a slave to a man and his family. Beaten every day. Raising his boys. Killing his girls.' She was silent for a moment. 'I chose a life that's lonely, sometimes, and hard. But it's my life.'

The strength that must take. Janani examined the patterns in the dirt around her feet, sick with shame at herself. She was that woman, the woman with no choice, pushed here and there by everyone else's desires. What a stupid fool Kamala must think she was.

She felt a hand on her shoulder.

'We women have hard lives,' Kamala said. 'But let's start making our own fate, hmm?'

The hand fell away, and Janani listened to the sound of stone grinding on stone in the early morning, crushing the pods into perfume.

Chapter Thirteen

The fifth month

*The skin on her fingertips swirl into prints. She begins
to move her limbs. Her mother feels her flutter.*

'You need to find a new place for your work,' Sanjay said. *And to
live*, he thought, but did not say.

They were strolling through the vegetable market between
aisles of fruit and vegetables. Strolling because, even at this
hour, the place was full of keen-eyed shoppers whose weekly excitement was snatching up the produce. Lavanika skipped along
ahead of them. The space and the pace gave them time. Time
for Sanjay to listen, speechless, as Janani told him of her friend's
near-death. It was the first time she'd spoken of it, though it
had happened weeks ago. He'd known something was wrong,
known by her forced smiles, by how much longer it took her
to relax into their conversations. When she finally told him,
she'd spoken in a monotone soft enough that he had to strain
to hear. Sometimes he thought he'd lost her words completely,
until he realised that she was halting, hesitating, to choke down
tears. He wished he could have reached out, put a hand on
her arm.

'Lavanika, wait!' Janani stopped in front of a huge pile of

green beans. Bending down, she began to sort through them, selecting some, discarding others. Sanjay was sure there was a method, but every bean looked the same to him. The vendor sat half-hidden behind the pile, watching them – an old man with a cloud-like swirl of grey hair, a smile beneath his equally grey moustache, legs wrapped in his lunghi and tucked beneath him. He leaned over and held out a steel bowl to Janani, who threw her handfuls of beans in, then placed the bowl on a scale beside him.

'Ten rupees, ma,' he said.

Sanjay watched her eyes narrow, her nose wrinkle. 'Eight is enough, Aiyan.'

The old man smiled, shook his head shoulder to shoulder. 'OK, OK.'

She handed over the coins and they moved on. Lavanika had returned for long enough to see the transaction complete, fidgeting with her faded, daisy-printed dress – she was off again as soon as they turned from the bean vendor, humming to herself, curls bouncing and anklets tinkling with every movement. It struck him then, how much she reminded him of Janani at that age, of the little girl he'd played hide-and-seek with so many years ago.

'I know,' Janani said quietly and Sanjay was startled back into their conversation. 'I'm saving. I'm sewing most days now. The women in the village mostly come to me – tightening and loosening blouses, stitching new blouses, skirts, everything.' She looked at him, and must have seen the blankness in his face, because she laughed. 'Usual tailoring work. Mamiyar knows I'm doing a little, so I have to give her some extra money, but I keep enough.' She paused. 'I'll have enough. Perhaps Shubha can come and work with me, when it's time. It'll spare her from the rice fields.'

They circled around a family with a mass of children, all exclaiming over a mango seller's wares. He was slicing up pieces of mango for them to try. They found Lavanika on the other side of the group, craning her head to glimpse the vivid, fragrant fruit.

'We'll go back there, Lavi,' Janani said. 'There are too many people now.'

'Have you found somewhere?' Sanjay asked quietly. 'A proper place you can set up?'

Janani looked at him. She laughed. 'Oh, Sanjay Annan, you always have the most wonderful ideas. But when would I get a chance to look?' she asked.

'We can make the chance,' he said, and regretted it, the *we*.

She didn't seem to have heard him. 'It's so hard.' She was frowning. 'How can I make sure they don't find out, Darshan, Mamiyar? If they did . . .' Her eyes moved to Lavanika, and one hand rose towards her rounded stomach. 'But I'll do it.'

They stopped again, before Sanjay could say a word. He was dismayed to see they were standing by a pile of bitter gourd.

'Do we have to get these?' he asked.

'Yuck, Amma!' Lavanika exclaimed.

'They're not for you,' Janani told her, then her lips curved upward and she said to Sanjay, 'or for you either. Your amma loves them. I'll make her pavakkai thokku during the week, when you're working.'

'They're such an old person's food,' he muttered.

'Amma likes them too, Sanjay Mama,' Lavanika said, grinning. 'Maybe she's an old person.'

He grinned back at her.

Janani was looking between them both, a smile tugging at her mouth too. 'Cheeky girl.' She handed Sanjay two of the nasty vegetables and he placed them in the hessian bag hanging from his left shoulder. Ostensibly, this was why he'd come, to be the vegetable porter. He tried not to think about how much he enjoyed the snippets of time he had with Janani. How many of the milling crowd around them thought they were a family, the three of them?

Pumpkins and onions. Tomatoes and carrots. Spinach, apples, okra, chillies, deep purple brinjal and smooth green plantains. By the time they had finished, Sanjay's shoulder was protesting.

'Mango, Amma?' Lavanika said.

'Yes, let's go and see.'

The mango vendor was now unoccupied. When he saw Lavanika, he smiled and sliced open a fresh fruit, cutting pieces into a little paper cup for her. Sanjay watched her chase the slippery chunks with her fingers, watched her bite into the first. Mango juice trickled down her chin. The unadulterated joy on her face, the bright laughter in her eyes – he hoped it would never fade. But how uncertain her future was. Or perhaps, it was too certain. Would she be married before she'd become a woman? Have her first child while she was still one herself?

Was there anything he could do about it?

Janani was picking mangoes up, squeezing them, either putting them back or to one side. In the end, she had six pieces of ripe fruit.

'You can take one with you tomorrow,' she said. 'Eat it on the train. The rest, your appa and Priya Attai can have.'

'Forty rupees,' the vendor said, but Sanjay jumped in.

'Here.' He fished in his pocket for his coin purse. 'Buy a few more. You take them home.'

'No, it's OK . . .' Janani began.

'Look at her,' Sanjay said with a laugh, pointing at Lavanika.

The little girl had two slices in her mouth, her cheeks expanded like a hoarding squirrel's. She tried to speak, but all that came out was a high-pitched grunt, and she grinned, a juicy yellow-orange grin.

'What is this, Lavi?' Janani said, and then she was laughing too.

Sanjay looked at her. The strain around her dark eyes had lifted, if briefly. The sun flashed off her silver nose-ring and gleamed on her jet hair.

'I like it when you smile,' he said. His thoughts had moved seamlessly, unchecked, from his brain to his mouth. What was he doing? He could have bitten his tongue in two.

As Janani's head jerked in his direction, he looked away, pretending to examine the fruit, ignoring the fiery burn in his cheeks.

They walked away with ten mangoes, Lavanika bouncing from Sanjay's arm, shouting, 'Thank you, Sanjay Mama! Thank you for my mangoes! Mangoes, mangoes, mangoes!'

The vegetable bag felt a little lighter.

They took an auto home, Lavanika sandwiched between them. Sanjay barely looked at Janani as he carried the vegetables to the kitchen. As they unpacked the bag, Lavanika ran to help.

'Wait, little one,' Janani said, 'go and wash your hands and your face. You're covered in mango, you sticky little thing.'

Lavanika scrunched her face into folds, nodded and trotted outside to the tap.

Sanjay watched Janani smile after her, and a thought struck him. He deposited the last bunch of green bananas on the kitchen bench.

'Can you wait here a moment?'

He hurried out before she could answer. Acha was thankfully not home. Amma's bedroom door was closed, and Vijay had

196

already left for a study session. There was a rare quietness in the house, a sense both of peace and loneliness.

Sanjay climbed the stairs two at a time to his room. It took him a while to find what he was looking for – the camera Acha had bought him for his eighteenth birthday, partly hidden from view by an engineering textbook on his bookshelf. It was miraculously dust-free, and even more incredibly, it was balanced on an unopened two-pack of Kodak film. Slipping a roll from the packaging, Sanjay unlatched the back of the camera without considering whether there was any undeveloped, unused film nestled inside. It was empty, and he ran back out of the room, still fumbling the roll into position.

Janani was in the living room, sweeping the floor with the coconut-reed broom, the air filled with its susurrations. Lavanika was sitting crossed-legged on the rug beneath the coffee table, her school books spread out in front of her, the familiar Saturday morning scene As he clattered down the stairs, Janani stopped, unbent and looked up at him.

'I'm still here,' she said, and smiled.

He shook his head. 'Very funny.' Now he was here, he wasn't sure what had seized him, why he'd been in such a rush. The camera felt strangely weighty in his hand. 'I thought . . .' What had he thought? He hadn't been thinking at all. 'I thought it would be nice, to take a picture of the two of you.'

Even as he said it, it sounded odd, unexpected, unwelcome. An intrusion. He waited for the heavy awkwardness, already searching for what he could say to dispel it.

He was expecting her smile to fade, not to stretch as it did, lighting up her face, her eyelashes flitting up and down like fans.

'A photo?' Lavanika was scrambling up from the rug. 'Do you have a camera, Sanjay Mama? Can I see?' She ran towards him and stood quivering on the balls of her feet, riveted to the camera in his hands.

Sanjay laughed, and his uneasiness disappeared like steam.

'Lavi, come here,' Janani said. 'Leave him alone, it is expensive.' There was laughter in her voice too. 'A photo?' she said to him.

'A memory,' he replied, not able to keep the grin from his face.

'Where should we stand?' she asked.

'Just here,' he said. 'Right here. Go and stand with your amma, Lavi.'

'Here?' Janani leant her broom against the wall and sidled back to the table. Lavanika went to her and pressed herself against her mother's legs. 'I haven't even finished cleaning.'

Sanjay rolled his eyes. 'It's always clean,' he said. 'Here is fine.' There would be time for other photos later, in the garden, maybe by the bougainvillea that she loved.

He raised the camera to his face and peered at them through the viewfinder. They stood there, looking at him.

'Punnakai,' he said and watched their smiles melt their stiff postures. He pressed the shutter button.

Later that evening, after Janani and Lavanika had left, after Acha had returned and wordlessly helped Sanjay feed Amma, after Vijay had returned, eyes ringed with exhaustion, Sanjay sat on the edge of the bed and flipped through his folder of job advertisements, one after the other. It had become an obsessive habit now. Why, he didn't know. He knew what he had to do. The details were scribbled on the company information he had printed out. It would be a different job, more technical perhaps than anything he had done since his studies, but perhaps that change would be good. It would help him, later. If there was a later.

When he'd spoken to Mr Ram Shankar, told him that he'd be unable to join Intel, he'd heard the disappointment in the man's voice. Now he looked at his handwriting, a scrawl, a mess like tangled string. The manager's name. The salary – almost as much as what he earned now. The address. Anna Nagar Street, Madurai.

Bittersweet emotion choked him, the feeling of being as safe as a parrot in a cage.

'So, has your dad found you a wife yet?' Praveen asked and Chaital rolled his eyes and put his head in his hands.

Sanjay sighed. 'No, and I hope he's not trying.'

'Of course he's trying, you fool,' Vijay said, shaking his head. 'For both of us.'

They were sitting in Sangeeth. It was busy as any Saturday night – not the most upmarket of restaurants and the service was minimal, but the food was excellent and it was crowded. They had demolished their thalis and now they sat sated, sipping scalding hot coffee. Sanjay wanted to redirect the conversation, but Vijay's comment had thrown him.

'What are you talking about, Vij?' he asked.

'I don't think he stopped looking,' Vijay said. 'He never thought it could work between you and Diya . . .'

Sanjay stayed quiet.

'Sorry, Etta,' Vijay said.

It was an effort to shrug, but Sanjay managed it. 'Better to know now that she wasn't the right one. You're right. Acha would have probably put out the fire if we tried to get married.'

'Maybe one day you'll be able to say you once dated a Bollywood star,' Praveen said and Chaital hit him.

'What about you two?' Sanjay asked.

'Done,' Chaital replied. 'A girl from Madras. My dad's old

school friend's sister's daughter. She studied microbiology. I've met her a few times. I like her.'

They all stared at him.

Praveen whistled. 'You kept that quiet!'

Chaital ducked his head. Sanjay thought he might have been flushed. 'I thought I'd tell you when the details were sorted. You'll have invitations soon.'

'Wow,' Sanjay exclaimed. 'Congratulations, brother!'

'Tell them about you, Praveen,' Chaital said, but when Sanjay and Vijay turned to him, eyebrows raised, Praveen raised his hands.

'I met a girl at college,' he said. 'She's an Andra girl, though. I haven't told my parents yet. I know they want me to marry a Malayali, but really, it's their fault they moved to Tamil Nadu.'

'Totally their fault,' Chaital agreed.

'Come, Sanjay,' Praveen said. 'You've been working so long. Up and down to Madras on that flight. Surely there's someone. Some girl in the office, some lady who always sits in the same seat every flight, trying to catch your eye . . .'

Sanjay threw a piece of pappadum across the table, earning him a weary look from a passing waiter. 'Idiot.'

'No one?' Praveen needled.

'No,' Sanjay replied. He looked down.

'Ah!' Praveen said, a note of triumph in his voice. 'There is! There is a lucky girl out there!'

'Shut up,' Sanjay said, laughing, but he must have waited a beat, because his brother was looking at him, and his narrow smile was more than just teasing. 'I have something else to ask you both. What do you know about renting a property? In Usilampatti taluk in particular.'

*

Vijay drove them home. He hadn't had a drink – he had to be up too early to study, he said, but Sanjay knew his brother was thinking of what their father would say. The statue of Ganesha Blu-Tacked to the dashboard stared at him, sombre as an elephant's expression could be. The god seemed unimpressed by the garland of flowers around his neck.

'What were you talking about, Acha looking for girls?' Sanjay asked.

'Of course he is,' Vijay said impatiently. 'What did you expect? He started looking as soon as you finished your undergrad. That's not what I want to talk about.'

In the corner of his eye, Sanjay saw Vijay twist his torso around to face him. He didn't look. Moths missed the car headlights and hit the windscreen.

'Etta. It's Janani, isn't it.'

This time, Sanjay didn't hesitate. 'I don't know what you're talking about.' Had he replied too fast, as though he'd been expecting the question, a batsman facing a fast bowler?

'The girl you've "met".'

'What rubbish, Vij.'

Sanjay could feel his brother's gaze, darting sidelong looks from the road to him. He kept his head steady, facing out the windscreen, until finally Vijay spun back around and slumped in his seat with a sigh.

'You're friendly with her. The grocery shopping and everything.'

'She's pregnant, Vijay. Amma can't do much. I'm just helping. We've been friends since we were about five.'

'Things change.' Vijay glanced at him again, and this time Sanjay turned too, catching his brother's serious brown gaze for a second before he looked back at the road. His little brother, always so serious. Always with his head in his textbooks, his glasses thick as concrete, on track to be the doctor their father so badly wanted in a son. 'I mean, she's married, of course . . .'

'I know.'

'She has a child and she's pregnant . . .'

'I know, Vijay.'

'And she's a low-caste Tamil cleaner. Kallar, right?'

'I know!'

In the silence between them, Sanjay realised his voice had risen. He looked out the window, trying to find some calm in the blackness outside. Somewhere below, the Vaigai was trickling along its course.

'Sorry, Etta,' Vijay said. At least he sounded chastened. 'I didn't mean to upset you. It's just that Acha always says . . .'

'Acha says a lot,' Sanjay interrupted. 'He's got a lot of strong opinions. That doesn't mean he's always right.'

But Vijay had always been like this, so much more pliable, so much more willing to bend to Acha's will. It could have been fear, or awe, or that he saw something in Acha that he aspired to. More likely it was all of those. Sanjay remembered that awed fear, that tall lanky man in his suit and his medical briefcase, always willing to deal out a slap if his marks weren't good enough. Thinking about it now, he realised it hadn't occurred to him that, given the disappointment Sanjay was to his father, it would have been harder for his younger brother.

And Amma, slowly weakening over these years, finding it more difficult to influence her stern husband, to temper him with her gentleness as she had always done.

The next morning, Sanjay came downstairs to find his mother at the dining table. Dressed in a pink sari that made her fair skin glow, she looked better than he'd seen her in weeks. Her eyes were outlined in kohl, her hair brushed and braided. Acha was handing her her tablets. He was dressed too, looking strangely casual in his beige trousers and loose blue shirt.

'Where are you off to?' Sanjay asked, sitting down and helping himself to still-warm dosas.

'Just your Priya Ammayi's house,' she said. 'Will you come?'

Sanjay had been planning on lazing around, perhaps watching the cricket, before his drive to the airport, but he already felt guilty for not being at home for dinner the night before.

'Sure,' he said.

She smiled. Taking the last tablet, she swallowed it down, grimacing.

They all went, all but Vijay, who, of course, was studying for an exam.

Priya's house was only a few minutes away, but they took longer, matching his mother's pace. Amma had insisted on walking. Her arm was looped through Sanjay's, her weight leaning into him. Her other hand was on his father's arm. Radhakrishnan was bearing the visit gamely, but Sanjay had noticed him scoop up the day's newspaper just as they left the house.

Priya was watering the red and violet flowers on her veranda. As they approached, she set down her watering can and hurried forward.

'All of you! Wonderful. I'm glad I bought so many bondas and samosas.'

'We've just had breakfast, Priya Ammayi,' Sanjay said, and she waved a hand.

'*You* have, you mean. Your amma and acha probably ate hours ago.' She insinuated herself into Sanjay's position beside his mother, slowly taking Amma's weight from him, helping her up the steps and into the house.

Inside, they settled into Priya's comfortable, cosy red cotton-covered couches. This room brought back memories that were now tinged with a sunny flow of childhood happiness. He and Vijay, Malini and Manoj, lying on mattresses laid out on this floor for sleepovers, watching *Star Wars* and *Indiana Jones*, *Betaab* and *Coolie*, telling ghost stories in whispers. The display cabinets with their photos and trinkets were all the same, souvenirs of Priya's travels around the world. Tribal masks from Tanzania, batik silk from Indonesia, Murano glass from Florence.

One day, he'd go to all those places. Malini and Manoj were already there, settled in San Francisco. Thousands of miles from their mother.

'When is your flight back, Sanjay kutty?' Priya asked. She had laid out huge samosas with mint and tamarind sauces, delicious onion bondas, their fried chickpea pastry skins crumbling in his mouth, and a plate of Parle-G biscuits. 'You should take some of these with you.'

'Not until seven o'clock,' Sanjay replied, 'and I don't think I'll ever be able to eat again.'

'It must be tiring,' Priya said. 'Back and forth like this.'

'So tiring,' Amma agreed. 'I told him he should stay in Madras for longer. Come back once a month. It would be easier on him. And,' she leaned forward conspiratorially, 'maybe he'd have time to meet a nice Malayali girl there, you know?'

'Amma!' Sanjay said.

There was a rustle from the newspaper.

'And how is that young girl, Parvati?' Priya asked. 'Janani?' Her eyes flickered to Sanjay.

'Such a sweet thing,' his mother said. 'Hard-working. I need her help now, to fetch the vegetables, to chop them for me. And that blouse she stitched – perfect, you know.'

What possessed Sanjay to speak now, he didn't know. Was

it the glow of pride he'd felt at Amma's words, as though he'd somehow had something do with earning that praise? 'I think she should do more of it,' he said. 'Tailoring, you know. Set up her own business, maybe. Get some independence.'

'A very good idea,' Priya concurred.

'Of course,' Amma said. 'The poor girl. It is very sad, how these people think.'

Sanjay's teeth set. He fought down the irritation. 'They're not too far off from being just like us, you know, Amma. I was born here.' He pointed at Priya. 'Malini was born here. A girl.'

'In Kerala, people don't do these sorts of things, Sanjay,' his mother said.

'You don't know that,' Sanjay retorted. It was the first time in longer than he could remember that he was angry at his mother. Not about her. *At* her, his annoyance directed towards her pale, thin face. 'And even if they don't, that doesn't mean we cross the border, settle here, and ignore it happening down the road.'

'Don't raise your voice to your amma,' Radhakrishnan said, lowering the paper slightly, although Sanjay hadn't raised his voice at all.

'It's OK, Krishnan Etta,' his mother said. 'He's right.'

'So why doesn't she do more of it?' Priya asked. 'Tailoring?'

'She's doing it mostly in secret at the moment,' he explained. 'At her friend's house . . .' An image came to him, of Janani sitting in a dark corner beside the woman whose life she'd saved, unable to stop looking at the mark around her neck. 'She can't keep doing that,' he said. 'And if her husband and mother-in-law find out, they'll want the money, you know?'

'The husband's probably a drunk,' Priya commented. 'They often are. I can't blame them, with their lives.'

Radhakrishnan snorted. 'Any idiot can drink himself into forgetfulness.'

'I think it's best if she rents somewhere,' Sanjay said, ignoring his father. 'Just something small, in Usilampatti. The rent will be cheap there, she'll be able to earn it easily if she has the time to build it up . . .'

'Does she have the money to pay until she has built it up?' Priya asked, her eyes narrowed.

Sanjay hesitated. 'I don't know.'

His mother reached for a Parle-G. She had not yet eaten anything. Sanjay felt a pang as she nibbled at the corner of the slightly sweet, malty biscuit. She'd always loved them.

'You know, I wanted to send that girl to school,' she said. 'Her parents, they couldn't afford it. They couldn't afford for her not to be at home doing housework. Her older sister they married to a man in Coimbatore. They were worried about Janani's dowry too.'

An image flashed into Sanjay's mind, clear as a photograph. Janani, begging to go to school with him. *Please, Amma. Please?*

'Why didn't you?' he asked. 'Send her to school?'

'Her mother wouldn't accept,' she said. 'She wouldn't accept any help. So proud, she was. And tradition is so strong for some people. She couldn't see that a girl could become educated, get a good job, support her family.' She sighed. 'In the villages, I suppose it's rare that that happens.'

'Why are we talking about this?' Radhakrishnan grumbled.

They looked at him, but he was still concealed behind the newspaper.

'We can help with this rent business,' Sanjay's mother said.

The newspaper came down.

'What is this?' Radhakrishnan said quietly. He was looking at Sanjay. 'What stupidity are you talking about?'

'Acha, I was just—'

'Who is this girl? She is a cleaner. An uneducated cleaning

woman. Does she know how to run a business? Does she know how to manage money? And you're asking your amma to just give her money from our pockets?'

'I didn't ask Amma anything,' Sanjay said. He felt hot, a prickling, pin-sharp heat. 'She asked about Janani, I answered. That's all.'

'Krishnanetta . . .' Amma and Priya said together, like a choir.

'And why do you care?' The newspaper was folded away as neatly as it had been compressed coming off the press. 'What business is it of yours, someone else's life, their work, their family? Why should you interfere?'

Sanjay should have said nothing, just looked down at the floor and said nothing, like Vjiay would have done. But all he could think of was Janani's face, of how every line, every curve had tilted down towards the earth like a wilting flower, as though the hope of a monsoon rain was just a prayer in still, dry air.

'Because I care,' he said. 'Because we played together when we were little. We're friends. You used to care about her too. At least, it seemed like you did.'

His father's eyebrows, angled down towards his nose like a film villain, relaxed in surprise. There was a moment of silence, as all of them waited for him to speak, because that's what they did. They waited for Radhakrishna, the renowned surgeon, the patriarch, to speak, as though he were a king.

To hell with that.

'And so I'm going to ask about her work, her family, her life. And I'll leave it to her to tell me to get lost, not you,' Sanjay said.

'So you plan to give her our family money, this girl you barely know, with no control over how she uses it?'

It had been so long since Sanjay had seen his father properly angry at him that he'd forgotten how loud he could be.

'OK, enough,' Priya said. 'Both of you.'

Sanjay blinked. He realised he was on his feet, and so was his father. He didn't know who'd stood first. It struck him, the way you'd suddenly notice a local shop had closed down or a neighbour had a new car, though it had been that way for months or years, that he could meet Acha eye for eye now. That the fear was draining away and was being replaced with something worse.

He looked away and saw the ladies of his family still poised on the couch. Priya, leaning forward, hands out like a bullfighter. Amma, straight-backed as always, eyes wide as a lost child's.

He crossed the room and sank down next to his mother. 'Sorry, Amma,' he said. 'I didn't mean to upset you.'

'It's OK, kutty,' she said. 'But there's no reason for shouting.'

Radhakrishnan had returned to his seat also. He looked calmer, if surly.

'Krishnan Etta, that girl has been coming to our house since she was a little child,' Amma said to her husband. 'Surely we can give her something to help.'

'But, Parvati,' Acha replied, 'we don't know how she will use it. We don't even know if this family of hers will let her keep it.'

'You don't have to, Amma,' Sanjay said. 'She can take care of herself. And I'll help her.'

'With all of your spare time?' Radhakrishnan said. 'You should be thinking about your own family. About finding a wife. Not running around after some village woman who might not even want your help!'

Silence had never been louder.

Sanjay felt a pain in his wrists and realised he'd curled his hands into fists around the material of his trousers and was squeezing as hard as he could.

It was his aunt, his brave, non-nonsense aunt, who broke the silence.

'Come,' she said. 'Let's watch a movie. Some nonsense drama. It will make us realise how loving our own family is.'

'Good plan,' Sanjay said. 'I'll drive you.' He wasn't enthused about sitting through three hours of some Tamil drama, but Amma loved them. He could fall asleep in the cinema.

Radhakrishnan picked up the newspaper. 'You all go,' he said. 'You know I don't like these movies. I will see you when you come home.'

That, at least, was a relief.

They watched *Enga Thambi*, which had enough action in it, thankfully, to keep Sanjay interested.

His mother and aunt seemed to enjoy it too. Every so often, he glanced sideways at Amma's face. In the flickering light, the play of colours on her skin, her face relaxed as the story took her mind away from the pain, she seemed almost as she did before.

On the drive home, they ended up in a far too in-depth psychological deconstruction of the killer's motives and the morality of the heroine's investigative methods. Amma seemed convinced that the movie was a clear indication of why it was dangerous for a girl to go into entertainment, which, by the time Sanjay had pulled into the driveway, had him laughing hard enough to cramp his stomach muscles.

Vijay appeared at the top of the steps as they walked through the hall past the drawing room and into the living room. The newspaper lay abandoned on one of the glass panels in the rosewood coffee table.

'Where's Acha?' Amma asked.

'He's gone to get ready for the temple,' Vijay said.

'Ah I'll go too,' Amma said. 'I'll just wash my face.' She retreated into the bedroom, calling for Radhakrishnan.

'Did you bring me any chocolate?' Vijay asked.

Sanjay threw him a block of Cadbury's. It flew up and over the banister like a purple rectangular frisbee. 'Don't forget to share.'

His brother caught it with a grin and disappeared back into his room.

Sanjay looked at his aunt. 'What a day.'

Priya settled onto the couch. 'You shouldn't try to make your father angry,' she said quietly.

'I don't,' Sanjay said, just as quietly. 'He makes himself angry.'

'He comes from another time. And . . .' She was silent for a moment. 'He had a very good friend, growing up. The son of a family who had worked for his family for years in Cochin. The usual, cooking and cleaning. When he went off to college, then university, they lost touch. Your father returned to Cochin one year and found that this friend had come to ask for a job and attached himself to your grandfather. He robbed him and ran. He'd had an alcohol problem for a few years, this boy. His family never told your father's family, because of the shame. After that, trust was broken, you know?'

'How do you know this?' Sanjay asked.

Priya gave him a withering look. 'What a question. You know how the Nambeesans talk. We all know each other. Anyway, by that time, your acha already had an eye on your amma.'

Sanjay shook his head. 'Just because it happened to him doesn't mean—'

'I know, kutty. But we don't always think logically about these things. And no matter how much people talk about the evils of the caste system, it is a way of thinking that is thousands of years old. It is ingrained into our identity. It will take some scrubbing to erase it.'

His parents emerged.

'Let's go,' Radhakrishnan said. He was in his white lunghi, shirtless, his janeu hanging across his body from his left shoulder.

He looked at Sanjay. 'Are you coming to the temple? It's been weeks since you came.'

'Next week, Acha,' Sanjay replied. 'I have some work to do before my flight.' It struck him that he had no idea where his own janeu was. He'd misplaced it at least twenty times since his upanayana. Almost once every year.

His father grunted.

'OK, kutty,' his mother said. She took a breath and stepped towards Sanjay. Back in the natural light, the illusion that the gentle darkness of the cinema had cast was gone. Still, she looked better than she had in weeks. Reaching out, she took Sanjay's hand and pressed a wad of notes into it. He looked from them, to his aunt, and back to Amma.

'Parvati, what is this?' Acha said.

'It's just a little money, Krishnanetta. It's so little to us. Whatever she uses it for, it will help her more than it could help us.' She turned away. 'Let's go.'

She walked out of the room.

Priya shot Sanjay a quick glance as she followed.

His father ignored him completely. 'Vijay,' Radhakrishnan called as he walked out into the hall, Priya following him. 'We'll pray for your exams, OK? Study hard.'

Sanjay stood in the middle of the room. In his hand, the crumpled stack of notes felt like drying flower petals, ready to be flung at the feet of the gods.

Chapter Fourteen

Madurai, 2019

The convoy heads back to where we started. There, I'm amazed that caterers have taken over the kitchen, directed with surprising firmness by Girija. Five men have set up in the courtyard, rolling chappatis, frying puri and stirring chana masala. The air's full of the smell of cardamom, cumin, turmeric, frying dough. My stomach grumbles.

Inside, the dining table's been extended to fit as many of us as possible, and Manju Ammayi's directing the younger generation to the living-room couches. I move to follow Arjun and Radhika when my aunt touches my arm.

'No, no, kutty,' she says. 'You come and sit here with us for some time – the ammayis and ammamas want to talk to you. It has been so long since they saw you.'

A jolt of pleasure. I'm reluctant to leave my cousins, but I'll have time enough for them. They could never tell me enough about what I want to know. They weren't there.

The older adults have all taken their seats at the table, in a priority order that seems to be by age. Or by interest in newcomers, I realise, as Manju Ammayi leads me to a seat beside Amma, opposite the oldest ammayi. She looks at me with interest. I'm mesmerised by her ears. The lobes are so long they must be less than an inch from brushing the tops of her shoulders.

That practice has faded away, of wearing earrings of gold heavy enough to stretch the small flap of skin like plasticine, into a giant needle head. Those ears were considered beautiful, once. Now they're markers of a life in another world.

In my peripheral vision, I see Amma sitting stiff and upright, on the edge of her chair, as she does when she's uncomfortable. It's good posture, but the stress levels behind it definitely aren't healthy. Her uneasiness is contagious. I realise I'm shifting in my seat.

Thankfully, the caterers appear with the food, providing an immediate distraction. Each has a different dish, and are enthusiastic servers – despite me shaking my head no, I end up with an extra chapatti and a mountain of rice. It takes a good ten minutes for the conversation to begin to flow, in a kaleidoscopic mix of Malayalam and English. It comes in a torrent that washes away anything I may have to say.

'So, Nila, what did you study?' Narendra Ammama asks.

'And you're working now?' An aunt whose name slips from my grasp asks. 'Is it good money?'

I barely have time to reply before the next question comes.

'It must be time now, surely?' It's the matriarch opposite me. Bindu Ammayi. She sits hunched over beside Acha, picking at her plain dosa, but her eyes are sharp as obsidian. My father looks startled out of deep thought. 'She is twenty-five, no? Are you looking for someone for her yet?'

My heart is starting to leap around like a wren trapped by a cat. Veliamma, sitting beside me, puts a hand on my arm. Acha produces an unintelligible murmur.

'Ah!' The obsidian eyes turn to me. 'One of these modern girls, is she? Independent. No marriage, only work. Isn't your acha trying to find a good Malayali boy for you?'

I don't know what to do except try a modest smile and look at my food. It's chana bhatura – oily and delicious – but sickening disappointment has drowned my appetite. The urge to leave the table makes my legs twitch. But also, hammering on the inside of my skull, is a mad scream. *I've found someone, all on my own. Definitely not a good Malayali boy. We're very much in love.* The thought of it conjures up the threat of a giggle, and I have to bite the inside of my lip to stop it.

'I think, Ammayi,' Acha says, 'girls these days are very capable of finding their own partners.'

'Ah, just like you did?' Bindu Ammayi says, and she cackles. An actual cackle, dry and hacking.

'Bindu Ammayi,' Veliamma starts, but the old lady carries on as though she hasn't heard her.

'Ask your amma, kutty,' she says. 'Ask her – what is most important in her life?'

It's the first time anyone at the table other than Acha or Veliamma have acknowledged Amma's presence.

The old woman doesn't wait for me to ask anything. Instead she fixes Amma with that crow-stare.

I look at my mother too. I don't know what else to do. I can tell she's startled.

Her eyes flicker to me. 'My children,' she says.

My face is on fire, as though I've eaten a handful of chillies. I think Amma's embarrassed too – she looks down at her hands and her lips are drawn into a line. It just makes me feel worse.

'See?' Bindu Ammayi says. There's a note of satisfaction in her voice that makes my jaw ache.

It's not her fault, I tell myself. She's an old woman. She means well.

In the corner of my eye, Amma takes a mouthful of chapatti and potato masala, and it makes me bite the inside of my lip.

It's her fault. She could say something, right now.

No, more than that. She could have said something, a lot of things, to me, a long time ago. Why was a marriage of love, a marriage that these people, Acha's own family, didn't want, OK for her but not for me?

There's laughter from the living room, where my cousins sit squeezed onto the sofas. I try to decipher their words, but Bindu Ammayi's still talking. I can't tune her out. I'm trying hard not to think of her as a bloody old crone.

'Yes, we have fun, carefree times during our youth,' she says. 'But the worthwhile things come later. A husband. Children.' She shakes her head and sits back. I can't help notice how tiny she is. 'There is nothing like a mother's love for her husband and child. Even your amma knows this.'

The emphasis is unmistakeable. Even *my amma*.

I feel, rather than see, Amma flinch, and then she retreats back into her chair, as though she's trying to melt into it.

Acha's hand comes down on the table, and his plate jumps and jangles. 'Ammayi,' he says, 'that's enough.' His voice is quiet, but it's the quiet between lightning and thunder.

A bubble of silence forms over our section of the table. It feels like we've been sealed off and the air has thickened. I'm angry and, somehow, I'm afraid.

Veliamma breaks the silence after a moment. 'Come, Bindu Ammayi,' she says. 'Tell me how Nikhil is doing.'

At first, I think the old matriarch isn't going to be distracted, but Veliamma adds a follow-up question and she's hooked.

The unspoken question hangs in the air between Amma and me, attached to a hundred more. It pulls my gaze to her.

She's staring at me, unblinking. The closest to that expression I've seen is when she's furious at me. My eyes stayed locked to hers momentarily, mesmerised by the intensity. Then she looks away, and the spell is broken.

Nikhil, apparently, is in New York and has married an American divorcee. It's a scandal. His parents aren't talking to him. They might never speak to him again. Bindu Ammayi is merrily shocked at it all.

I wish Rohan were here. I wish I were back home, feeling the temperatures cool and the autumn winds kick the scent of eucalyptus into my nose, bush-walking with Iphigenia through the Royal National Park.

I'm tired of secrets and talk. So I avoid the family for the rest of the afternoon, hiding in the shade of the balcony after lunch. The fan is on, its blades whirring air directly into my face. I like it out here. The trellises of jasmine and bougainvillea hide the street from view. Hercules lies next to me, his tongue hanging from his mouth, twitching in a half-doze. There's a paper I should be reading, about rehabilitating meniscus tears in older patients, but my head has started to feel tight again.

I miss Rohan, suddenly and acutely. Fishing for my phone, I send him a text.

How you doing, dork

There's another message. Not from Rohan.

I'd left my phone at home during the funeral. At some point between now and then, this had appeared.

Hey, love. Hope today goes okay. Thinking of you. As always.

For a moment, there's nothing in the world but those words. 'Nila.'

I jump so violently, Hercules jerks out of his sleep. Amma is at the door, blinking in the sun.

'Hi, Amma.'

'I didn't know you were here.'

'I'm just reading.' The phone screen blanks.

'Can I get you some biscuits, or fruit? There's mango. Or a coffee?'

When she worries about me, when she's penitent, she makes peace offerings with food as though it's gold.

'I'm not hungry. Thank you.'

'You don't want to nap? It's nice and cool upstairs, and I've closed the shutters. We had an early start.'

Irritation scratches at me, mosquito-like. 'No. Thanks, Amma.'

She stands for a minute. I keep my eyes on my book, even when she moves forward, even when she eases herself into the chair beside mine. Hercules looks up, the pink ribbon of his tongue hanging from one corner of his mouth, and his tail rises in a lazy wag.

'It's nice to see your veliamma,' Amma says. 'She is one of the best people I have ever met.'

'Then why don't you ever visit her?' I ask before I can stop myself. The words are like a door slamming. *Shit*, I think into the silence that follows, but I don't know how to undo it.

'It was hard for me, here,' she says finally. 'For all of us.' Her voice is quiet, almost as though she's not speaking to me.

But it's more than I've heard her mention about those days in a long time. My anger shifts slightly, towards whatever unknowable thing it was that's brought that pain to her eyes.

I wait for her to continue, but there's just silence.

'Maybe we can go for a trip somewhere tomorrow,' Amma says, finally.

'Great.'

The cicadas have started up, rasping like tiny chainsaws.

Usually I find their conversation calming, ambient sounds of life. Now they grate against my eardrums. But it's just the two of us here, for the first time since before we left Australia. I could tell her, now. Ease it into the conversation, as gently as Amma slips puri into boiling oil to fry. Maybe she'd tell me something in return.

'It's a good thing that we came,' Amma says. 'Good you have seen your family.' Her voice has changed. She sounds like she's trying to soothe a wild animal. 'You know, Manju Ammayi is looking for a wife for Arjun.'

The moment shatters. The disappointment makes me feel sick. Closing my eyes, I let my head drop back against the wall of the house. 'Poor thing,' I mutter under my breath. Sweat is dampening my back where it makes contact with the chair.

'He is the right age.' I sense her turn to look at me. 'And he's got the right attitude. That's very important. If you don't have a positive attitude, how will you find someone?'

We listen to the cicadas and I try not to cry.

'You should be looking for someone too.'

'Oh God, Amma.' It feels like there's a laser burning into my temple. 'Thanks, Bindu Ammayi, for bringing that up.'

'You need someone to look after you, Nila. To be with you through your life, so you are not alone, you know. Not lonely.' She looks away. 'It's a terrible thing, to be lonely.'

Loneliness. I imagine a life without just that one person, and the thought coats my mind like thick black oil. I watch Amma's profile. She looks small and sad, and it makes me furious. It's her fault. Her fault I can't be who I am. Her fault I know so little about who I am.

'So you were lonely, were you? You were younger than I am when you married Acha. How lonely could you have been?'

She looks surprised. Her mouth closes, opens, closes again. Her lips draw into that obstinate tightness that Iphigenia tells me mine do, when I'm feeling stubborn. She's not going to answer, and it makes me angrier.

'I'm not going to be alone. I've got friends, unlike you. I've got Rohan. I've got Iphigenia. I've got people I love in my life, and I can look after myself.'

I'm so close.

Tell her. Just tell her.

'Your friends, Rohan, they all have their own lives,' Amma says. 'Iphigenia is a lovely girl, she will find someone soon. Rohan will get married too, and anyway, he is a boy and boys are different.' She has turned her whole body sideways. Hercules is looking at us.

'Really?' I say. 'Boys are different? That's your justification for thinking he'll be fine and I'll be alone, friendless, not able to look after myself?' I say it, but it's the thought of Iphigenia, happy and laughing with someone while I'm shut out, alone, that makes my head drum harder.

Amma looks exasperated and stricken at the same time. Her knuckles on the arm of her chair are as pale as they can be, the veins on the top of her hand bulging. I didn't realise arms as thin as hers can have that strength.

'That's not what I mean,' she says. 'It's just . . .' Her eyes roam wildly, searching for the word. The sun's moved to lap at our faces and her pottu glitters in its touch. 'It's different.'

'It was different for you, too,' I reply. 'You found Acha, you said it yourself. Moved to Australia, got yourself a job. Sounds like you took care of yourself.'

Amma stares at me, her mouth slightly open.

My anger's firing my courage, and I ride it. 'I think it's time I do the same,' I add. 'When we get home, I'm moving out.'

I've said it, just a part of the truth, the smallest part. *Keep going, keep going*, but I can't, because already her face has contorted and speaks of a fear I just can't understand.

My head is pounding now, a drum beating in my left temple, *da-dum, da-dum*, as though there's something struggling to escape. Irrelevantly, I remember the myth of Zeus, Athena leaping out of his migraine-struck head, fully formed and armoured.

'Nila.' Amma's out of her chair. Her hands are outstretched, almost in supplication, and a bullet of guilt hits me. 'No, you're not. I'll never . . . You're not moving out, not until you are married. Not until you have someone to look after—'

I stand up, chair legs scraping against the tiles. 'I'm going for a run.'

'A run? Where? No, Nila, it's dangerous to . . . Nila!'

I'm already jogging through the house, swinging around the end of the smooth wooden banister, thumping up the stairs two at a time. In our bedroom, I rummage through my suitcase, pulling out an old marathon finisher's shirt, a pair of leggings, my shoes. I'm glad I've brought running kit. Even putting it on brings a moment of relief, as though I've shed a skin that isn't mine and I'm free, just me and my body, which can carry me anywhere.

I'm about to bound back down the stairs, my trainers hanging from a couple of fingers, when I hear voices. The words are jumbled beats of sound, strained and deep, rough as a dog's bark. Down the stairs I continue, casual and measured, as though I can't hear, as though I'm not interested. And I'm not. I just want to get out of here.

By the time I've reached the second-last step, I can make out syllables, sentences, coming from the half-closed door to the living room.

'Do you have no self-pride? Is all of this meaningless to you?

I don't understand.' It's Kochachan's voice, in a mix of English and Malayalam, his voice rougher than I thought it could be. There's a pause.

I tiptoe as quickly as I can past the gap in the door, just as there's a baritone mumble in reply.

'What?' Kochachan says. 'I can't hear you.'

'Of course I have self-pride!' Arjun, shouting. 'That doesn't mean I care about any of this!' I hear something hit the floor with a sloppy slap. 'But you don't seem to understand that!'

I've stopped, just out of sight. I can't help it.

'Don't shout,' Kochachan says, calm as the calm before fire bursts through bushland. 'You'll upset Amma.'

'She upsets herself,' Arjun says. 'She's neurotic.' He's stopped yelling, but now he sounds bitter as overripe lime. 'I can't not live my life just because of you two. I can't.'

I hear movement towards the door and start walking immediately. My heart's dancing the tarantella, bouncing off my ribs. I don't stop until I'm just outside. Through the window, I can see that my father's standing with my mother. Bending down, I insert my feet into my shoes and lace them up.

'I just got home and you're off?'

I loop the last knot, draw it tight and stand up to face Arjun. He's watching me, his face as sardonic as ever under his carefully side-swept hair.

'I'm just going to go for a run.'

He looks startled, stands up out of his slouch. He's wearing a Nirvana shirt over his jeans. It surprises me.

'You're not serious, are you?' he says.

'Serious about what?' I start down the veranda steps. The heat hits me like a steam-cooker.

He snorts with laughter and follows me out. 'Where are you going to run?'

'I don't know,' I reply, annoyed. I like to run without a route, just let my feet find a way.

'You'll be murdered,' Arjun says. He's shaking his head, and I realise he's laughing in disbelief. 'You'll be hit by a car. You'll get heat stroke. We'll find your body somewhere.'

'Nila.' We both turn to look at my parents. Amma has pushed herself out of the chair. 'You can't just go for a run. It's not like home.'

'Would you be saying the same thing to Rohan?' I say, trying to keep my voice below a shout.

'Janani Ammayi's right,' Arjun jumps in. 'The traffic's mad. And, well, you're a girl, on your own, and so, yes, it'd be different for Rohan.'

'Oh, for God's sake.' I can feel myself vibrating, with anger, with the urge to take off. 'It's a run. I'll be back in half an hour, I've got my phone.'

'Nila!' Amma exclaims, taking a step towards me. She looks almost as though she's on the verge of tears. 'Stop being so stubborn!'

'If you're going to run, run around the house. You can go through there,' Acha says, pointing to the tiny corridor between the house and the garden wall. The ground there is dense with fallen fruit and moulted dried palm leaves.

I look at them. Then I turn and begin to jog up the driveway, slow and steady, letting my ankles and knees warm up.

Amma calls after me, but I ignore them.

'Nila.' Arjun is jogging up behind me, his sandals flapping in the dust. 'At least share your live location.'

We've reached the top of the driveway. I stop and glare at him, but I pull out my phone and do it.

'Half an hour,' Arjun says, and I turn and run, ignoring

the sight of Amma coming up the drive towards us, one hand outstretched.

It's hot. Hot like a kitchen with a kettle that has boiled for an hour, hot like a bathroom after a scalding shower. I embrace the heat, feel it soaking into my pores.

I've turned left at the top of the driveway. Part of me is aware of my surroundings – the impenetrably dark pond, the supermarket that smells like masala and sugar, the decaying outsides of a bank building – but mostly I'm just running, taking the path of least resistance. I wish Iphigenia were here with me.

'Look, Nil,' she'd say. 'A bakery. Let's stop there on the way back.' She'd point out the five-star hotel whose sign I barely notice, lush trees flanking the steep drive sweeping up behind the ornate gate – '*Look* at this place, I'm booking a night here immediately, we can escape the family.' I take imaginary notes for her as I dodge around dried cow shit and try not to breathe in petrol fumes. The tightness in my chest has forced its way up into my throat and is burning my eyes.

It's only now dawning on me what I've done. Just the first step, a small step. I've told her in anger, but I've told her that I'm leaving, and right now I realise I don't know if I care what my mother thinks. That maybe I'll lose her if I want to live my life, and that I might be able to live with that.

I turn left again as I hit the highway – the thought of crossing it is not appealing. The air becomes noxious; even the sky ahead of me seems tinged with grey. I run as far as a restaurant that declares itself 'Krishna Veg!' and loop around with the smell of masala dosa and idli clearing out my nostrils. By the time I turn back off the highway, I need to stop. Coughing, I stand with hands on knees, waiting for my lungs to clear. My phone vibrates, and I pull it from my pocket. Five kilometres.

There's a bakery beside me. From the corner of my eye, I see a family selecting cakes. The young son's a round beaming thing with terrible posture, lordosis curving his lower back.

'Hoy!'

I look up. A woman passes by, raising an eyebrow at me. A bag from Saravana stores dangles from one hand. She's wearing a bracelet-ring, fanning gold threads stretching across her hand to attach to the engraved piece around her wrist, like an Arabian princess, a little girl tugging on her other hand, and as I watch them, the kid says in Tamil, with typical childlike subtlety, 'Ma! What's that girl doing?'

'Hoy!'

The woman is not the source of the shout.

I gaze around. There's a group of men, four or five of them, maybe a few years older than myself, gathered around a coffee shop. Two sit at the top of the few steps leading up to it, the others standing at their feet. Cigarette smoke creates an unsteady haze around their heads, joining the steam rising from the plastic white cups of coffee they're sipping. All of them have turned to stare in my direction. They're smiling. I must look ridiculous, sweaty and as red-faced as I can ever be.

I look away and push myself up to stand. My tongue has stuck to the roof of my mouth, but I just want to get home now. I double-check the route – straight on and a right turn past the pond – and slip the phone back into its pocket.

Shaking out my legs, I break into a trot.

'Hoy! Where are you going, so quickly?' Laughter. I ignore it, ignore the blood that's beginning to pump a little faster into my legs, and keep my steady pace.

A little later comes the clink of gears and too-loose bells, and then the grinding sound of bicycle tires on dusty dirt. 'Hey! Nayanthara!'

Maybe they've mistaken me for someone else.

I've picked up speed now, adrenaline pulsing through me, the heat forgotten. The bikes are just behind me. I don't turn, just pound my feet into the street. Everyone I pass is looking up in surprise.

'Slow down!'

'Where are you going?'

'Talk to us!'

'We just want to chat!'

And the laughter. Snickering laughter, the kind a cat would make if it could laugh.

There is a bike on either side of me now. With the tiniest flicker of my eyes, I can see that the men are not pedalling as fast as they could be. I'm hyperconscious that at any moment one of them could speed up and cut me off. If that happens, I'm ready to run straight into him, send him flying.

'Hey, Nayanthara!'

'Such a pretty lady.'

I am boiling, my anger is hotter than the air around me. I turn my head.

'Fuck off,' I growl at the man to my left.

The smile leaves his face – he looks as shocked as though I've slapped him.

'Ohhhhhh!' the other guys crow.

I want them to stop. I want to turn around. I want to punch them in the face. I'm so angry I'm sprinting now, leaving them behind. They are falling back, their inane voices repeating their magpie calls, now dwindling into the distance, now disappearing into the roar of an oncoming motorbike.

'Nila!'

I turn ready for a fight, and come to a halt, dust flying up at my heels.

It's Arjun, sitting on his scooter, one foot on the ground as the engine rumbles beneath him. He's looking at me with concern. 'Are you OK?'

'Yes,' I pant. I become aware of a stitch in my right side and dig my fingers under my rib cage. 'I'm good.'

'Those guys . . .'

'Immature idiots,' I say.

'Come on,' he says. 'Jump on. You've been well over half an hour.'

'I'm pretty sweaty . . .'

'Just get on.'

My legs feel like jelly now and the remnants of adrenaline and fear and anger have left me shaking. Trudging to the side of the scooter, I swing one leg over. I look back as I do – the gang of child-men have disappeared.

'Did you come looking for me?' I ask as Arjun throttles forward.

'Yes. I was checking your dot and I saw you'd stopped. Your amma was pretty freaked out. I figured I'd come make sure you hadn't fallen into a well or something.'

'Ha,' I say. 'Could have used the drink. Thanks.'

'You'd have got dysentery. No problem.' He hesitates. 'Are you sure you're OK? They were following you.'

'Not for long,' I reply. 'Any idea who Nayanthara is? They kept calling me that.'

He snorts. 'Idiots. She's a Kollywood and Mollywood actress. Malayali, actually. You do look a bit like her, but you're darker.'

I glance down at the back of my hand. My mouth opens, but Arjun is not finished.

'Be careful,' he says. 'People still think of girls differently here, you know? It's not like Australia, or Europe, or the US. It's not just talk.'

It's not always just talk anywhere, I want to say, but I'm still trembling, so I hang on to his waist and watch the houses slip by.

Chapter Fifteen

Madurai, 1993

The sixth month

Now she hears the lullaby her mother sings to her sister.
It soothes her. She has hair and lashes of white.
Her skin is flushed pomegranate-red.

'You'll look after Ma, won't you.'

It was the most animated Janani had seen Darshan in weeks. In the old, stained mirror, Janani could see him grinning, his teeth gleaming below his moustache in the lamplight. He turned to her, expectant.

She nodded, and dropped her eyes to the sari she was folding so he wouldn't see her face. Darshan gone for five whole weeks. It had been a while since he'd been gone for so long. She wasn't sure if it was relief or apprehension that she most felt. Darshan had the ability to temper Vandhana, to draw her attention away from Janani's faults, from her ever-growing belly.

But with him gone, it was one person less to cook for, one person less to have to prepare a meal for. She could spend a bit more time with Shubha. She could stay a little later at the Nambeesans' house. With Sanjay.

'Well, good,' Darshan said. She couldn't help a guilty start. But he looked at the foot of the bed, where Lavanika was lying on her stomach on her sleeping mat, thumbing through the already-worn pages of the comic Sanjay had given her. 'Lavi, little bird, can you go and sleep with Patti tonight?'

Lavanika looked up. 'OK, Appa,' she said. She kicked her legs, her anklets chiming, and pushed herself up. 'Can I take my comic?'

'Yes, of course,' Darshan said.

Janani watched her go as she finished folding the sari and placed it neatly in the cupboard. Her heart was settling into her stomach. She shouldn't be surprised, she thought. Of course, if he was going for five weeks, he'd want to have sex. He knew she wouldn't protest. And of course she wouldn't – how could she? Maybe if she lay with him properly tonight, he wouldn't have sex with the women he met on this job, as he drove his new employers from temple to temple on their pilgrimage. Strange women, unclean women, coated in disease that he might bring back.

As she blew out the lamp and crept into bed, she hoped for a vain minute that her stomach would stop him. Surely, her bulk couldn't be attractive? But he didn't seem to care as he rolled over her and rucked up her nightdress. At least he supported his weight a little on his forearms as he thrust into her, otherwise she thought she might have panicked, might have tried to push him off her. Closing her eyes, she gritted her teeth and tried to breathe as his movements quickened, until finally, thankfully, he slowed and stopped, panting, sweat dripping from his forehead onto her shoulder. As he rolled off her, he patted her arm.

Minutes later, he was snoring.

Janani lay on her back, looking up at blank darkness above her, listening to the hum of mosquitoes. And she found herself wondering how very different her husband was from Sanjay, what she had done in her past life to deserve one and not the other.

She turned on her side, away from Darshan, longing for her dawn bath and fighting the burning in her eyes.

She had been right. In the first few days after Darshan was gone, Vandhana's comments became more biting, her slaps and pinches more frequent. She began to push Janani at any hint, real or imagined, of a transgression – the tea was not hot enough, there wasn't enough salt in the avial, the goat wasn't being milked early enough. The pushes were often timed to catch Janani off guard. She'd feel those strong, scarred, bony hands in the middle of her back, and then she would be stumbling into the wall or off the back step and into the dirt on her hands and knees.

The second push had sent her stomach first into the storage cupboard by Vandhana's sleeping mat. Janani had caught her breath and righted herself, then turned and found Vandhana staring at where her hand had come to rest protectively on her belly. Realisation struck her like a knife in the chest – Vandhana was trying to kill her unborn granddaughter. Janani had stood and looked back at her, feeling sick. And stupid. How could she have thought that Vandhana had stopped trying? Would stop trying?

From that moment, Janani ate only what she'd prepared herself, or poured herself, and tried to keep Vandhana in her eyeline as often as possible. It left her feeling drained, exhausted and afraid every evening.

Surprisingly, it was Lavanika who softened her grandmother's anger. She *was* soft. Soft hair, silky dark ringlets bouncing around her face even after Janani had tried to plait them, soft cheeks, and the big air-stealing, full-body hugs that made even Vandhana's riveted face melt a little.

But no matter how she wished she could keep her daughter with her, for smiling company, for a bright little light during the hours she was at home, Janani made sure she was at school every day, that she was with her friends in the evenings, running around, playing game after game of nondi or anchangal, coming home dusty and smiling. She would have to work hard all her life. This time, these sugar-sweet days of childhood – at least Janani could give her those.

The Saturday after Darshan had left, Janani walked to Usilampatti bus station, the morning air still cool. The bakery on the main road was open and she breathed in the smell of fresh sweet bread and cakes. One day, she thought to herself, she'd buy one of those cakes for Lavanika's birthday, her first cake ever. She was missing Lavanika today, but she was safe, happy, playing with Nandita under Shubha's watchful eyes.

The bus was starting its journey, so she was able to find a seat, up the front. It filled to the brim in minutes, people streaming in like rice grains poured into a bowl.

Sanjay would be home today. At least, she hoped so. The thought brought the warmth of pleasant anticipation. It was so vitalising, that the friendship they had had as children still stayed. The kindness between them. The laughter.

I like it when you smile, he'd said. The memory made her cheeks flush as she looked out the window at the flat green carpet of rice fields. The softness in his eyes, in his lean face, the relaxed curve of his lips. It was just kindness, of course, a friendly, brotherly kindness.

She wondered about the woman he'd marry one day. A Nambeesan, of course. She would have gone to college. To university. She would know all about the things Sanjay talked about – the government, the big cities that she dreamed about visiting, other countries that she had never heard of before. He would be good to his wife, she was sure of that. Caring. Loving.

Once, when she was little, Amma had taken her to the temple during Navratri. It had begun to rain, and by the time they left, torrents of thick, warm droplets were splattering into the ground like angry tears. They had cut through the rice fields, balancing on the raised, rounded tracks of dirt that bordered each paddy field square. Normally she'd loved to walk like this, watery rice-lings on each side of her. That evening, the mud was slippery, the sky was iron grey and thunder clapped them on – and Janani was scared. Scared enough to wobble as they walked past the overflowing irrigation canal, to lose her balance, to fall in.

In the few seconds before Amma's desperate hands had pulled her, gasping and coughing, from the muddy water, Janani had felt a darkness roll through her. A seething darkness, that took everything away from her so that she was as powerless as a lizard in a crow's beak. She'd felt that darkness a few times since that night, times that reminded her of trying to scramble through wet blackness, clawing for air. When Rupini had married and gone away, far away, to Coimbatore and her husband's family. When Amma had told her that she couldn't go to school any-more. When she was told she would marry.

When her babies were taken from her.

Now she felt it again, the dark helplessness, when she thought of Sanjay married, Sanjay gone to start his own family, far from here, from her – because why would he stay?

She pushed the thought away, actually shaking her head, which earned her a startled glance from the woman sitting next to her. This was ridiculous thinking. Of course he would go, but she didn't need him. She couldn't need anyone.

The house was quiet, a calm oasis, all morning. Radhakrishnan Aiyan left for work soon after Janani arrived. Neither of the boys were at home. Parvati Amma seemed brighter, strong enough to come into the kitchen and ask Janani how she was, to offer to help stir the sambar.

'When will you stop coming?' she said, gesturing to Janani's belly. It seemed to grow rounder every day. 'You must take care of yourself now. And if you are not working here, you can at least spend more time with your tailoring work.'

'I still have some time, Parvati Amma,' Janani replied. 'I feel very well. 'And I don't have that much tailoring work. Not yet.' The truth was she had plenty, but she needed this money, needed every rupee, every paise she could save if she were to get away. And she enjoyed it here, especially the times Radhakrishnan Aiyan was away and only Priya or Parvati Ma – or, even better, Sanjay – were in the house. She loved this gentle woman for her kindness, for her caring eyes despite the pain she must always be in.

Sanjay returned home just as Janani had finished dusting the living room. She heard the front door open as she was drawing the cleaning cloth over the ceramic elephant sitting atop the small square table in the corner of the room. His eyes under the sweep of his thick dark hair found her as he came into the room and his face lit in a smile.

She smiled back, until he looked and away and glanced around the rest of the room, up the corridor into the main house.

'It's quiet,' he said. 'Is my acha home?'

'No,' she said, 'not yet,' and she saw him relax.

'How are you?' he asked.

'I'm well,' she replied. 'You? You were up early today.'

'Yes,' he said. 'Too early.' He hesitated. 'Do you have some time tomorrow? There's something I want to show you.'

A shiver ran through her. He wanted to spend time with her. With an effort, she pushed down the spark of excitement and forced herself to think. With Darshan away, her chores had lessened slightly, but still there was a pile of tailoring work that had to be done.

'It's in Usilampatti,' Sanjay said. 'It won't take long.'

That was enough. She nodded. 'I'll have to bring Lavanika along.'

Sanjay laughed. 'The little moonbeam? I wouldn't be without her.'

Seeing him like this, relaxed and light, made her want to reach out, as though she were freezing and he was a fire.

What he saw in her face, she didn't know, but he stilled, and the silence that settled was heavy, the silence of bated breath.

'Sanjay?' Parvati Amma appeared in the doorway of her bedroom and the moment was gone. 'I thought I heard your voice.'

'You heard correctly,' he said, walking to her as she emerged into the living room, and wrapping her in a hug.

Janani found herself with the cleaning cloth half-raised and smiling at them, through the ache she felt for Amma. As she settled the elephant back in its place, she thought, *Moonbeam*. That was what Lavanika was. Her light in the dark.

The glimmer of a scratchy, uncomfortable thought – that it could describe Sanjay too.

'What is it he's going to show you?' Shubha asked, the next day. They were sitting at the back of Shubha's house. The children were playing hide-and-seek around them, the beat of Janani's sewing machine accompanying their running footsteps and their shrieks of laughter.

'I don't know,' Janani said. She turned the blouse material under the needle. She was enjoying this – it was a new pattern, one of a stack that Priya Amma had given her. 'It could be anything, really. A different temple? Someone else he knows who needs a tailor?'

'Come, Janani,' Shubha said. 'It must be something more interesting.' She was grinding dosa mixture, pestle grating against lentil and rice and stone. 'Perhaps a new bakery.' A pause. 'Or a restaurant.'

Janani glanced over, startled, to see Shubha was grinning at her. Not smiling, grinning, in a way Janani had not seen since *before*. There was a mischievous, knowing look in her eyes.

It was such a relief to see that Janani could do nothing but grin back. 'What are you talking about, you donkey?' she said.

'He's very friendly with you, isn't he, your Sanjay Annan?' Shubha said.

'We've been friends since we were children,' Janani replied.

'Maybe it's more than that,' Shubha said. 'Maybe you should run away from Darshan and that witch and marry him.' She laughed.

Janani felt as though cold water had been thrown in her face. Run from Darshan and marry him. Marry Sanjay. Shubha's voice had been lighter than it had been in weeks, but her words felt heavy as iron chains. The impossibility of them, of that future.

Digging her fingernails into her own wrist, Janani forced herself to smile. 'Oh, don't you start saying rubbish like that!' she said. 'That's all these people need, could you imagine if Rani heard?'

'All of Usilampatti would know in ten minutes,' Shubha laughed.

'All of the world,' Janani said.

She watched Shubha laugh again, her bubbling, infectious laugh, and it warmed her, distracted her from the shock of those words. The scar of the rope was still there, the raised welt pale against the smooth skin of her neck, but this was the first sign that it was truly fading.

They'd never spoken of that day. But Janani came here, every day, and every day she saw another piece of Shubha returning.

Janani turned the blouse and began to hem just below the bust. For a few moments, there was nothing but the sound of the machine between them, *tat-at-at*, the children laughing somewhere out of sight.

'Janani, it was a jest,' Shubha said. 'I hate how that man treats you – Darshan, I mean. At least you have a friend in your Sanjay Annan.'

'I know,' Janani replied. At least she had that, until he married and left. She stopped and looked up. 'Come with me, today. Your mamiyar will be here to watch the children, won't she?'

'Yes,' Shubha said. 'I'd like to come. I'm very curious. Are you sure?'

'Of course,' Janani replied.

Shubha stopped grinding and clasped her hands together. 'Oh, I'm going to meet your Sanjay Annan.'

They waited for him by the Canara Bank branch on Usilampatti Main Road. Janani held Lavanika's hand tightly. The road was busy both with traffic and with people, families returning from the market laden with vegetables, flowers and sacks of rice detouring into the restaurants for masala dosa and chicken chettinad. Thick grey cloud shielded them from the sun, but Janani could smell the rain in the air. Peacocks wandering the undergrowth now would have their tails spread, warning of the monsoon, adding their iridescent colour to the storm.

Sanjay appeared before the first drops fell.

Janani recognised the car as it drew up beside them. She felt Shubha take an instinctive step back as the spotless, gleaming red vehicle stopped. A moment later, Sanjay emerged. Lavanika was jumping up and down beside her, waving. Sanjay came around the front of the car to meet them, his teeth gleaming in a smile that lifted his moustache. Janani couldn't help but notice that he smelled of incense and something else, the scent that permeated his room, a fragrance of wood and flowers.

'How are you, little moonbeam?' he asked.

Suddenly shy, Lavanika shrank into Janani's sari pleats.

'Good.' The word came out muffled.

Sanjay put a hand in his pocket and withdrew it to reveal a purple-wrapped bar. Janani recognised the image of two glasses of milk being poured atop a square of chocolate. When Sanjay looked up at her, a question clear in his eyes, she smiled and nodded. Lavanika gasped when he held it out to her; she took it with hesitant little fingers and pressed it to her chest.

Sanjay straightened and smiled at her before his eyes flickered to Shubha.

'This is my friend, Shubha,' Janani said. 'The one I've told you about.'

Their eyes met for a second, and she wondered if he'd question why Shubha was there, if he'd insist they leave her. For an instant, she regretted bringing her friend at all. But then he turned that warm smile back to Shubha and they were exchanging a respectful 'vanakkam'.

'Come, come, all of you,' Sanjay said. 'It looks like the heavens are about to open.'

Janani felt herself relax. She cast a glance around, scanning the road for faces she knew, but there were too many distractions for anyone to be paying attention to passers-by.

'Amma, can I sit next to Sanjay Mama?' Lavanika asked.

'Quickly, then, little flower,' Janani said, and Sanjay opened the passenger door to lift Lavanika in.

Janani and Shubha slid into the back.

'Where are we going, Sanjay?' Janani asked, realising as they pulled away that she should have asked this some time ago.

'Not very far,' Sanjay said. 'You can walk from your home. I didn't want to give you the wrong directions though. I've only been here once.'

It was not far. They drove back up Usilampatti Main Road, passing the hospital at a crawl that was barely faster than walking speed. The rain had started to come spattering down and the shoppers with baskets of papaya and green bananas atop their heads were hastening their pace. Two little boys were leaping up and down in a tight circle, palms and eyes raised to the sky, snatching at droplets. Janani watched them until they fell away from view as Sanjay sped up to cut in front of a lumbering vehicle emerging from the bus station.

'We don't want to sit behind his smoke,' he said.

They turned onto the highway, joining the stream of lumber and petroleum and granite lorries. Only minutes later, Sanjay was pulling in to the side of the road, just after a roadside tea stall.

'Here we are.'

Janani looked out the window. Where? She could see nothing extraordinary. The tea stall was nestled under the shelter of a peepal tree, leafy and dark green in the storm's half-light. Directly beside them was a large white building which Janani remembered was a hotel restaurant. She had wandered this far in the months after she was first married, exploring the area.

Sanjay had already slid out of the car, and was now unfastening Lavanika's seat belt. Janani found Shubha looking at her, eyebrows raised. She shrugged and opened her own door.

They joined Sanjay as he stood, staring at a row of small buildings past the restaurant – flat-topped shops and houses with both the slanting, overhanging roof of Janani's own as well as thick thatch. She gestured Lavanika over to her and pulled her sari pallu around them both to shelter from the rain.

Sanjay turned to her. He was still smiling, but now Janani sensed a tinge of nervousness in the tilt of his eyebrows. At his sides, his hands curled into fists and opened, curled, opened.

'OK,' he said. He was looking directly at Janani, as though they were the only ones there, standing at the side of the highway in the afternoon rain. 'I think . . . I think I've found a shop to rent. For your clothes.' He shook his head, ran a hand through his hair. 'That doesn't make sense. I mean your sewing.'

At first, the words seemed to have no meaning. It was as though she were hearing for the first time that she was getting married, or that she was pregnant – so unexpected that she felt she'd been pinched.

'Rent?' she said.

Sanjay nodded. His smile was fading. She recognised the expression on his face. She'd seen it when he'd come home from school and faced his father with exam grades, school reports, a tense, hunched look as though he could already hear the shouting, feel the slaps. 'It's not much. Enough to store your sewing machine, your materials. Enough to hang up your clothing . . . and other things you might need . . . I asked the landlord, he said it would be big enough . . .'

She was still staring at him. The metallic taste of rainwater was on her tongue.

'Let's see it!' Shubha said.

Janani started. She'd forgotten her friend was there.

Sanjay's shoulders relaxed, his lips quirking.

'Yes,' he said. 'At least we can get out of the rain.'

He led them to a little free-standing brick-and-concrete room – it was too small to be called a building – metres back from the edge of the highway. Here was a peepal tree too, the fruit still small and green. Behind it, and off to one side, stood an automobile repair shop and a general store with piles of fruit and vegetables looking waxy in the murky afternoon light. Sanjay produced a key and inserted it into what looked like an actual metal door. There was a rasp and a grind, and it opened to reveal darkness. Reaching inside, Sanjay pulled what seemed to be a string, and the room was bathed in a warm yellow glow.

'The previous tenant has moved now to Madurai,' Sanjay said. 'He used to sell rice, dahl, spices. The man who owns this – that is his shop there.' He pointed at the automobile shop.

Janani was half-listening, her eyes travelling across the white-washed ceiling and brick walls, the slim gas pipe that ran like a rigid snake along their adjoining border. There was a little shelf in the back of the room, another at the side. A bed could fit in here, and a sleeping mat. Pots and pans for cooking, water urns in one corner, her sewing machine in the other.

She took the few steps into the centre of the room, Lavanika still pressed to her. In her mind's eye, she saw it transformed. She saw space for a clothes rail and a shelf for materials and her picture of Meenakshi Amman, a table in the front for her to mark down measurements.

Blood was pounding in her ears, her chest so tight she had to remind herself to breathe. She could see it there, close enough to touch, the open door of her cage.

Footsteps sounded behind her, and she heard Shubha gasp. 'Oh, Janani,' her friend whispered.

Turning, she saw Sanjay silhouetted in the doorway.

'What do you think?' he asked, shifting from one foot to another. 'It's not much. The space might be too small.'

'It's wonderful,' she told his shadowed face, and saw his smile grow slowly, wider and wider. It was wonderful. It was perfect: small and perfect, just like her daughters – and like them she couldn't have it. 'I can't afford this, Sanjay Annan. I don't have enough yet. Maybe not ever.' Suddenly, her legs felt weak, as though the exhaustion of it all had drained into them. The urge to sit down almost overwhelmed her. The warmth of Shubha's fingers grasping at her arm almost brought tears.

'Can I talk to you for one moment?' Sanjay asked. 'Alone?'

She looked at Shubha, who nodded encouragingly.

She left Lavanika inside with Shubha and followed him back out into the rain and under the tree, its leaves shielding them from the larger drops.

Sanjay cleared his throat. Then he frowned.

'The rent is paid,' he said. 'And the deposit. One year.'

'Iraivan,' Janani whispered. 'You . . .'

'Not me,' he said, his hands waving as though he were brushing something off a table. 'Amma.'

'It's too . . . too much . . .' And it was, far too much, what would her mother say? They didn't accept charity, they were Kallars, they worked hard for what was theirs . . .

What he saw in her face, she didn't know, but he brought his hands up to scrub them through his hair. Water flew everywhere. 'Please don't argue about this, Janani,' he said. 'Please. You and your amma have given so much to our family, and you should spend more time tailoring, you're *good* at it, and . . .' He turned around and she watched his back, the water slicking his pale blue shirt to his skin, speechless. When he turned back, she was shocked. Surely not. Surely it was just the rain moistening his eyes, clinging to his thick lashes?

She felt her arm lifting, pulled up like a puppet. Fought to stop herself reaching out to touch him.

'Amma is dying, Janani,' he said. 'I don't know how much longer she has. This is one of the last things she can do. I think she knows that. She tried to help your amma, but you know what happened. Please don't refuse her now.'

The memory came flooding back, the pain of that day, the

ache of her chest as she cried and cried. She wouldn't be going to school anymore, Amma had told Parvati Ma. She would no longer be going to the Nambeesans' house. She was getting older, she had to learn how to take care of her own home, prepare herself for marriage. Sanjay had been there, and his face had been drawn, his lips twisted in a way that she knew meant tears were on the horizon.

And Parvati Ma had said, *Send her to school, Geeta. I'll pay the fees. She is so bright, so hard-working. Let her keep learning.*

It had taken Amma a long time to speak, but Janani had known the answer, even before her mother pressed her hands together, thanked Parvati Ma, and said no.

She'd always been proud of how hard her parents worked, of how they needed help from no one. Proud, until her mother's pride had sliced through her chance of another life, and left her hurt and bewildered. Aching at the disappointment in Parvati Ma's face.

Now, though, she could understand what Amma had felt that day. The shame of not having enough. Of not being enough.

The baby inside her kicked, one tiny limb flailing against her insides, and then another.

'This can't be a gift.' She could barely hear herself over the raindrops hitting the leaves, *sh–sh*-ing like cicada wings. 'I can't accept it.'

Sanjay looked as though she'd shoved him backwards. 'What . . .' The rain dripped into his eyes, making him blink; he wiped them on the back of his hands like a frustrated child.

Don't, Janani wanted to say. *Don't cry. I'll make it OK.*

'A loan,' she said. 'I'll take this as a loan. You tell Parvati Amma that I will pay her back. Every rupee, every paise. I have to do that.'

He looked at her. Somewhere above them, a crow shrieked

from where it sheltered beneath the leaves of the banyan tree.

'A loan,' he said. 'You have it.' He frowned, the smooth skin between his eyebrows creasing into a valley, just as it had done when she beat him at a game when they were children. 'But interest-free.'

She laughed, the sound high-pitched to her own ears, pealing in her throat. Without thinking, she reached out and took his hands, both of them, in hers. They were lean, wiry, slick with rain. A callus here, a callus there, gifts from the cricket bat. Warm, strong. He gripped her fingers.

They were so close to each other now. His body was sheltering her from the rain. He smelled like lemons and jasmine.

'Amma?'

They dropped each other's hands as though they'd been burnt.

Janani turned to see Lavanika running towards them, chocolate bar still clutched in one hand.

'Can we go now, Amma? I'm tired.'

'OK, little one,' Janani said, bending to her, wrapping her arms around the warm little body, kissing the wet curls. 'Let's go.'

She could think of nothing but the little shop – hers now, *hers* – as they climbed back into the car for the short drive back. The shop, and the feel of Sanjay's hands in hers. But she didn't need to speak – instead, it was Shubha whose voice filled the car, exclaiming about the shop, thinking of all the ways they could tell everyone – but Vandhana – of Janani's services. Another miracle – Janani had not heard so much life in Shubha's voice since *before*.

'I'll take you home,' Sanjay said as they turned back on to Usilampatti Main Road, but Janani shook her head.

'No, no, that's OK,' she said. 'It's still best if no neighbours see us with you. They'll talk, they'll ask questions.' Vandhana would find out. Even that thought couldn't bring Janani's mood down from its heights.

Sanjay pulled up once again further beyond Canara Bank. They scrambled out into the rain. Janani was the last to slip from the car.

'Tell Parvati Amma,' she said quietly, and stopped.

Sanjay looked back at her and smiled. 'I will,' he said, 'if you stop calling me "Annan".'

She laughed.

By the time they waved him off, the rain was coming down harder, but the road seemed just as busy. The wind blew droplets diagonally into their eyes, turning the world into a blurry, wet mess.

'Stay close, Lavi,' Janani said as they walked down the road. 'It's very slippery.' Her daughter's hand in hers was slick as a fish. Shubha walked on Lavanika's other side, the two of them shielding her as best they could.

The traffic was not slowing. It blared past them, a mass of horns and headlights, throwing up sprays of water and mud. Janani was regretting asking Sanjay to leave them here now; she was close to soaked through and could think of nothing but getting home, drying off, getting into her nightdress, even if it meant returning to close quarters with Vandhana, hemmed in by the rain.

'Amma, look!' Lavanika said. She'd slipped her hand from Shubha's and was pointing down the street. 'It's Manasi!'

'Where?' Janani asked distractedly. It was hard to focus on anything other than putting one foot in front of the other, waiting for the turn off this awful road.

'There!'

Janani squinted along Lavanika's outstretched, pointing arm, and could just make out a woman and a girl, the child waving back at them, her pink pattu pavadai bright in the gloom. If Lavanika hadn't called her friend's name, Janani didn't think she'd have recognised Rani and Manasi.

'I'll go and say hello!' Lavanika said.

'No, Lavi,' Janani said, 'we'll walk there together . . .'

But Lavanika wasn't listening, or maybe she couldn't hear, over the *thrum* of the autorickshaws, the honking, the squelch of their sandals in the mud. Her daughter's hand slipped through Janani's fingers like air, and she was gone, running down the road with the speed that had always caught Janani by surprise.

'Lavanika!' Her voice twinned with Shubha's, and still their cries were lost in the rain.

Lavanika ran.

The motorbike came towards them, two young men hunched atop it, their black hair matted to their heads. Janani only saw the autorickshaw as a rounded flash of black and yellow, a giant bee, and perhaps the young motorbike driver saw the same, just a flash, too close, far too close, because he shouted, or at least Janani saw his mouth gape in a shout, and he swerved, and the boy behind him flailed, and then the bike was careening at a wild angle, and Lavanika was running, running, and now Janani was too, running and screaming . . .

Lavanika turned just before the bike hit her.

Janani's eyes followed nothing except the green of her daughter's skirt. She barely dodged the fallen bike, the motionless bodies tangled beneath it. Pain jolted through her legs as she fell to her knees beside Lavanika.

Her child's eyelashes were fluttering, delicate moth wings in the rain. From her lips came little whimpers, like those that escaped her when she was trapped in the web of a nightmare. She was in the mud, there was mud everywhere . . .

Janani slipped her arm under Lavanika's neck, her shoulders, pulled her out of the filth of that water-soaked earth and up into her lap, stroking her curls, patting at the dark stain on her blouse that kept spreading, turning green to ugly maroon. Her blouse, that she'd watched Janani stitch, her head on Janani's shoulder, her breath warm against Janani's cheek.

There were people all around now, around the bike, around her and Lavanika, shouting, touching her shoulders. She could hear them. She could hear voices she thought she recognised. But all she could see was Lavanika, looking up at her, the flutter of her eyelashes slowing, the voice getting softer, slower.

'*Rock, my little peacock.*'

Back and forth, they rocked, rocked until her baby fell asleep, her cries quietened, her nightmares gone.

Chapter Sixteen

The seventh month

Now she twists and turns in her mother's womb. Her tiny fists open and close at the sound of her mother's voice. Her heartbeat calms.

For the first week, Janani was mute.

Amma had wanted to send her home.

'I told her to take some time off,' she'd told Sanjay when he returned from Madras on Friday evening to the news that the little moonbeam had been lost. He'd been wordless himself for several long minutes. It had been a long time since he had been so close to tears.

It had been Priya Ammayi, his mother said, who had taken Janani's limp-as-rags hands and told her she could stay as long as she needed, do whatever she wanted, say whatever she had to. And so she came every day, at her usual time, an hour or so after dawn, and dragged her feet out of the back door in the late afternoon.

Sanjay forced himself out of bed very early on Saturday morning. He'd struggled to sleep. Imagination plagued him, conjuring up the spectre of Lavanika, jasmine flowers tangled in her hair, skipping ahead of him, of Janani, the sun-golden glow of her smile as she looked down at the little girl clutching her hand.

The house was still silent, Vijay asleep after a late night squinting at his textbooks, even Acha not yet up and ready for work.

A few pieces of mail sat beside the phone, on the carved wooden side-table in the hall. Sorting through them, he found one addressed to him. Clearly, Amma had been well enough to collect it – Acha would probably have opened it. Still, Sanjay had been nervous having it sent to his Madras address, although there was no logic behind his fear. There was no way anyone at work would see his mail. That they would even care was doubtful. And yet, it had felt to him that he would have been cursing himself in some way, sending this marker of a change in his life to that chaotic, confusing place.

He opened it quickly, heart beating a little harder, just enough to make the paper tremble in his hands. The contents were thicker than he expected and in his haste he ripped the rough material of the envelope that had housed them.

Contract of Employment: SKT Engineering LTD.

A feeling of finality flooded through him. Of door chosen and path accepted. Was it a good feeling? He wasn't sure of that, but it felt right. And for now, that was enough.

It was silent enough that he could hear the footsteps that sounded at the side of the house. A minute later, the back door rattled, and opened.

Bells, high as birdsong, chimed faint but clear.

Sanjay stood in the hall, uncertain which way to go, feeling absurdly like a thief in his own house.

You need a coffee. Just go and make yourself a coffee.

Clutching the contract to him like a shield, he walked past the living room, through the dining room, into the kitchen. The house breathed around him, peaceful, quiet.

By the time his hand had touched the kitchen door, he could no longer pretend to himself she wasn't there. Pots rattled to running water as the gas hob hummed. He had to force himself to tap lightly on the door and ease it open.

She was already turning his way as he entered. They both stopped, Janani with a carrot in one hand, while the water ran into the pressure cooker in the sink, ran until it overflowed.

Janani rushed to the sink to turn off the tap and Sanjay took the opportunity to step inside, easing the door half-closed behind him so he could reach the coffee tin.

The water stopped. Janani was once more gazing at him. Sanjay realised she'd had to lean well over her rounded belly to reach the tap. Exhaustion and pain and grief were painted mercilessly on her face. All of her seemed to sag towards the ground.

I'm so sorry, he wanted to say. My deepest condolences.

He held up the tin. 'I'll just make some coffee,' he said. 'Can I make you some?'

Janani's eyes widened and they stood frozen for a long moment. Then she turned away from him. Both hands went to her face, the carrot pressed against her cheek as though it were trying to comfort her.

He took two steps towards her and stopped, not sure what he was trying to do, what he was going to do next.

In the end, he didn't have to make the decision. Janani turned around and her arms wrapped around his waist, the side of her face pressed against his chest.

Sanjay held her without thinking. He remembered, years ago, when they'd played at the end of the driveway, the stray dog that had loped its way towards them. He remembered Janani running towards it, remembered it snapping at her leg, drawing bright beads of blood that gleamed gem-like on her smooth dark skin. Radhakrishnan had sat her down, cleaned the wound, given her a tetanus shot that made her grimace. But only afterwards did she cry, just like this, their arms around each other and her hot tears soaking through his shirt.

They stayed like that for a long, long moment, until the smell of the gas forced Sanjay to gently detach himself.

'The kitchen will catch on fire,' he said.

She nodded, wiped her eyes on her sari pallu.

They talked for an hour, until the rest of the household began to stir. She told him of Lavanika's burial, a quiet, unbearable day, Shubha at her shoulder, Vandhana scowling in the background. She told him that she'd left Lavanika with the comic he had bought her, and the chocolate bar. He had to turn away then, stand at the back door and look out beyond the bougainvillea.

'I want to tell you something too,' he said.

'What?' The kitchen smelled like sambar. Janani was grinding the coconut chutney. She had to shout over the mixie's growls.

Sanjay turned. 'I want to tell you something!' he half-yelled. 'I found a job in Madurai.'

The mixie rattled on for a few more seconds, then died.

'What?' she said, much softer now. 'Why?'

He shrugged, very conscious of the sudden quiet. 'I won't have to travel to Madras every week,' he said. 'And I want to stay. Because of Amma, you know.'

The silence hung between them – silence and everything else.

Sanjay broke it by walking over to the fridge and extracting the milk, creamy and fresh.

'I'll make coffee,' he said, just as the mixie started again.

Radhakrishnan came into the dining room just as Janani was laying the table for breakfast.

'You're up early, for a change,' he said to Sanjay. Pointing to the papers Sanjay still held in his hand, he asked, 'What's that?'

'Just some work I was reading through,' Sanjay said, and darted out of the room before he was asked anything further.

Upstairs, in his room, he flipped quickly through the contract, turned to the final page, signed and dated it.

Done.

He stayed in his room until he heard his father call for him.

'Your amma's awake,' Acha said. 'Can you help her take her medication?'

'How is she feeling?' Sanjay asked. He could ask her himself, but she never told him the truth – it was Radhakrishnan whose duty it was to bear the burden of her pain, who understood what the nausea, the cramping, the endless fatigue meant.

'Not so good this morning,' his father said. 'Make sure she's resting.' He hesitated. 'And don't leave her alone with the girl. Janani. What happened was horrible, of course, and it is only natural it might distract her from her work, from your mother.'

A flare of anger made Sanjay open his mouth, but his father had moved on as though he were dictating notes rather than having a conversation.

'Your Priya Ammayi will be along soon – stay here at least until then. Vijay will need to go to the library to study.'

'Of course I'll stay,' Sanjay said. His voice sounded cold and tight in his own ears. 'But Janani's perfectly capable of looking after Amma. She does it more often than you do.'

Radhakrishnan froze. He'd already begun walking away, down the hall, briefcase in one hand.

Every muscle in Sanjay's body tensed. He crossed his arms over his chest and waited.

His father took a breath heavy enough for Sanjay to see his shoulders rise and fall, and kept walking.

Sanjay stayed where he was, listening to his father retrieve his shoes, collect his keys, and finally close the door behind himself.

Even then, he felt rooted to the spot, until he heard a clatter behind him.

'Are you OK?'

He turned to find Janani standing at the entrance to the dining room, a coconut palm broom in one hand and a bucket of water, carpeted with soap suds, in the other.

'Yes,' he said. 'Everything's fine. I'll just check on Amma.'

He walked away before she could catch any of the anger, the guilt, he knew must be drawn on his face.

By early evening, Amma wasn't feeling much better and Sanjay could think about little else. With much persuasion, he had been able to coax some food down her – rice and yoghurt, with a little sambar to flavour it, as though he were feeding a toddler. Janani had stayed well past her usual time, stroking his mother's back as she sat up in bed and sipped the water he held for her. Only when Amma insisted did she finally go home, looking exhausted.

They'd been alone most of the day. Vijay had come down, scoffed breakfast, given Amma a kiss and a worried look, then disappeared to meet his study group. It was the swell of relief Sanjay felt when Priya arrived that made him realise just how afraid he was.

Priya took over with brisk efficiency, brushing his mother's hair, helping her bathe, talking at her as though she'd never run out of words. By the time Radhakrishan came home, twilight had dimmed the windows enough to turn on the lights. Sanjay and his aunt had managed to help Amma into the living room, and the three of them were sitting together with a crossword puzzle book. His mother was engrossed – every laugh she emitted released a tiny puff of Sanjay's worry.

'How are you feeling, Parvati?' his father asked after he'd deposited his bag and gone to scrub his hands.

'A little better, Etta,' she replied, smiling.

'You're late,' Sanjay said. 'Long day in the clinic?' His voice sounded flat to his own ears.

'Yes,' Acha replied. 'There were a few walk-ins who were too ill to turn away.'

'Amma was feeling quite ill.' Sanjay kept his head bent over the crossword. *Tropical flightless bird. Nine letters.* 'I'm glad Priya Ammayi was able to come.'

'I'm better now,' his mother said. He felt her hand on his arm.

'I'm glad Janani was here too,' he continued, looking up at his father. 'She was perfectly capable. Not distracted at all.'

'Sweet girl,' Amma remarked. 'She stayed too long.'

'It starts' with "c", Amma,' he said as his mother began to write 'peacock' beside the clue. 'And nine letters.'

'I'm sorry I didn't come earlier,' Radhakrishnan said. 'I just couldn't get away.'

'This word, here, this is "serenade", isn't it?' Amma mused. '"To sing in the open air, usually a man to a woman"?'

'Yes, you're right,' Sanjay agreed. 'Nice work.' He was distracted by his aunt, who had stood up, facing Acha. 'So the third letter of the bird word is an "s".'

'Of course you could, Krishnan Etta,' Priya said. 'You could easily get away, there are so many young doctors at the clinic now. You just didn't want to.'

'Oh, I know this bird,' Amma said. Sanjay could almost feel the strength of her desire to end the conversation, to dispel the gathering of the storm clouds. That's who she was, the calm, the tranquility. What would they be when she was gone? 'Come, Priya, and play the game.'

'I'm coming, Parvati,' Priya replied, twisting to look down

at her. She turned back to Acha. 'You're hiding in your clinic. Hiding from this.' She swung an arm around in a semicircle that roughly encompassed Sanjay and his mother.

'I'm not—'

'You care about your patients, I know. But what about your wife?'

Sanjay realised he'd got to his feet too. He took a step forward, sliding his body between his mother and the rest of the family.

'Priya,' Amma said from behind him, a hint of iron in her voice now.

Sanjay had never seen his aunt like this. Rarely seen any of his family like this, shoulders angled, head down, poised like an angry bullock. She looked so tiny in front of his towering father that it should have seemed ridiculous, but it didn't.

'When will you tell her? When?' she pressed.

'What is this, Priya?' Radhakrishnan said.

Part of Sanjay wanted to go. Wanted to let them speak the words they hadn't let themselves say. They were his seniors. This was their discussion, their business, not his. But at the edge of his vision he could just see his mother, back straight with dignified, fragile grace, only her head tilted down to the crossword, and he knew she was listening and trying not to hear all at once. And so he spoke.

'Priya Ammayi,' he said.

They all turned to him, in one moment, like deer at the smell of a tiger's approach. Sanjay realised he didn't know what to say.

'Amma's almost finished the crossword.'

There was a heartbeat's pause as the words registered. Then he felt his mother's hand curl around his fingers.

'Cassowary,' she said, the syllables soft drips of gentle rain.

Priya's head dropped. She nodded and turned back to the couch.

Sanjay looked at his father.

'Let me get your dinner, Acha,' he said.

They left his mother and aunt to the crossword.

In the kitchen, Sanjay put the freshly cooked sambar and avial on the hob to heat. The rice was still steaming in the rice cooker. He heaped food on the plate, balanced a pappadum on the side and took it out into the dining room.

Radhakrishnan was sitting at the table, his head in his hands. Sanjay paused at the door, watching him. It was rare for his father to look old, but here, at the rosewood, glass-inlaid table he was so proud of, surrounded by the equally beautiful carved cabinets filled with his sons' awards and souvenirs from overseas, with carved marble elephants and Murano glass, Radhakrishnan Nambeesan looked ancient, bowed down by the struggles of reaching this place in which he now sat.

And at this table, he'd helped Sanjay with his homework, taught him poker, read him Enid Blyton and Tolkien and *Tinkle Digest*.

Acha.

Walking around the table, Sanjay placed the plate in front of his father. Radhakrishnan's head came up and he looked at his dinner, then at Sanjay, as if he didn't know what they were doing there, or even where he was.

'Thanks, moné,' Radhakrishnan said.

Sanjay watched his father pick at his food. *Moné*. He hadn't used that word in years. It was as though he'd reverted back to a lifetime ago when the decisions and the actions that weighed him down today were just a dark tangled path before him. Before he, Sanjay, was just a rolling stone of slight disappointments. Before Amma had become sick, begun to die too quickly for any of them to accept.

'I've taken a job here,' he heard himself say. 'An engineering job, in Madurai.'

His father looked up at him. There was a long moment.

'Hmm,' Radhakrishnan said, and he nodded. 'Your amma will be happy.' He glanced away, eyes directly ahead of him, gazing at something not physically there. 'It won't be too long that you'll have to stay.' He sighed and took another mouthful.

Sanjay left his father to eat in whatever peace he could find.

Priya put his mother to bed, then hugged Sanjay and retired to the guest bedroom beside his parents'. For a moment, he thought about going to sleep too. He was exhausted, despite the relative earliness of the night, despite the fact he'd been trapped at home all day.

Vijay still wasn't home. His father had finished his dinner and walked without a word to the drawing room to bury himself in a book.

Praveen, Sanjay knew, would be out in Madurai, in one of the hotel bars, drinking, laughing. He could head into the city to find him. The thought of harmless, pointless banter, of an ice-cold, burning whisky almost had him running out of the house.

Instead, he found himself tapping gently on his parents' bedroom door.

A murmur from his mother reassured him she was still awake.

She was sitting up against the headboard when he entered. The lamp on her bedside table was on, yellow light shining through the clear glass peacocks that arched their necks against their frosted backgrounds. She was holding a book – or resting it open in her lap. The *Bhagavad Gita*, Sanjay saw.

'Sanjay, kutty,' she said. 'Come here.'

He went to kneel by her bed. She smelled of sandalwood and jasmine, like she always did.

'Are you OK, Amma?' Sanjay said. 'I'm so sorry about earlier.'

'Why, kutty?' she asked. 'I'm sick, but I'm not a child. I don't need to be hidden from the truth, do I?'

He didn't know what to say.

'I know, kutty,' she said. 'Your acha wants to protect me. Maybe he thinks it will sap my strength, if he speaks it out loud. But I know my body.'

She placed her hand on his, where it rested beside her on the bed.

'It doesn't matter, moné, what it is or isn't. We'll take one step at a time, won't we, along our paths?' She tapped the cover of the book. On it, the famous image was etched in gold – Arjuna kneeling beside his chariot on the Kurukshetra battlefield, listening as Krishna stood calmly beside the horses he would drive into war, coaxing the doubts out of Arjuna's mind. *There is nothing greater than understanding your duty on this earth, and doing it.*

He wanted to hurl the book across the room. He wanted to bend his head and cry. Instead, he forced himself to his feet.

When he left the room, Amma was sitting content, nestled amongst her pillows, engrossed in the ancient text. She was smiling.

Chapter Seventeen

The eighth month

*Now her eyes can focus. Her wrinkles are smoothing over
her baby fat. She is the size of a cabbage.*

For days, Janani could not sleep. For weeks after those days,
searing, vivid dreams woke her. Dreams in which she walked
Lavanika to school, her daughter skipping beside her, curls dancing; dreams that left her lying in bed, for a few floating seconds
before the weight of her loss fell back upon her like boulder
of iron. Dreams in which she saw, again, the motorcycle, saw
Lavanika fly out of sight, felt the warmth of her blood, which
left her crying in her sleep. She woke to a sodden pillow and
burning eyes, reaching for her child.

The hours dragged, every moment painful, as though her soul
were being tugged across the coconut grater. Vandhana barely
spoke to her but to curse. When she had heard the news, she had
flown at Janani, slapping her about the head and shoulders, wild,
swinging, open-palmed slaps.

'You can't even look after your own child,' she'd screamed.

Janani had let her, standing motionless, still sodden from the
rain, until Shubha and Narendran had pulled her mother-in-law
away. Vandhana had turned away, hunching in on herself, and

they had heard her mutter, under her breath. 'All the bad luck on my head, Iraivan,' she had said, and Janani's chest had twisted itself into an impenetrable maze her breath couldn't penetrate.

She found herself lingering at the Nambeesans', the work consuming her mind. Parvati Ma's gentle understanding, her soft hands wrapping around Janani's, or resting against her wet cheek, was a slight relief from the constant, gnawing ache. And Sanjay . . . During the week after she had first told him, she thought often of his arms around her in the kitchen. The solidness of his chest, the smell of his aftershave. Of how, just briefly, she had felt as though she wasn't alone, that someone else was sharing the weight of her grief. They hadn't spoken of it since, but she could see it, in the warmth of the smile that stretched his thin cheeks, that lit his dark eyes.

On the days Sanjay wasn't there, Janani completed her cooking and chores as quickly as she could when she returned from the Nambeesans' house. Then she walked to Shubha's and sat in the corner with the sewing machine, until long after darkness fell, until after the children were in bed. She couldn't look at them, at Nandita, at Raman. She focused every ounce of concentration on the stitches and the eye-hooks, squinting at the measurements she scribbled down on scraps of paper through sore, swollen eyes. Shubha sat beside her, singing to her, reciting stories she remembered from childhood. They had to stop, every ten minutes, for Janani to scrub the ceaseless tears off her cheeks.

Darshan returned two weeks later. Drunk, of course. It was Vandhana who told him, sounding more gentle than Janani had ever heard her. He had looked at her, looked at Janani, and laughed.

'What are you talking about?' he slurred. 'Little bird?' His voice rising to a shout. 'Where are you, little bird?' Stumbling to the bedroom, he peered under the bed, opened the cupboards, lifted clean clothing, craned his neck out of the window into the thick night. 'Come and give Appa a kiss, Lavanika.'

It was like fiery salt on Janani's raw soul.

'She's dead!' she said, and she ran to Darshan and turned him around by his thin shoulders, smelling the cheap whisky on his breath. She shook him, or tried to – he barely budged. 'She's dead! Like all of our other girls. She's dead.'

He pushed her, blindly, unthinkingly, and she stumbled back. They stared at each other. What Darshan saw she didn't know, but Janani watched as her husband's face, skin flushed and eyes bulging, crumpled slowly.

She'd never seen a grown man cry like Darshan cried then. He howled like an injured dog. Sinking to his knees, he curled up, head in his hands, tears dripping through his fingers onto the floor. There, he rocked back and forth, his wails muffled by his palms

It was Vandhana who went to him, squatting slowly and painfully down beside him. She murmured to him, stroking his hair, as she'd done so sparingly with Lavanika. Janani watched them and felt so sick she had to leave. Stepping past them, she walked to the back of the house and busied herself soaking rice and dahl, chopping vegetables she wouldn't need until the next day, washing plates and spoons and knives. She boiled tea for her husband and mother-in-law and tried not to think about throwing it in their faces.

Finally Vandhana was able to coax Darshan into bed, un-washed, still dressed in his driving clothes, his trousers and shirt. Within seconds, he was snoring loudly enough to drown out the cicadas outside. Janani heard Vandhana emerge from the bedroom, but she ignored her until she felt a hand on her arm. She pulled herself free and turned around to see Vandana's drawn face.

'Stupid girl,' Vandhana said. There was weariness, not anger, in her voice. 'How could you tell him like that? She was only a girl-child, but he loved her.'

Janani just looked at her. Her head was starting to pound. How tired she was.

'Maybe you should go back to your parents,' Vandhana said. 'What a useless wife you are.'

The thought sent a thrill through Janani. Oh, to be back there, to feel Amma's hands on her face, her arms around her. To hear Acha's gentle voice telling her stories and the gossip from the quarries. But she wasn't a child anymore, and they weren't young. How could they endure the shame, to have her returned to them, a damaged, unwanted object, not even able to do the basic duty for which she'd been born?

'I'm going to sleep, Ma,' she said. It was the safest thing to say. 'You should too. We're all tired.'

Without waiting for a reply, she walked away, back to the bedroom, closing the door behind her. She was gentle, but she needn't have been – Darshan's snores didn't falter.

She went to the corner of the room, dark but for the milky moonlight dripping through the window shutters. The bamboo mat stood leaning against the cupboard. Unrolling it, she laid it flat and straight at the end of the bed. The sheet was still rolled within it, and the thin pillow.

She lowered herself down. As the weight came off her legs, she was suddenly aware of how much they ached. Her anklets were tight against her swollen skin, her feet throbbing. Her lower back twinged in sympathy.

Closing her eyes against the discomfort, she breathed in the smell of Lavanika that lingered on the sheet. Surrounded by that smell, she drifted off to sleep, the sheet clutched to her breast, the pillow under her cheek wet with tears.

*

Janani woke early the next morning, unsure if it was the rooster crowing or Darshan's snores that had disturbed her. The sun had barely begun to stir.

Still in a daze of sleep and half-remembered dreams of Lavanika, she crept outside, past the curtain hiding Vandhana's sleeping body, to bathe and dress. The water was cold, clearing her head as she sluiced it over her hair. The cooling relief of it splashing against her legs and back and stomach was delicious, if temporary.

She judged she had about an hour before her chores would call her, so she walked – or waddled, her body swaying from side to side behind the weight of her baby – up the road to Shubha's house. The streets were quieter than she had ever seen them, only the animals stirring, young goats calling out for feed, the gentle cluck of chickens tucked out of sight. A lone cat, mottled brown and white, darted across her path.

It didn't occur to her until she had been knocking for a few minutes, until Narendran opened the door with sleep still dragging at his eyelids, that she might not be welcome. She saw the concern in his eyes before he asked if everything was all right. By then, Shubha had appeared behind him.

'Janani,' she said. 'Are you well?'

'Yes,' Janani replied, hearing the uncertainty in her own voice. 'I just . . .' She couldn't help looking to the corner of the room, where her sewing machine sat hidden beneath and behind piles of clothes.

Shubha followed her gaze. 'Oh,' she said. 'Now? It's very early, Janani, you should rest.'

The concern hadn't left either of their faces. Janani didn't know what to say. She had three sari blouses, two pattu pavadai and two salwar kameez to stitch. Salwar kameez were new to her – she had stitched a few of them to her own measurements from material that Priya Amma had given her. They were orders from the village, orders from friends of Priya and Parvati Amma. She had to get them right. And today Malini and Ponaal were coming, with more sari blouses.

Shubha was murmuring to Narendran. He nodded and moved out of her way, letting Shubha step outside to join Janani, closing the door gently behind him.

'Janani, you're working too hard,' Shubha said, taking her hands.

'No, no.' Janani shook her head. 'It's fine. I have . . . more time, now.' Now there were no walks to and from the school, no curls to brush, no meals to coax into a reluctant little mouth.

'Then just come and sit with me,' Shubha said, squeezing her fingers gently.

Vandhana believed that was exactly what she was doing, when she noticed Janani's absence in the hours she should have been back from the Nambeesans'. She had no idea of the money Janani was storing in the pouch in the folds of her oldest sari, concealed at the back of the cupboard.

'I like the work,' Janani said.

'Yes,' Shubha replied. She paused. It seemed as though she were hunting for what to say next, her eyes flitting away from Janani, searching the street behind her, to either side. 'It's hard for you to sew now, my love,' she said finally. 'The children are sleeping. And Mamiyar and Mamanar. They're old now. They need the rest.' Pity softened her face.

Sparks of embarrassment shot through Janani, warming her cheeks. 'Of course,' she mumbled. Of course. She was using Shubha and Narendran's house like a workshop. It wasn't much bigger than her own, with one more adult and two more children. And her, clacking away on her machine, taking up that space, taking away their privacy. Why hadn't she thought about it? She cast her eyes around too, as though a solution would materialise. It was only just dawn, she realised. She'd disturbed them all. She could have cried with the shame. 'I'll take it away, soon,' she said. 'I've got the shop now. I won't keep coming here, getting in your way.'

'No, Janani!' Shubha said. She shook her head. 'You can come here for as long as you want. But you have to look after yourself. And the child.'

I can't look after any of my children, Janani thought, but she couldn't say that. If anyone understood her pain it was Shubha, and she didn't want to remind her of that.

'Can I take the machine outside?' she asked. 'It will be quiet there.'

Shubha looked at her, worry etched over her face. 'OK.'

'And I promise, soon I won't bother you with it anymore.'

They crept inside, where Nandita and Raman slept on mats, almost hidden behind a curtain. Janani slung her bag of material over her shoulder and slipped out of the back door, Narendran, who insisted on helping, following her with the sewing machine cradled in his arms. There Janani sat, as dawn broke and the sky lightened to palest blue streaked with the glow of wispy orange clouds, the sewing machine tapping along to the rhythm of her breathing.

Later, Janani went to collect water from the pump, Shubha alongside her. They spoke little – Shubha seemed to sense that producing words was still slightly beyond the limits of Janani's energy. But the comfort of having her there eased the hollow feeling in her chest and stomach that had stuck obstinately in the weeks after Lavanika's death.

'Come this evening,' Shubha said as they stopped in front of

Janani's house. 'Or, if you don't want to, I'll come here. I'll come, OK?'

Janani looked at her. Shubha seemed as animated as she had before that last, lost child, as though Janani's grief seemed to have made her forget her own. Somewhere, beyond the numb sensation, outside the hollow in her chest, she knew she was glad to see the life in her friend's eyes. She nodded.

'I'll come,' she said.

Shubha nodded and walked away, water buckets balanced carefully atop her head and in her hand.

Janani circled around the back, depositing a pail by the kitchen door, beside the pans she'd washed, and another by the half-empty bucket by the bathroom. Her back had begun to ache again – she hadn't been able to fill the pails to their brim, the weight too much for her pregnant, sweating body.

As she stepped towards the front of the house, she heard voices.

'Yes, yes. Another girl. Always girls, with this one – those she has given birth to, at least. The only boy was a miscarriage.'

It was Vandhana's voice, low-pitched, sounding even rougher than usual. She was close, very close – just at the front of the house. She must have just emerged.

'Well. And now the first girl gone too, the poor little thing.'

Janani couldn't quite recognise this second person's tones. Old Radha, maybe. Or Nalini. One of the women Vandhana had grown into her married life with, as Janani had grown with Shubha.

'She's still young,' Vandhana said. 'Darshan too. A son will come. You know how long it took me? I survived, and I have two sons.'

'Will you . . .' The second voice had dropped even lower. Janani found herself creeping closer, pressing her body against the side of the house, too nervous to peer around the corner. 'Will you keep this child? Another girl, but with the first one gone . . . One girl in the family is good.'

The baby was weighing heavily on her; she needed to urinate badly, but she bit her lip and ignored the discomfort.

She heard Vandhana laugh. There was a bitterness in it that Janani had rarely heard. 'You remember what happened after my third girl? My mamiyar did this.' There was a pause.

The other woman clucked. Radha then. 'I remember. The oil everywhere. Madhu Ma said you'd spilt it, the old cow.'

Another pause.

'Ah well, maybe the child won't survive,' her mother-in-law said. 'Maybe Iraivan will have some pity for us.'

'Maybe.'

Janani backed away. She crept back to the kitchen door, unlocked as she had left it the night before. Two coconut halves sat on the bench just inside, drained, the water poured into three glasses. She'd not drunk it yet, had forgotten with Darshan's appearance that they were there.

Picking up the coconuts, she went back outside. The coconut grater was waiting for her. She put a steel bowl beneath the wicked blade, sat down with difficulty on the very back of the block of wood and began to grate. The smell of fresh coconut began to rise from in front of her, from somewhere below the curve of her vision-obscuring belly.

With each rasp of the shell against the blade, her thoughts swirled. A thought flickered into her mind, a wish that it were Vandhana against this blade. But then she remembered her mother-in-law's mottled, scarred hands, and imagined her screaming, shaking, trying to fling the droplets of boiling oil from her skin and the thought melted, leaving the aftertaste of shame.

*

'Mamiyar,' Janani said. 'I want to go home to have this baby.'

It was nearing the middle of October and she had maybe two months more to carry this child. She had waited this long on purpose to broach this subject. The hours she'd spent at the Nambeesans' house had barely dwindled. She hadn't let them make her stop working, and that had been easy too. Parvati Amma was weakening. She hadn't the strength to cook, or to clean. Radhakrishnan Aiya had hired another cook, a hard-working woman about a decade older than Janani, pleasant but with few words. Still there was a lot of work, more now that Sanjay had come to stay the whole week in Madurai.

She hadn't been prepared for the surge of emotion that had left her breathless when she arrived for work on Monday and he had appeared for breakfast. It was his first day in the new job – his shirt and trousers had been ironed into sharp angles, his thick black hair brushed back. The sight of him made her skin tingle, as though her whole body was trying to smile. When she was not working, or even when she was, if he was home, they talked, about his work and her village gossip. About his amma, and her Lavanika. He and Shubha were the only ones she could speak about Lavanika to.

Now, however, it was leading to the time that she would have to stop working. Her back ached incessantly. Even Radhakr-ishnan Aiya had looked at her two days ago and said that a woman in her condition should not be scrubbing floors. He didn't want her, he said, to give birth in his drawing room. She could afford to stop now. The money she had saved up from her sewing had become a heavy sum, enough to keep her fed for months. And Parvati Amma had given her a stack of folded rupee notes for the months she couldn't work. She hadn't had a chance to hide these before Darshan saw them. He had grunted in rare approval, taken most of them and left Janani with what she needed for the week's dahl and vegetables. She didn't want to stop working, Janani realised. Parvati Ma's soft voice and Priya Ma's blunt jokes soothed her, drew her thoughts away from Lavanika, from the weight of her belly. And Sanjay . . .

When she stopped work, she would stop seeing Sanjay.

'Home?' Vandhana said, the rasp of her voice tearing Janani from her thoughts. 'This is your home, stupid girl.'

Janani kept the expression of her face. She half-wanted Vandhana to try to slap her, just so she could slap her back. 'To Amma and Appa,' she replied.

'Why?' Vandhana asked. Her eyes were flat. She knew damned well why, Janani thought, a bitter laugh threatening to bubble up from her throat. She swallowed it down. It wasn't the reason it had been. With Lavanika's death, she had no girls now. None.

'I haven't seen them in a long time,' she said. 'And . . . since Lavanika . . .' She couldn't finish.

Vandhana was silent for a long time. Then, 'Darshan!' she called.

A few minutes later, Darshan appeared, wearing a lunghi, still bare-chested, his hair damp from his bath. 'What?' he asked.

'Your wife wants to give birth at her mother's house. I say let her.'

Janani felt her eyes widen in surprise. There was no change in Vandhana's expression. What was beneath that granite-hard surface to the woman?

Darshan looked at Janani. She wasn't sure if it was lack of comprehension or lack of interest in his face. His eyes were sunken; he didn't look well.

'OK,' he said. 'So?' To Janani, he said, 'You'll come back afterwards?'

Janani nodded. In some ways, she was lucky with the man

she had married. He could have been brutal and controlling, the way some men were, refusing to allow her out of the house, to make any of her own decisions. Instead, he was a gormless, apathetic fool.

Vandhana's face relaxed. 'Go, then,' she said. 'I have had enough of the troubles of your births. The mess.'

The words burned like poison. The *trouble* of birth, the *mess* of it. The only mess Vandhana ever cleared up was that of the existence of her granddaughters.

'Don't expect Darshan to take you there,' Vandhana added. 'You can take an auto.' She glanced at Darshan and took a step closer. 'And if you bring a girl baby back into this house, I'll throw it into the street.' She prised open the snack jar and began to chew on a murukku, grinding it between her teeth.

Relief accompanied Janani's anger. The smells of her child-hood, the warmth of her parents. She was going home.

Chapter Eighteen

Madurai, 2019

It feels strange to carry on in the days following my grandfather's cremation as though nothing had happened. It's a different strangeness for me, of course. I feel it reflected off the rest of the family. The meals for which Manju Ammayi sets the extra place at the head of the table, and we all stare at the additional plate and tumbler, none of us sure what to do, until she realises and clicks her tongue and puts it all away. The mornings Kochachan says 'I'll just check on . . .' and his sentence peters out into silence and a shake of his head. The evening Radhika hunches over her chemistry homework and her tears spread dark circles on the page about covalent bonding.

Amma and Acha and I get out of the house, escaping together. But there's a different strangeness between us. We're all on our best behaviour, navigating through a forest of crystal towards each other.

The shouted words before my run didn't end in silence. Instead, Amma's every word to me is delicate, sweet, like storm-washed blue sky. We don't talk about the fight. We don't talk about what happens next.

Two days after the funeral, we visit Thirumalai Nayakar Palace. It seems bizarrely out of place, surrounded as it is by the frenetic activity of the city. As we cross the road from where

Kochachan's driver, Mahesh, drops us off, Amma grips my hand as though I were five again.

I gaze up at the ornate entrance, its curved Mughal-style arches making it seem as though it's been transplanted from a far-off kingdom. Rajasthan maybe. The creamy-white exterior is marked with dirt and moss.

Inside, I stand and look up at the gorgeous multiplicity of carvings at the top of the pillars, the painted ceilings, the immensity of the halls.

'It's seventeenth century,' Acha says. 'Apparently the king recruited an Italian architect for it. It's a mishmash of Dravidian, Rajput and Mughal styles.' He smiles when I stare at him. 'Amazing, isn't it? Globalisation, four hundred years ago.'

The curve of his eyes reminds me of when I was child, and he would weave stories for me at my bedside. It's the first light in his face I've seen since we landed in India. I smile back, and reach to kiss his cheek.

Amma walks beside me. There's a dreamy look in her eyes as she gazes up at the kaleidoscope of colours adorning the ceilings above us, as she runs her fingers over the painted brickwork of the pillars, before pulling her hand back as though she's been burned.

'You must have been here so many times,' I say to her.

'No,' she replies. 'Only once.'

'Why only once? You didn't come on school visits?'

'No. Nothing like that. It is beautiful, isn't it?'

'Very,' I say and she smiles.

Tell her. In this big open space, in this beauty, she'd understand. You shouldn't have to hide who you love, Iphigenia had said, and Iphigenia was right.

Amma's already wandered away, taking her thoughts with her.

I could follow her, of course. But my fear's already surged back, sickening, viscous, coating my thoughts, and I let the moment pass.

The next day, we go to the Gandhi Memorial Museum. Artefacts and relics of his life stand poised behind glass – his sandals, his walking stick. At the end of the exhibit, I find myself standing in front of the bloodstained clothes Gandhi was wearing when he was shot dead in the street, the famous white dhoti and shawl painted with rusty red.

It's a world away, that moment in a street in Delhi, seven decades ago.

Acha appears next to me. He and I tend to navigate these things at the same speed. I turn to see that Amma's still several exhibits back.

'Do you remember the assignment you did, in primary school?' he says. 'About the Salt Walk?'

'Yes,' I reply. It was a history competition, run by the local council. I'd won second place, and five dollars. 'It's about as much Indian history I studied at school.'

The museum's quiet and my words hang in the air like dust. It's the first time I've really considered them. I feel a weight settle on my chest, as though I've just remembered someone I've loved, and lost.

'I'm glad you did that,' Acha says. 'We should all know our history. It makes us who we are, doesn't it.'

He states it as though it's a universal truth. I don't think that when he speaks he realises the irony of it. Or maybe he thinks the minutiae of our individual histories is insignificant, single grains of sand in a moving dune.

'I don't know my history,' I say.

'That's why we're here.'

'Not this.' I wave a hand around me. '*My* history. The black hole on Amma's side. Isn't that important?'

Acha looks at me. There's surprise on his face. I'm surprised myself, at the bite in my tone.

'Of course it is important, molé,' he says. 'But you have to ask her about that. You know that. It is her story to tell.'

It's my story to know, I think.

A man and a woman, about my age, walk past. She's looking up at him, lips curved in a shy smile, and he keeps fiddling with his glasses. Their shoulders are so close they almost touch.

'What do you think Amma would say, Acha, if I told her something about me she really didn't like? That she might think is wrong?'

He's looking at me. There's concern in his eyes and I know that his mind is whirring, whirling, but it never shows.

'I think she would say she loves you anyway, sundari kutty. Both of us would.' *Beautiful child.* His gentle words soothe me like a lullaby.

Maybe she would, I think, but maybe it would break her. Break us.

Amma's coming towards us and her face is bright with her smile. She looks as delighted as a child, and I know then, like I always have, that I can't lose her. I don't say anything, but I link my arm through hers when she reaches us.

'How's the holiday going?'

We're back at the house. The late-afternoon sun is slowly fading; the buzz of mosquitoes is in the air and I can smell the mosquito coils Girija's switched on. My feet itch for a run, but instead I've curled up on the end of the green sofa in the living room, an old *Tinkle* comic in hand. I'd loved these as a kid.

Arjun flops down on the sofa beside me. He must have just showered – his aftershave wafts towards me. His hair's spiked up into what must be the latest Bollywood trend. It glistens with gel, like a damp echidna.

'It's not really a holiday,' I say. 'It is nice to see you all though.'

'Yeah.' He sighs. 'But I've been a pretty terrible host. Shall we do something?'

I'm surprised at how pleasant the thought of getting out of here is, of getting away from my parents.

We locate Radhika, finishing her homework at the dining-room table, and drag her away. 'Playtime,' Arjun says, and she rolls her eyes, but I see the dawn of her first real smile for days.

We pass the parents in the drawing room. There's some awful, screechy Tamil serial on the TV, but they're not watching it. They're chatting instead, cradling cups of hot tea, a plate of Parle-G biscuits on the Taj Mahal table in the centre of the room.

The youngest of us is seventeen, but it doesn't stop our parents' questions. Where are we going? How long will we be? When will we be back?

'Just the three of you are going?' Amma says. She sits up, back stiff, turns to Kochachan. 'Will they be safe? It's getting late.'

It's six-thirty. I can feel my face burning.

Arjun raises his eyebrows at me, then says, 'Mahesh Annan will drive us, Janani Ammayi. It will be fine.'

I watch Amma look anxiously at my aunt, but I don't wait for her to respond. Instead I walk quietly to the shoe cupboard, pull my sandals on and step out the front door. There's a murmur of voices, and then my cousins follow, a step behind. Mahesh is leaning against the car, hypnotised by his phone, but when he sees us, he bares his gleaming teeth in a smile and waves.

We go bowling. Mahesh drops us off at a huge indoor games complex that shouts about its virtual paintball, cinemas and arcade games. We wear giant clown bowling shoes and slide over the floor under fluorescent lights. Bollywood R 'n' B mash-ups lullaby us along. I haven't been bowling for years and I'm surprised at how much fun it is.

'I need the bumpers!' Radhika grouses between bowls as we sip vase-sized cups of Diet Pepsi. Arjun's bought a carton of fries, too. The grease seeps into the cardboard.

I laugh. 'You're a little old for bumpers.'

'You're not doing a thing I tell you,' Arjun says. 'You're going to put a hole in the lane soon.'

We're all laughing then. It's the most fun I've had since I left Australia.

Afterwards, we walk down the main road, past vendors selling bangles and pottu and the last vegetables of the day, to a cute restaurant that amazingly serves wine. Arjun orders a bottle of red and a couple of glasses as I stare at him in surprise. He grins at me as Radhika asks for a lemonade.

'Just don't tell the parents,' he says. 'They'll be furious I gave a girl alcohol.'

'A girl,' I state.

Radhika rolls her eyes. 'It's still a complete scandal when girls drink,' she says. 'Forget all the nightclubs in Chennai and Mumbai and Bangalore and Delhi. All the old people just pretend it's not happening.' In her soft, accented voice, *nightclub* sounds surreal.

I shake my head and take a sip. The wine's not great. It's silty with hangover. Right now, I don't care.

We chat about nothing over our dinner – Arjun and I dredge up memories from childhood of stealing sweet sharkara upperi from the pantry and eating so much we felt sick, of Rohan dropping Radhika on her head onto a fortuitously located cushion. We talk about dreams of travel, of being Indian in Australia. We talk about our family. We finish the wine. Arjun looks at me and I shake my head, so he orders himself a glass. And then another. And, after we call Mahesh, he asks for a whisky, then settles the bill.

By the time we make our way to the car, the sky's a hazy mix of star and splotches of dark cloud. The heat of the day's barely drained away. The contrast from the air-conditioned restaurant is startling. I shiver and sweat and feel tipsy at the same time.

'Do you guys go there often?' I ask as Mahesh twists and turns his way out of the car park.

Radhika laughs. 'Definitely not. Etta never spends time with me.'

Arjun cranes his head back from the passenger seat. 'Hey. I'm studying. Studying medicine. I'm busy.' There's a strong smell of mediocre wine.

'Failing medicine, you mean,' his sister says.

Surprised, I wait for him to snap at her. He smirks and twists back around.

It strikes me how little I know about him, outside of film-snippet memories of us as children, on the intermittent visits with Acha to Madurai, playing hide-and-seek, squealing down the water slides at Athisayam Water Park, the pen pal emails we sent to each other for a few years afterwards. I know less about Radhika. She was a drooling toddler when I saw her last. Who are these people now, my closest family outside Acha and Amma and Rohan?

There are a few beats of silence, a friendly, comfortable, thinking silence. I look outside – we're trapped in a slow snaking line of city traffic, full of blinding headlights and an incessant cacophony of horns.

'I'm sorry for being so boring during your visit, Nila Chechi,' Radhika says. She's fiddling with the end of her braid, twisting it around her left index finger.

'Don't be silly,' I say. 'It must have been hard, with Achacha not well, and now . . .'

I've never talked to someone about death before.

'She was his favourite,' Arjun says, not turning.

'No I'm . . . I wasn't,' she says. 'Well, not until you started all your rubbish.'

'My rubbish?' he laughs. There's a bitter edge to it, and just like that the peace in the silence of just seconds ago is gone, split into shreds.

'You're always out, you come home in the middle of the night, stinking—'

'You sound like Acha. Congratulations.'

'. . . You're failing all your classes . . .'

'Because I fucking hate them.'

Radhika gasps and claps a hand over her mouth. She turns to me, eyes wide. She looks so young. I notice the butterfly clip in her hair. Its glittered lavender wings tremble at every shift of her head.

'Come on, Arjun,' I say.

He runs a hand through his Shahrukh Khan hair. It barely moves, frozen into its gelled peaks. 'Do you know what I wanted to study when I finished school?'

'No.' I'm wishing we hadn't had the wine.

'History.' He twists back. The light-soaked city is reflected in his eyes. 'Indian history. And politics.'

Surprise makes me forget my discomfort. 'That sounds great!'

Arjun looks at me. A shy smile begins to draw the corners of his mouth upward. 'Thanks. When I told the parents, Amma looked like I'd grown another head. Acha laughed. And then I told them I was serious. I insisted. Amma started crying. Acha was angry. Furious. And Achacha – it was as though I'd told him I'd come to kill him. Do you remember, Radhika?'

Radhika sighs. Nods.

'In this family, it's medicine. Engineering. Finance,' he explains.

'So medicine.'

'I had the marks.' He snorts. 'One-hundred-percent-Arjun. That's what they used to call me, at school. One-hundred-percent-Arjun would never do *history. Politics.* These days, film stars go into politics. And ex-cricketers. Achacha,' he says, 'he was so disappointed. I couldn't disappoint him. He's been so good to me, you know? I did medicine, and pretty quickly I wasn't one-hundred-percent-Arjun anymore.' He points to Radhika. 'She's taken up the challenge. Haven't you, Radhi? Achacha ignored you until then, and now you're his favourite.'

'Be quiet, Etta.'

'He ignored you?' I ask Radhika, before I can stop myself, then bite my tongue.

Radhika shrugs. 'A bit.' She looks out the window, and I think about how to change the subject.

'She's a girl,' Arjun says, and his laugh is not nice. 'That was Achacha for you.'

'Can we stop talking about this?' Radhika says. Her voice has crept up in pitch.

'Definitely,' I reply, but Arjun's not finished.

'Nila, you got the same treatment, didn't you? Even worse, I guess, because . . .'

He trails off, into a silence that is not silent, it's the chaos of too many people outside and it's a thick block of iron in the car, heavy and cold.

I shouldn't pursue this now. I can sense the onset of Radhika's tears.

Mahesh, who might even be younger than Arjun, has his eyes on the road, and I know his English is almost non-existent, but he doesn't need to understand our words to feel them. His shoulders have inched closer to his ears.

But I have to ask. 'What do you mean?'

Beside me, Radhika's pressing herself against her door, chewing on a fingernail, her eyes huge.

'Just . . . because . . .' He's drunk, but aware enough of a line he's stumbling over, an imaginary boundary someone's placed before him. 'You know, your amma. She's just not . . . who Achacha would have chosen, I guess.'

I do know. My father a Keralan Brahmin, my mother a Tamil Kallar. She's married so far above her caste that it's like a mortal marrying a god.

A dull pulse of anger starts in my chest. This family, so stuck in an older India. No choice, no freedom, only sanctioned fun. It's like we're all poured into a mould from the moment we're born, that if we don't stay there, perfectly frozen, perfectly formed, we'll break.

But I've been broken from birth, because of who Amma is.

'Nila, it's just old-people shit,' Arjun says.

Somewhere in the whirlpool that's my mind I realise expletives sound strange in his accent, as strange as if it were my parents swearing.

'OK,' I say. 'Let's talk about something else.'

We don't, though. We don't talk at all, until we get home.

The car pulls into the carport and I can see the tension rise from Mahesh's shoulders as he switches the engine off. Hercules' deep barks herald our arrival. Mahesh is the first to get out of the car. He bids us farewell and disappears into the darkness like a scared wraith. He's followed almost immediately by Radhika.

'I need to . . .' she starts, but she's already running to the front door, and the rest of her words whip away too quickly to hear

The jasmine's blooming again, as though it's worshipping the night. The air is heavy with the scent. Somehow, it's given Arjun back his speech.

'You know,' he says, 'Amma's trying to find me someone.'

I want to run, too, but Arjun's ambling, his steps uneven.

He takes a cigarette out of his pocket and leans against one of the carport's supporting poles. Balance uneven, he almost slides off it before he catches himself. 'She was thinking about you. About us. I heard her speaking to Achacha about it. He said it might be a good thing. It'd bring you closer to the family. Isn't that weird? Like, just because your amma isn't a Nambeesan, and just because she wasn't married when you . . .' His voice tails off. The air is so thick it seems to hold the echo of his words.

'What are you talking about?' I say. My voice is very quiet. It shakes. I feel my hands shake too.

Arjun holds his hands up. 'Ah, shit, I talk too much when I've been drinking,' he says.

The front door's shut behind Radhika. I'm not sure if it's locked, and knocking is the last think I feel like doing. So I hold out my hand. 'Give me the keys.'

'Oh, come on,' he says. 'It's just a chat. Some family gossip.'

'Arjun, just give them to me.'

The molten darkness presses over us, moulding the world into this nightmare.

Above us, a window lights up with flickering electric yellow.

Arjun doesn't seem to notice. My words seem to be filtering with honey-like viscosity into the recesses of his drunken awareness. And my anger is contagious.

'You think you're better than me, don't you?' He nods, answering himself. 'Perfect Nila, top marks in her degree, it's not medicine but close, great job, sports trophies . . .' Sliding his hand into his pocket, he pulls the keys out. They dangle by his side, hanging from the Ganesha key chain he is holding by the curling elephant's trunk. 'You must think I'm useless too, like all the rest of them,' he says. His voice rises with every other word.

'How pathetic you sound.'

His mouth opens, and his face contorts, but I'm disappointed, so disappointed that the night's ended like this, that I'm raging. Warmth trickles down my cheeks, tickles at my jawline.

'Give me the fucking keys.' I shake my outstretched hand.

He drops the keys into them. Ganesha's trunk digs into my palm as I squeeze my fist over them and run up the stairs onto the veranda. In the corner of my eye, Arjun throws his cigarette onto the concrete and walks after me.

As I open the door, I'm aware of the light above us switching off.

The living room's dark. Ghosts and house lizards lurk in the corners.

'I'm going to bed,' I say. My skin's prickling despite the heat, as though I'm rolling in grass dotted with farmers' friends, as though I can expect to find the barbed tips of the daisy seeds clinging to my clothes when I undress tonight.

Arjun steps into a moonbeam and that's when I realise he's crying too. 'Why am I the one who's never good enough?' he says. 'You're the one whose dad married some village woman. After they had you.' It's not spite in his voice. It's the shadow of a plaintive wail.

The light turns on, flooding the room. They emerge into the light, four of them, hair sleep-tousled, pyjamas and nightdresses rumpled, eyes squinting like emerging prisoners – his parents and, almost hidden behind them, mine. I wonder what we must look like, grown adults, weeping at each other.

'Arjun!' Manju Ammayi speaks first. I've never imagined she could sound like that.

It brings Arjun up short too. He stands at the door, breathing heavily, staring at her, tears staining his face. Then he bends down. We watch him wrestle with his shoes, tugging at the laces, almost falling over as he wrenches them off his feet. He opens the shoe cupboard and hurls them in. The door slams. Without a glance at me, he walks down the corridor. He's expressionless but for the gleam of moisture on his face. The older adults part to let him through, as though they're a ceremonial guard. We listen to the heavy tread of his feet on the stairs, and then the shuddering slam of his bedroom door.

I'm frozen. We stand, the five of us, in the new silence. The shoe cupboard door inches open, choking on an ill-fitting shoe. Amma's mouth opens to speak, and that's what releases me.

'It's nothing,' I say, and then I run, out of the drawing room, up the steps, into my room, into aloneness.

Not my room.

Acha's.

I sit on the bed. A knock sounds on the door, which I've locked. Of course they'd come. I wait until they knock again, until Amma calls my name, until they fall silent, until the light on the landing goes out.

There's a vibration against my leg.

My phone.

I wrench it out of my too-small pocket. Stare at the screen. It illuminates the room with its harsh, cold light. Flashes an image that usually tugs the corners of my mouth up. A name.

I want to pick up. I need to hear that voice. I can't. I feel sick.

Standing up, I begin to pace, my eyes on anything but the phone I've thrown screen-down on the bed.

It's the first time I've really looked around this room. It's too hot up here during the day. In the evening, jet lag and humidity send me into a sticky slumber. Besides, Acha, or whoever cleared up after him, has left little behind. Textbooks, reference books, an obese hardback Oxford English Dictionary. Files and folders of bank statements and engineering industry magazines and ancient issues of *National Geographic*. There are no posters on the walls. There's a vase of flowers – the flowers are fresh, the vase is chipped. The narrow bookcase against the wall holds well-read paperbacks and creased spines of mainly fiction authors – Isaac Asimov and H. G. Wells and Arthur C. Clarke. A picture arises in my mind, of the gangly, glasses-wearing, teenage Acha in the family portraits downstairs sitting at the worn wooden desk, reading *Foundation*, and I feel a sudden, trembling swell of affection for my father.

There's also a dusty, red-covered *Bhagavad Gita*, and slightly newer-looking *Bhagavatam*.

I stand up and step over to wiggle the *Bhagavatam* out of its niche. Krishna was always my favourite god, whether I believed in him or not. The stories about him are an endless series of adventures. He's Acha's favourite, too. It's lovely to think of him thumbing through this when he was a child, absorbed in the hopeful reality of a god who lifted a mountain with a finger to save a village from drowning rains.

When I open it, though, I see that it's in Malayalam. The swirls and lines and dots dance their way across the page. Unintelligible, hypnotic. Page after well-turned page, wrinkled with love.

I let my body pitch back onto the bed, the book suspended above me, shielding my eyes from the yellow glow cascading from the bedroom light. As I turn the pages, somehow it doesn't matter that I can't read this. It feels like a code I must be able to decipher. I know this story. This language is in my blood. Surely there's meaning in this for me.

Something drops onto my face.

I flinch and close my eyes just in time. It's harder than the book's pages, lighter than cardboard.

A photo.

Sneezing in old-book dust, I turn onto my stomach, closed *Bhagavatam* in one hand, the photo in the other.

It was taken here, in this house. The living room hasn't changed much, although the pictures on the wall are different, and, even in the faded ink, the sofa looks newer. There's a broom against the wall, strangely. The coffee table is the same, dark wood, thick legs carved with floral designs.

Beside it stands my mother, and me.

Amma's wearing a sari and a tiny, shy smile. Her head is slightly lowered, and she looks up at the camera as though she's ashamed to have been caught by it. I'm clinging to her skirt, and unlike her, my chin is so high, my face is barely discernible. What can be seen is a huge, gap-toothed smile and a mop of black curls that end just above the shoulders of my pink blouse. There's a shine around my mouth, my lower cheeks, as though they're stained with juice.

That blouse is familiar. So is the sari draped around Amma. So is the broom leaning against the wall, so close that Amma could have stretched out and picked it up, a traditional one formed from coconut leaflets. Girija has one just like it.

The photo must have been a surprise, because my mother hasn't had a chance to push away the metal bucket at her feet, or drop the white rag she holds in the hand that isn't clasping me.

I'm already feeling my mind tatter and fragment when something else catches my eye.

Pale yellow in the corner of the photo, barely discernible against the cream of the rug. But legible.

The date stamp.

I stare at it, at this impossible photo.

The world recedes away, like the ocean before a tsunami.

Chapter Nineteen

Madurai, 1993

The end of the ninth month

Now she is chubby with fat and her bones have hardened.
Her home is too small for her, holding her close and warm.
She reaches for the world's embrace.

The golden shower tree outside the window had shed some of its blossoms overnight, leaving a dusting of bright button flowers on the ground. Janani stood in the early-morning breeze, feet bare and hair unbound, and breathed in the fresh familiar air, filling her lungs with it. A pair of crows, glossy-winged in the sunlight, took flight from the roof of the tiny free-standing storeroom at the back of the house.

Despite the strain of her seemingly unendingly growing belly, she felt as though she were more rested after the four days she had returned home than she had since that long-ago day when she had left. She was back in the curtained-off space where she and Rupini had grown up, sleeping sometimes side by side and sometimes in a slumber-messed tangle, playing anchangal or telling ghost stories on the floor during the monsoon rains. She remembered the moment she had left it all behind. A lifetime had passed, but she could still feel the heat of the marriage fire and the weight of the gold in her ears and around her neck.

'Janani, child,' her mother called from inside. 'Come and eat.'

Dosa and chutney and sambar, Amma's sambar, awaited her when she stepped back inside. Appa had pulled over a chair for her – it was near impossible for her to get her swollen body down onto the floor and back up without a significant amount of effort and a helping hand.

She ate in comfortable silence, listening to her parents talk about the neighbours, about the village, even about Jayalalitha's promise of quotas for backward classes. Much good that would do her. But her children. This child.

By the time she'd arrived, Amma had had time to hide her grief for Lavanika. All she had done was hold Janani, in a long, tender embrace. Just being here was a balm on the still pulsing wound of Lavanika's loss. For the first time since the accident, she was sleeping through the night. She felt that now she might be ready for this new baby, ready for what this next step along her path would bring.

'Are you OK, Janani?' Amma asked her. 'It has been a hard time for you, child. Lavanika – I wish we could have come to you then.' She looked at Janani over her half-finished dosa. 'And the other children.'

Her mother's sweet, kind face, lined now in a way that Janani couldn't remember, made her throat tighten.

'I'm here now,' she managed to say.

Amma reached out and put a hand on her knee, and Janani felt her sore muscles relax under the familiar, beloved touch.

The following morning, she stood outside in the warmth of the sun, slinging the washing onto the line hung between the corner of the roof and a coconut palm. There was an animated discussion happening between two ladies at the back of the neighbouring house, about what seemed like an impending marriage. Janani listened to it, to arrangements of jewellery purchases and catering, gossip about the girl's family and criticism of the venue, her mind pleasantly blank.

A cramp rippled through her middle, making her gasp. She stopped, arms half-raised, one of Appa's shirts dangling from her hands. When nothing else came, she slung it up over the line and continued with the other clothes.

The second cramp forced her to hunch over, clutching at the bulge of her stomach. She stayed there, bent into a right angle, until the pain eased and she was able to straighten and take slow, careful steps back inside.

The house was empty. The water buckets were gone – her mother must have gone to the pump. Somewhere close by, water splashed onto hard floor – Appa was bathing.

Janani went back outside and finished hanging out the clothes, carefully, calmly. Then she walked slowly up and down behind the house, waiting for her parents to return.

Another cramp came, longer and more painful than the last, and when it subsided, she was aware of sweat trickling down her face, forming rivulets between her breasts. This seemed faster than the last time, than any of the other times.

She heard Amma's voice around the front of the house and waddled back inside, braced for the next contraction. Amma had appeared at the front door, a pail of water in one hand. Relief flooded through Janani, so strong that she felt the prick of tears at the corner of her eyes. It must have been painted thick on her face. She saw her mother's smile fade into concern. In the briefest moment, the pail had been set on the floor by the kitchen and warm, strong fingers were grasping Janani's arms.

'Come, child,' Amma said, and Janani followed her gratefully.

Her mother helped her change from her sari into a long cotton nightdress which hung loose and comfortable even over the baby. They paced together around the room. Amma's soft voice was in her ears as she walked, telling her about her sister, her nephews and niece, about cousins and aunts and uncles she hadn't seen in years, stories she'd never heard and memories of times past.

Her father emerged from the bathroom, but he didn't stay long. Amma was barking orders at him immediately, to fetch food, water, to get in an auto and bring Kamala Amma back. Janani could have cried at the sound of Kamala's name. When she had first come, her mother had asked her if she wouldn't rather go to the primary health centre closest to them. Perhaps she should have done, but it was Kamala she trusted with her delivery. The thought of the primary health centre just raised memories of Shubha's baby, there and then gone. The thought of the hospital made her think of the sour-faced nurse who'd betrayed her baby to Vandhana.

When her father appeared with Kamala, Janani clutched at her as the old midwife kissed her forehead and took her place on the other side, opposite Amma. Appa disappeared

'We won't see him for some time,' Amma said, smiling.

'Good,' Kamala grunted. 'They just get in the way.'

They walked and walked, and talked, and ate lunch together. Perhaps it was hours later, or perhaps it only felt it because the sun still hung high in the sky, but finally Janani felt a trickle, and then a gush as her waters broke.

Here you come, little peacock.

She wished Sanjay were here. *You'll be OK,* he'd told her once, when she'd fallen and split her head open on the edge of the concrete wall bordering the driveway. *You'll be OK.*

It was late afternoon by the time she was resting on the old woven mat in the bedroom. They left the shutters open so the sun filtered through the leaves of the coconut palms, reaching fingers across Janani's face. It was warm, but she didn't care – the fresh air, the light, was more important than the discomfort of sweat prickling her temples.

Amma stroked her brow and wafted air at her with a plastic hand fan with a picture of Ganesha on it. In the corner of the room, Kamala was mixing herbs in with water and melting coconut oil over a candle flame.

'It'll be over soon,' she said, 'sooner than the last. Rupini's third one came so quickly she barely had time to push.'

'I miss Akka,' Janani said. Her sister wouldn't know about Lavanika yet.

'Me too. Coimbatore is far. But we'll go there soon. All of us.'

Janani looked into her mother's face and realised, for the first time, how old she seemed. The lines and crevices around her eyes and mouth had spread, lengthened, deepened. Her hair was more steel grey than black now, and her shoulders were beginning to hunch, as though the years of cleaning and carrying water were just beginning to bear down on her.

Then her body tensed with another contraction and she forgot about anything else.

'The little one's ripe for the world,' Kamala said, gently massaging warm coconut oil into the skin of Janani's stomach.

Hours later, her face was wet with sweat and tears. Nausea gripped her, but she had already thrown up her afternoon meal and even retching was too much effort. The light from the window had faded and it sounded as though someone was beating a parai outside, drumming that got louder and louder, like a marriage procession growing closer. Then the breeze drifted the faintest spray of water through the window to settle on Janani's face and she realised it was raining. With a low groan, she bore down and bore down and bore down, forgetting even to breathe until Kamala cupped her cheek and ordered her to. She focused on imitating the way the midwife inhaled, exhaled, inhaled, exhaled.

The day blended into the rhythm of her straining body and the pulse of pain. Kamala gently coaxed a warm kasayam down her throat, water mixed with the pulp of bitter-tasting medicinal leaves. And finally, her mother gave a shout – Kamala was holding the baby's head in her hands.

A few moments later, a new, thin, beautiful wail sliced through the thump of the rain on the roof tiles.

'A girl,' the old midwife said.

Of course it is, Janani thought, and glanced at her mother.

Amma's mouth was tight, as though she were still in the midst of the labour. When she saw Janani looking at her, her lips twitched into a half-smile.

Kamala ran a warm, wet cloth over the tiny body. She cut the umbilical cord, sprinkled a white powder on the stump, and tied a small rag around it. She rubbed coconut oil into the flailing little limbs. Then she leaned over and carefully placed the baby on to Janani's ribcage, into her waiting arms.

Janani gazed at the wrinkled red face. She hadn't thought that she would ever feel this mindless love again, after all the others, after Lavanika. Surely there was a limit to this sensation, of fierceness and helplessness, of joy and terror, all so strong that once again she had to struggle to breathe?

The vestiges of the afterbirth pushed out of her, but she was barely aware of it, of Kamala and her mother carefully cleaning up.

'Put her down for a moment, child,' Amma said and Janani almost snapped at her, her hands closing tightly over the soft skin.

'Just for a moment,' Kamala said. 'Let us clean you.'

Janani watched her carefully place her daughter on the bed,

then let them wipe her down with a wet cloth and change her nightdress. They helped her onto the bed and Amma lifted the little wailing body and placed her back on the comfortable shelf below Janani's breast.

Amma disappeared with the bamboo mat and the mess of labour. She would bury the placenta somewhere, in the back, away from where the animals could get at it, to ensure the health of the child it once carried. By the time she returned, the baby had fallen asleep. Janani ran a finger over the soft, feather-light hair. Then she slept too.

She woke a few hours later to the baby's cries. The rain was as hard as ever, but over it she thought she could hear her mother's raised voice, and then Kamala's. She couldn't quite make out the words, then the front door slammed, and there was quiet. Delirious with tiredness, Janani sat up and took her new daughter into her arms. In a second, the baby was nursing hungrily. How light her little body was in Janani's arms.

Amma appeared soon after, carrying a plate of rice and rasam and fresh, steaming vegetables.

'Ah,' she said, 'I was just coming to wake you. You should eat.'

She looked as exhausted as Janani felt, her face flat and wooden, as though she couldn't spare the energy to engage those muscles.

The warm weight was lifted from Janani's chest. She felt the loss immediately, but her mother sat close beside her, on the floor, her new granddaughter cradled in her arms.

Janani watched the baby as she ate, scooping the food quickly into her mouth, too hungry to notice the taste. Her daughter dozed comfortably, tiny fingers splayed as though she were waiting for something to be handed to her. Amma's face was mostly hidden, her head turned to the baby.

When she'd finished, her mother rose with the baby and carefully placed her on the bed beside Janani. She took the empty plate and poured water on it from the pitcher for Janani to wash her hands and mouth. She looked blank, as though she were in an unfeeling daze.

'Ma?' Janani said. 'Ma, are you OK?'

Her mother started. 'Yes, kulantai. I'm just tired.' She smiled. 'Not as tired as you. Rest now,' she said. She settled the baby on the mat. Janani was asleep before she drew the curtain across the room.

The next time she woke, the sun was streaming onto her face and the sounds of morning activity filtered through the window. Janani lay blinking in the light as awareness slowly returned and, with it, the soreness of her body.

She turned to where her baby lay beside her.

There was not even a depression in the bed where her little body had lain.

Janani pushed herself up onto one elbow. Perhaps Amma had taken the child out for some fresh air.

'Amma?' she called, but there was no answer.

She levered herself slowly out of bed, ignoring the aches and pains of overstretched muscles, and out into the main room. The smell of warm dosa and fresh sambar reached her.

She could hear raised voices, somewhere outside, but her bladder forced her to head directly for the bathroom before it burst. She clung to the wall as she squatted, her body aching, and relieved herself painfully.

Washing herself clean, she stumbled back into the daylight and took a slow, dragging walk around the house. The ground was already drying back into hard-baked mud. The chickens were squawking in their pen, and her parents' cow, Thulasi, was grazing on a pile of hay.

'It's done!' Amma's voice.

Janani had reached the back of the house. Her mother was sitting on the ground, green chillies spread out on a cloth before her to dry in the sun. She was looking up at Appa. He was standing just at the corner of the house. Two big hessian bags sat next to him – he had clearly just returned from the ration shop.

'Amma?' Janani said, blinking in the sunlight.

Their heads whipped to her. When she saw Janani, her mother's eyes widened, then dropped back to the steel container of chillies she'd yet to spread out.

Janani's hands went to her head. She felt herself twine her fingers through her hair and pull.

'Where is my child?' she asked. Her voice sounded thin and reedy to her own ears, the words coming out on a painful breath.

Silence.

'Where is she?' Janani said and she had more breath behind the words this time.

Amma had risen to her feet.

'We took her away,' she said. Quietly, as though the neighbours were listening with bated breath.

Janani stared. *Took her away.* She felt caught between laughing and being sick.

'Took her where?' she urged

'We are . . .' Appa took a step forward, glancing at her mother. 'We are worried, Janani. About what will happen if you go back with another girl-child.'

There was a buzzing in Janani's ears, as though a fly had slipped its way in and was circling her head. 'What have you done?' she said.

Her mother's silence burst like a dropped papaya. 'You can't take back another girl, Janani,' she said, each word sounding as though it were pushing through clenched teeth. 'You can't. They won't allow it. That boy comes here. Darshan. He asks us for more dowry, because you keep having girl children. No boy. No living boy.'

The shock of the words was like a kick in the ribs when she was already sprawled in the dust. Darshan had done what? When? She was shaking. 'I don't care,' Janani said. 'Don't give it to him. She's my daughter. Who are you to take her away from me?'

Amma's face crumpled. Janani had only ever seen her mother cry at her daughters' weddings. 'What if they hurt you? We don't have money to give, and they'll hurt you.'

'I don't care!' Janani said again, her exhausted stomach muscles clenching. 'I'll leave! They won't touch me.' She thought of the sewing machine, of the little pouch of money that kept growing. She felt like howling. She had been so close. 'I was going to leave.'

Her parents looked stunned.

'You can't leave your husband, Janani,' her mother gasped.

'What a ridiculous thing to say,' Appa said at the same time. 'Where will you go? Who will look after you?'

'A woman doesn't need a man to look after her,' Janani said, 'if she is prepared to work.'

'And what?' Amma said. 'Live like the midwife? An outcast?' Distaste twisted her mouth even as tears filled her eyes. 'People will beat you. They will destroy your house. Your life.'

Silence fell.

Janani watched them, this beloved family of hers, her sanctuary, and knew they were thinking of how old they were, if she came back to them with a daughter. Of the horror they felt, of her being beaten or burned. Her heart writhed with rage and pity, but she didn't have time for it. She needed to find her baby.

'Where is she?' she said, to Appa this time.

'I don't know, kulantai,' he said. He shook his head, turning away, wiping the back of his wrist across his eyes.

Amma dropped her face into her hands and tears leaked through her spread fingers. Speech seemed to have escaped them, even if they would tell her.

It didn't matter. She didn't need them. All she needed was her daughter.

Janani searched the house first. It didn't take long, looking in the sink and the pots and pans, under the beds and sheets, inside the rolled-up mats and chests, under the piles of laundry waiting to be washed or folded.

No sign.

She felt like she was trapped in the seventh circle of hell.

Outside into the sunlight. She retraced her steps to the bathroom, looking carefully around for the sickening sight of broken ground. There was nothing, and the bathroom was equally empty, no baby lying lifeless in the full water bucket.

Exhausted and thirsty, Janani began searching outside, looking desperately for some sign – a scrap of rag, an overturned box. She glared back at passers-by in the street. They stared at her in alarm, as though she were a madwoman.

As she rounded the corner, she saw where the back of her parents' tiny patch of rented land gave way to the treeline of coconut palms and tangled undergrowth. It stretched out until it abutted the nearest rice fields. Janani remembered a story from just a few months ago, of a baby girl who had been found by a farmer ploughing his fields, squalling and alive. Bhoomi Devi, they had called her. Goddess of the Earth.

Janani stood and looked at the trees under which her baby could be buried now, imagined the moist, waterlogged earth on which she might be lying, and her heart sank into her womb.

Think.

They always lost things around this tiny house, she and Rupini Akka. They'd find a new toy, or make one out of sticks and mud and coconut shells, play with it for a while – weeks even – and then forget about it, and when they sought it out again, it was gone. Always because Amma or Appa had packed it away, out of the house.

In the grain room.

Janani looked at the small outbuilding, concealed behind baby palms and under fallen foliage. Her aching body protesting, she hurried towards it. Amma might have looked up at her. She didn't care.

The door creaked as she opened it. Shutterless windows a hand's span beneath the roof's edge let in a stream of light as the smell of dusty hessian and rich scent of uncooked rice and lentils overwhelmed her. She coughed, put a hand over her mouth, and listened.

There was no sound but her own breathing, uneven through her tears.

She moved forward, looking behind the sacks and pieces of broken furniture, watching where she placed her feet.

Nothing, nothing, nothing.

The back of the shed was looming and with it her despair. She had no choice – she had to go back to Amma and beg.

But what if she was already dead, her little one?

Nausea was becoming an undertide to the ache in her stomach and loins.

There was a short weak cry, like a newborn pup.

Janani stopped breathing.

It could have been anything – a cat on the roof outside, a mouse much closer, a crow at the window.

The cry came again, somewhere ahead of her, and to the right.

She moved forward again, as fast as she dared in the dimness, until the back wall was only a step away. A sack full of old clothes hid the back corner. Janani recognised the material of one of her mother's old saris. She always kept them, did Amma, passing them to Dalit families if they were still wearable, or turning them into towels or cleaning cloths.

Janani pushed it away and edged past it.

There she was.

She was wrapped so tightly she couldn't move. Her eyes were half-closed, in sleep or semi-consciousness.

Janani let out a gasp of terrified relief. She gave the clothing bag another shove, and threw herself to her knees beside the tiny, still body as her own body protested with a stab of pain.

She picked her daughter up.

The first touch made Janani cry out. The cloth enclosing the little limbs was wet through, although the ground around was dry. For it to be so damp for so long, it must have been soaking when she had first been wrapped.

Janani unwound the cloth as quickly as she could. There was the bitter smell of urine. Under it, the baby's skin was cold and clammy. The child stirred as her limbs were freed into the warm, dry air, emitting another one of her soft, short cries, as though too weak to manage anything more. Janani turned to sit with her back against the wall, put the baby on her lap and began to rub her arms, legs and chest, trying to draw out the cold.

It seemed to take hours, but only minutes must have passed before, thankfully, the little mewling cries became longer and more frequent.

The cotton of Janani's nightdress tore as she struggled out of one arm. Leaning back against the wall, she gathered up her daughter and brought her to her breast.

The newborn wails stuttered, then faded, as the little mouth found and latched on to the nipple.

Janani's face felt dry enough to crack, caked with salt. She watched her daughter, the delicate spiderweb lashes, the thick thatch of gently curling hair, the slowly flushing cheeks. When the light from the doorway was blocked by another figure, Janani shouted it back out into the sunlight, away from them.

Time slipped past unnoticed as Janani sat, not speaking, half-dozing as the morning heat grew, until finally the baby fell asleep, her mouth slipping from the breast. Grasping her with one arm and bracing herself with the other hand on the floor, Janani painfully pushed herself first to her knees, then to her feet. She rooted around the old, tired cloth in the hessian bag and managed to find a cotton petticoat to loosely wrap the baby in.

Taking a deep breath, she stepped carefully through the store-house and opened the door to the daylight.

The front door of the house was open. They were still there. Ma sat in a chair, her face still wet with tears. Appa had been stalking up and down the room. He stopped as Janani appeared in the doorway. Both of their eyes moved from Janani's face to the wrapped bundle in her arms.

She didn't say anything. She couldn't think of anything to say. All she knew was that she couldn't stay here a moment longer.

As her mother rose from her chair, one hand outstretched, Janani hurried past her to the bedroom. She closed the door behind her.

Her bag was where she had left it, the few saris she had brought still inside. She pulled the remainder of her nightdresses from the pile of clean laundry in the corner and shoved them into the bag.

Not bothering to change, she slung the bag over her shoulder, picked her baby daughter up and pushed the door open.

'Janani,' her mother said at once. 'I'm sorry! Where are you going? What are you going to do?'

Janani ignored her. There was no space to think while she was still in here, in this house, with this danger to her child. A danger she could never have imagined, that should have been impossible.

So she kept moving, past her parents. They seemed rooted to the spot – in shame or guilt or horror, Janani did not know or care.

'Child, you can't leave. Not like this.' Appa urged.

'Please, Janani,' her mother said. 'Where are you going?'

She stepped outside. A bullock cart rolled lazily along in the road, filled with mud bricks. 'I don't know,' she said, her breath coming in short spurts. 'Maybe home. At least there they don't lie to me. They tell me "no more daughters" and take them from me. I'm never coming back here.'

Her voice broke on the last words.

'What have we done?' Appa said to Amma, quietly.

Her mother's faced crumpled.

Janani turned away from them.

'Janani!' her mother cried, calling her name like a prayer.

She kept walking, out into the street, past the carts and the goats and the blaring horns of jeeps and autorickshaws. She didn't know where she was going. But she would walk until her feet bled to make sure her baby girl was safe.

Chapter Twenty

Madurai, 2019

I show them the photo in the morning. My head pounds, because I haven't slept. Instead, I've spent all night, until darkness leached into dawn, reviewing every memory. Every smell, every touch, every recollection I have from before today. My fingers have scratched at my phone, desperate to call Rohan, or Iphigenia, or . . . But I can't.

Now the night is over and we are outside. Hercules stands at my feet, looking up at me, his tail swinging so hard his entire hindquarters move. Mahesh and Veliamma's driver, Shankar, are squatting by the cars. The sky is lapis-lazuli blue, and the coconut palm fronds fan out against it. The morning is saturated with colour.

And against it, Amma is as ashen as she can be. Her eyes are wide and fixed on me. She is hunted-animal still. I can almost sense her, almost every cell in her body, poised for me to say something, to move, to breathe. Acha is looking at the cement of the veranda beneath his feet. He's blinking rapidly, the way he does when he's thinking hard.

I let the air out of my lungs in a short gasp and suddenly I'm aware of how thirsty I am, the dryness of my tongue sticking to the roof of my mouth.

There is a sense you get, when you watch your elders, that

they have done something wrong. Unspeakably wrong. It could be forgetting to buy a concert ticket, burning a meal, going awry in the birthday present shopping. It might be not getting the bullies expelled, or not having enough money for more than one meal on the table. It's there when their shoulders slump and their faces wilt and their necks sag. When they speak and there is utter defeat in their voice. When you're a child, it fills you with a fear that's just as unspeakable. That fear picks you up and turns you from safety to danger.

I feel it now and it freezes me.

The front door is open. From the drawing room, the clock chimes and the tinny rattle of one of Bach's preludes fills the air.

Amma draws in a breath and I look at her, and will her to *open, sesame*.

'Where did you get that?' she says.

Something in my face answers her, because her head turns towards Acha.

His throat moves. The curve of his jaw tightens.

'It's mine,' he says. He's angled himself somewhere between us, but his eyes flicker towards my mother.

'It's a mistake,' she says, and flinches, because it's such an obvious lie.

'What is?' I ask. 'This?' I look at Acha. Shake it at him, the flimsy rectangle of coated paper. 'You took the photo, didn't you?' Because who else in this house would have ever wanted to capture Amma like this?

Acha looks up at me, and then over at the bougainvillea creeping bright against the wall. His face wears the same expression it did when Vijay Ammama told him his father was dying. He is in his mundu. We're going to the temple soon, for the next puja for Achacha. Soon the rest of the family will join us out here. Their voices dance off the walls and drift outside.

Amma still isn't speaking. She's looking at the photo, tight-lipped, her arms pulled into her sides like a soldier standing at attention.

'This isn't me,' I say. There is no question of it. They know it, of course they do, but still I point at the date stamp in the corner.

July 1993. Four months before I was born. I am there, in the photo. I am the round of my mother's stomach, draped in the fall of her sari.

Acha looks at Amma. No. He's looking *to* Amma. Waiting.

'Who is this, Amma?' I could guess. Throw my thoughts at her. But I wrench back my words, let the silence between us stretch.

Then Amma crosses her arms. 'It's not you.' Her cheeks are a flushed maroon. The look on her face makes me sick, a thread of nausea coiling through my stomach. 'It's not you. It's your sister. Your akka.' Her eyes are steady on mine. 'She's gone now.'

There's the sound of movement from indoors, and the thin echo of voices.

Acha lifts one hand, rubs his temple. 'Molé, can we talk properly about this later?'

I can't believe it. I have just found out I have an older sister. How can he feel like this is a moment to be postponed? I take out my phone, swipe through my photos, and hold it up.

'I want to go here,' I say.

They squint at the image in a way that is so familiar that I ache for everything to be normal again.

Amma recognises them first. Her eyes widen.

There she is, in the same sari as in the photo I have just found. There I am, pressed against her side, the pink of my blouse and the deep green of my skirt even brighter than the Pongal kolam behind me. But it's not me. It's the other girl, in the same pink-and-green clothes that jar with the muted tones of the living room. In the sunlight, with the knowledge I have, I can see a detail or two. The girl in the picture has a tiny circle of a mole, just above the right corner of her lip. Her nose is slightly wider than mine, her curls slightly tighter.

Acha's back straightens in some sort of realisation and his eyes go to Amma.

'I want to know who these people are,' I say. The photo trembles in my hand, and the people in it too – the old woman with her basket of snake beans, the tall, lean, moustached man. 'I want to know who I am. And maybe they'll tell me, if you won't.'

Amma takes a step towards me. 'This doesn't change who you are,' she says, and her voice is low and intense.

The voices are nearer now, and then at the front door, and the rest of the family pile out. Veliamma is first. She's smiling at something Radhika is telling her as she emerges, but then she looks at us and something she sees drains the lightness from her face.

'Is everything OK?' she asks in Malayalam.

'Yes, yes,' Acha answers, while his tone says *no*.

'OK,' she repeats, although her eyes are still probing our faces. 'Breakfast is ready.'

'Excellent,' Acha says. 'Nila, let's talk after we've eaten.'

I shake my head. 'I'm just going to sit here for a moment.' Forcing a smile for my great-aunt, I tell her, 'I'm not feeling too well this morning.'

When my parents say nothing, Veliamma nods and they all traipse inside for breakfast.

I let them go. My breath is rasping in and out and the thought of being in that dim dining room, with all those people, makes every nerve end scream at me to flee. Instead, I sit on the bottom step of the veranda with Hercules, and he licks my bare toes as I stroke his cobalt fur.

Manju Ammayi re-emerges ten minutes later, bringing with her the smell of fresh sambar and ishtu and idli. She asks me to come and eat, and I tell her I'm not feeling well. Hercules has rested his head on the step by me and I run my hand over the velvet-soft tips of his ears as he drifts in and out of a doze. The front door closes quietly behind my aunt.

They leave me for a while. Then I hear the murmur of voices above my head through the open drawing-room window, but I don't try to make out the words. There's enough already tumbling through my mind.

Mahesh appears, garden hose in hand, a spray bottle and giant yellow sponge in the other. He sees me, grins and waves. I wave back.

I think about running, a long, exhausting, dehydrating run, outstripping stray dogs and mangy cats and gently grazing cows, idiots on bikes and families piled into autorickshaws. But my running gear is inside. So instead I look at the sun filtering through the fronds of the palm trees and try to count the coconuts clustered at the base of the leaves.

It's Amma who comes to find me. Hercules stirs when she emerges and lowers herself slowly onto the step beside me. She watches the dog, wary, as he circles around us, thumping us with his solid black tail, until I persuade him to sit down and put his paw in my hand.

'Where did you find the photo?' she says.

My breathing's shallow with anticipation. At first, I don't want to say anything. But there's too much writhing, seething thought to stay silent.

'My room. Acha's old bedroom.'

'Is that so?' She looks at me, a long, searching look. Then she reaches out and tucks a strand of my sweaty hair back behind my ear.

'Yes,' I say. Reaching into my bag, I pull it out. A corner of it has creased, and I feel a shooting sense of guilt. Poor Acha, he'll be upset . . .

She takes it. Smooths it out. Holds her palm against it. Then she hands it back to me.

'You weren't even married then, were you,' I say. 'So who . . . what were you doing in this house?' I don't wait for her to answer. My eyes are irritated. I blink, and feel my lashes dampen. 'You've lied to me my whole life. Both you and Acha. And now . . . this.'

'Nila,' Amma says. 'Don't say that.' Her arms uncross and she rubs her hand over her face. The sun is starting to creep around the side of the house, casting her half in light, half in shadow. She reaches out to pet Hercules' head. 'It just . . . After all the years, it doesn't seem helpful. Those were bad times.' She shakes her head. 'It's not an important thing. It doesn't change anything.'

'Maybe it's not important now to you,' I say. 'Did you . . . work here? Did Acha . . . Were you . . . before you were married?' I'm struggling to get the words out. 'Is that why Achacha couldn't stand any of us?' Even as I say it, I can't believe a word of it, not of my loving, gentle father, not of my steely, spirited mother. I don't know if the alternative is worse. Because if they weren't together, then who's my father?

Amma's face crumples. 'No, molé. Don't say things like that.'

'What else am I supposed to think, when you don't tell me otherwise?'

Silence. Somewhere, a crow calls. An autorickshaw overladen with cackling young men drives past the gate. There's a hard stone pressing into the back of my throat. Swallowing, I hold up my phone. The other picture is on the screen, of Amma and the girl who isn't me and the man and woman who could be anyone. 'Where is this?'

There's a pause. 'Usilampatti,' Amma says. There's a tear making its way from the instep of her eye, moving in a graceful curve towards her lips. 'That's where I lived then.'

I breathe out, a long, amazed breath. She's taken a step. Finally.

Usilampatti. I've heard of it, seen it written on road signs.

'I was the cleaner, here,' Amma says. 'And before that, my mother. Your aacchi.'

The front door opens, closes. There's movement on the steps above us. Hercules raises his head and his tail thumps the floor. I can smell my father's aftershave

'I'm going there,' I say. 'If you don't want to go, fine. Tell me how to get there. Who to ask for.'

'Nila,' Acha says from behind us, but Amma cuts him off.

'You can't go by yourself,' she says quietly. 'It's not safe. You can barely speak the language.'

'I'll be fine, Amma. I'm a grown woman, do you understand?'

She looks at me. 'Yes,' she says. 'Yes you are.' Her shoulders are hunched; she looks exhausted. 'We'll go together. It's Iraivan's will, isn't it?' Sitting there, her bangles loose on her wrist, her arm tiny against the banister, she looks so vulnerable, as though a gust of wind would knock her over into the dust.

Hercules, wise in a way only dogs can be, moves away from me and lays his heavy black head on her lap. She looks down at him. She doesn't gasp, or back away. Instead, she runs her palm over his fur, and I feel in that moment how much I don't know of her and how much I love her anyway.

'OK,' Acha says. 'We all go.'

I look at him, and I wonder how hard it must have been for him to stay silent all these years, about everything Amma never wanted to speak of.

He nods. 'Tomorrow.'

Amma runs a finger over the photo, as though she's revisiting this place, that time. She puts a hand on my arm, then slowly shifts Hercules' head from her knee and stands. I don't. But I turn and watch as they climb the steps, my parents, Acha's hand going to the small of Amma's back, fitting there as though it were made to.

It feels like I've been asleep for minutes when my alarm rings, but I almost fall out of bed, the sheet tangled like a spiderweb around my legs. For an instant, I panic that I've slept in, that I'm late, as though my phone doesn't declare it to be seven a.m., or that I'm not the reason we're leaving.

I dress in my most traditional salwar, dark green with golden embroidery down the front and along the short sleeves, the loose navy kameez trousers billowing around my legs. The green cotton glows against my neck and arms.

The first thing I notice when I appear in the dining room is my great-aunt. She looks up at us with a smile. I am stupidly relieved to see her.

'Veliamma's taking us,' Acha tells me. He and Amma are sitting with their heads close together, Amma peering at what appears to be a map on Acha's phone. Acha's perched his reading glasses on the end of his long nose. Manju Ammayi has a plate of dosa and ulli chammanthi waiting for me before I even notice her. I sit down and begin inhaling my food.

'Tchh,' Veliamma says. 'There's no need to rush, kutty. Eat slowly.' Her voice is gentle. I don't know how much Amma has told her, but she knows more than I do. She always has.

I can't eat much. My stomach won't stay still enough. It writhes and flails like a fussy baby. I take a swig of coffee and one of water.

'I'm finished,' I say. 'Let's go.

Amma rises last. She doesn't look at me. Her face is drawn and sombre, almost ill. I hate myself, but the need to know drowns that out, a tsunami over a slum.

The old Maruthi is outside, as is the equally old Shankar. When he sees us, he grins and bows like a cheerful unwrapped mummy.

Veliamma sits between Amma and me in the back, a calm airbag, small, firm, solid, cushioning us all against the thick awkwardness that's following us like a noxious cloud. I don't even mind the added heat.

The Madurai–Theni highway is dusty and grey, but still hot air shimmers above it as we hurtle down behind huge petroleum trucks with WARNING: INFLAMMABLE wrapped in a red semicircle on the back and pictures of Ganesha adorning the sides.

I crane my head out the window. Mostly all I can see are rice plantations and open fields of golden-brown, stretching out, sometimes bumping against slender coconut palms and denser forest. Cows graze incuriously, and the odd goat-owner wanders through the long grass, watching their charges.

It's another world. I could be on another planet. It's not just the wing-like leaves of the palms, the rich dark green of all the other unfamiliar trees, so different to the silver-barked eucalyptus of home. It's not just the never-ending rows of baby rice that carpet the ground until they reach the infinite blue of the sky. Or the slumping, mud-brick buildings that look half-lived in, half-loved, like solitary mausoleums. It's the smell of the place, so different, vibrant and moist and warm. It's the people, the kids splashing in the canal, the women walking along with sacks balanced with one hand on their heads, the workers in the fields, lunghis and saris hoisted up out of the water, living a life I can't imagine.

Amma's life, once.

Along its length, the highway is dotted unevenly with shops and eateries, schools, and then an impressive-looking set of symmetrical sandy buildings set back behind a long drive and a shrouding fence of trees. 'Madurai Kamaraj University', a sign set at the side of the highway proclaims it.

Questions for my parents throw themselves against my ribcage, but I can't ask them. Pride and resentment have sewn my lips shut. I can see Amma gazing out of the other window, her hair in its long braid draped over her left shoulder. Her head is twisted so I can't see her face. One hand is clenched around the hold above the window, although Shankar is driving quite placidly. I try to remember her telling me about her schooldays and realise I've never probed. Only brief snippets come to me, of tight, blue-ribbon-bound plaits, of school meals of thayir sadam, of chasing the boys around the dusty schoolyard and being smacked for not memorising her Tamil alphabet quickly enough.

The question comes despite myself. 'Where did you go to school, Amma?'

'We'll pass it soon,' she says. 'That way.' She points across Veliamma in the direction of my window. Her finger levels just before my nose, short-nailed and slender, accusing. I can do nothing but turn my head to follow it.

Ten minutes later, 'There!' she says, almost throwing herself across Veliamma.

I press my face against the glass.

'The blue building,' she says, and I can just make out, beyond a thick clump of trees, the outline of blue walls, the colour of rain-wrung sky, a roof of curved rust-red tiles. There's another building alongside it. Even together, it's tiny.

'It's grown since I was there,' Amma remarks.

I turn to her and see her still leant over, still gazing out the window, as though she can still see that little concrete building with its dawn-blue walls.

The school has already passed us by.

'And that was it,' Amma says, sitting back. 'I stopped going when I was twelve. Akka – my older sister, Rupini – she got married. Amma needed me at home.' She looks at me. 'Your aacchi.'

I'd known she'd never gone to high school. *Many girls back then didn't*, she'd told me. I'd felt a wave of sympathy and accepted it without a further thought. That, for ten-year-old Nila, had been explanation enough. Now I'm having trouble with the expression on her face. She looks almost angry. My fingers start fidgeting with my bracelet, undoing the clasp, redoing it. One foot is tapping on the floor of the car; I press it down, hard.

'Here,' Amma says suddenly.

We travel at the same velocity for a couple of seconds before Shankar manages to slam his foot on the brake. All of us lurch forward. I'm glad I'm wearing my seat belt. Veliamma's not – she braces herself against the back of the driver's seat.

'Careful, Shankar,' she says in Tamil.

'Yes, *ma*,' he replies.

A couple of cars, an autorickshaw with at least six people crammed in the back and a granite lorry trundle past us before Shankar turns off the highway, into a small village street.

There's a tiny grocery store at the corner. I make out bottles of orange-flavoured Miranda and packets of crisps. Then the houses come into view, each painted a different colour, some with tiled roofing, some with thatch.

I turn my head from side to side as we inch up the narrow road. A couple of young men, barely out of their teens, come past on a bicycle, towards the highway. One's pedalling and the other's perched impossibly on the back. They both look at us, squinting curiously through the windows. *Keep your eyes on the road!* I think, glancing away. I don't want to see them crash.

'Go slowly here,' Amma says, although a lazy koala could match our pace. She's leaning forward too, intent, eager, the seat belt straining at her right shoulder. Her braid's caught in it. She doesn't seem to notice. There's a sheen of sweat on her forehead. Everything about her seems on the edge of manic. I'm starting to prickle with it, my heart picking up into a trot, the heat of the day feeling claustrophobic.

In the rear-view mirror, I see Shankar's head wobble, wobble, calmly ignoring or acknowledging or agreeing with Amma's request.

'That school is new,' Amma says, pointing past me. It's another sky-blue building, *Fatima Convent School*, the right half of the building obscured by a robust, luscious tree, the foliage spreading in a radius well beyond the segment of trunk, arching down towards the red, red mud. It's a planted metaphor, a tree of knowledge.

'You see that tree?' Acha speaks for the first time. 'It's a kadamba tree. A . . . What's the English? A burflower tree. Sacred to Meenakshi. Madurai was famous for them once, but they're quite rare now.'

'Kadambavanam,' Amma says, so quietly I'm sure she's speaking to herself.

'Yes.' Acha smiles at her, at me, his face tender. 'One of Madurai's names. The kadamba forest.'

The tree is decorated with globular orange flowers, mini suns dangling like baubles beneath leaves of a rich, dark green. The mud beneath it reminds me of gold-panning in Bathurst, of dry New South Welsh soil. Red as vermillion.

I feel homesick, and just a little bit at home, and so confused I can't think.

When we come to a junction, another tiny street coming from an angle at the left to meet us, Amma tells Shankar to keep going. She hasn't moved, her eyes fixed on a point beyond the windscreen.

The houses to our left give way to more rice fields, and I watch the swaying saplings pass us, aware that I'm starting to feel a little nauseous. I've just relaxed into the motion of the car when Amma moves, her left hand coming up off her lap, slapping into the back of Shankar's headrest. I don't understand what she says, the Tamil's too quick, or too local, but Shankar spins the wheel right and we're manoeuvring into another street, even more cramped, hedged on both sides by tiny houses, the paint peeling, the mud fissured, thatch hugging tile hugging thatch. The colour catches my eye, the greens and blues and pinks of the walls, bright saris and skirts alternating with the sober white of lunghis on ropes strung between trees or roofs. I imagine Amma growing up here, running barefoot and scrawny-armed between the houses, walking what must be at least half an hour to the primary school we passed.

'Here.'

The car stops, just before the road narrows to the point where we'd have had no choice but to stop. The only sound inside is the air conditioner, sounding like a furnace, and the slow inhalation, exhalation of five adults cramped together in thirty-six-degree heat and three times that in humidity.

Acha moves first. I hear the click of his seat belt, then Veliamma's, and so I undo mine and we open the doors. By the time we're standing blinking in the morning sunlight, Amma's door has opened as well. She clambers out. I've never seen her face like this.

'That tree.' She points at a gnarled old thing at the end of the road. Its grey-brown bark peels away from it like a shedding snake. 'We used to play hide-and-seek around it.'

It's as though now she's decided to talk, she can't stop, a burst dam, an unplugged barrel. I'm happy to let her overflow, but I don't know this amma. I don't know what else will emerge.

Amma starts walking. Acha and I and Veliamma fall in beside her like loyal disciples.

Shankar leans against the car, watching us with his yellowed grin.

We don't have far to go. The house we are aiming for is one of the last in the street. It's green and stout, with a thatched roof. I can see smoke curling lazily from somewhere behind it and smell frying mustard seeds.

Amma's hand, somehow cool despite this heat, finds my wrist. She pulls me closer.

'This is my parents' house.'

'My grandparents,' I say.

'Yes. We grew up here, your attai and I. We didn't have much, but we were happy.'

It's hard for me to imagine, because I'd never thought I'd stand here, that I'd even know of its existence.

'It's a lovely house,' I say. It's the only thing I can think of.

She turns, and the smile she gives me is a shy, beautiful thing.

I feel like we're at the first shrine on a pilgrimage. I'm burning to knock on the splintering beige door, or even peer through the unshuttered windows.

Before we have time to do any of that, the door opens.

The morning sun falls on a woman, framed in the doorway. Her hair is iron grey. She's as slim-boned as my mother. Her face is more lined, but the resemblance is unmistakeable. She squints at us in the light.

There's a frozen instant.

Amma's eyes have widened, are still widening.

'Janani?' the woman says.

'Rupini Akka,' my mother says.

My aunt – for who else could she be? – takes a step forward, then another. I can see the tears form in her eyes by the way the sunlight makes them glisten. Her hands come up, palms together, reaching for my mother's face. They're trembling. Amma reaches too.

They're too close now for words to carry. My aunt brings Amma's head down, kisses her forehead.

They stay like that for several long moments while the rest of us shift our feet. I feel like I'm watching something too revealing, too stripped bare.

When they break apart, my mother introduces us, one by one.

When she hears my name, Rupini stares as though I am an alien lifeform. She walks towards me. How small she is, I realise, when she stands in front of me. Smaller even than Amma, the slight bend of scoliosis in her back forcing her earthward. But I can see Amma in her, in the curve of her ears, the sweep of her lips, the curl of her eyelashes, the kind eyes.

She places one palm against my cheek. I feel her rough, lean fingers, stroking once, twice. Then she reaches for my hands with both of hers. I take them, feeling the swell of arthritis in her knuckles, feeling a lifetime of labour. How different they are, to Amma's hands. The difference of a lifetime.

Fresh tears tremble at her lower lids.

'Bless you, kulantai,' she whispers. 'God bless you.'

*

315

Only my mother, my aunt and I enter the house. It's tiny and dark and spotlessly clean. It's even cool, the thick mud-brick walls and shuttered windows keeping the mid-morning vigour of the sun from us. But there's no escaping its modesty, this tiny house where Amma grew up.

The kitchen utensils are split between the back of the house and outside the rear door, where Rupini Attai has been cooking on her small gasoline stove. She makes us tea. She brings us murukku.

She tells us that when her in-laws passed away, and then her husband, she had come back here, to look after her own aged parents. And then, when they too passed away – Amma draws in a tight, sharp breath – she preferred to stay. Her son – my cousin – lived quite close. He was away now, working in the city.

'Nila,' Amma says to me. 'Come here.' She's speaking in Tamil. One hand rises, palm out, to stop her sister from following us.

I take the few steps with her across to the only other room. She pushes the door open, revealing a space much smaller than the one we're standing in. A rope is tied from one end of the ceiling to the other. It supports a curtain which, pulled to, would split the room in two. A pallet lies on the floor. Another rests against the wall beside some rolled-up bamboo mats.

Amma closes the door behind us. 'We used to sleep here, all of us,' she says. 'Amma and Appa, there,' she points to the left side of the room, 'And me and Rupini Akka there.' She points to the right.

It's a bare little space. The pallet looks worn, stained, thin.

Amma grasps my hand, surprising me. She takes a deep breath.

And then she says, 'This is where you were born.'

A second punch to the gut. At first, the words don't mean anything. I have to repeat them to myself, slowly, one by one, ruminating on each, as though I've had five glasses of wine and my mind's swimming in a whirlpool. *This is where you were born. This. Is. Where. I. Was. Born.*

I'd never imagined seeing the place I'd come into the world. I thought it would have been some linoleum-floored, slightly run-down rural Indian hospital. It strikes me I've pieced that vision together from scraps of TV news reports and documentaries.

But it wasn't. It was here.

'What does that mean?' I don't realise I've spoken out loud.

Amma takes my hands, turns me to face her. Tears spill over onto those still baby-soft cheeks, like a physical accompaniment to her words.

'Amma,' I say. My chest is tightening. Damn. Every time. 'If this is too much for you, we can go.' My throat's constricting and I have to force the words through. 'I don't want to upset you.'

'No, no,' she says. 'I upset you. I hurt you. Those photographs – you shouldn't have to learn about it all like that. And you are right. You should know.'

We stand looking at each other in the dim light. I realise we're both squeezing each other's hands, that the pain feels right.

And there, in the room where she fought to bring me into the world, she speaks.

He's waiting for us, outside. For me. He stands with his hands clasped behind his back, still straight and strong despite the grey hairs Rohan and I have planted in his head. The sun's beating down on his head, and I wish he'd brought his Akubra.

He's not my father. And, of course, he is.

What he sees on my face, I don't know. The tears, of course. But anything else? Does he see grief, betrayal? Does he see love and faith?

Whatever it is moves him immediately, his long strides

317

consuming the space between us. There's no hesitancy. There's no uncertainty. One moment, he's there, and the next, his arms are around me and my face is pressed into his shoulder and the smell of his aftershave, that comforting smell that's seeped into my mind since before I can remember, is all around me.

'It's OK, little one,' he says. 'It's OK.'

We squeeze into the car. I sit wedged between my mother and great-aunt. As we pull away, Amma cranes her neck, keeping her childhood home, and her sister, in view until she can't. She grips my hand as though she'll never let go, and I cling to hers just as hard.

Chapter Twenty-One

Madurai, 1993

*Now everything is new, frightening, forbidding – everything, until
the sound of her mother's voice, of her mother's heart.*

Sanjay drummed his fingers on the steering wheel. One of the
cows in the herd now crossing the road in front of him looked
up, its lazy head swinging in his direction as though it could
sense his impatience. Beside him, Priya Ammayi seemed so
calmly still it was almost irritating.

The radio was crackling again, jumping between an aggra-
vated man talking about corruption within the AIADMK
and the crooning music from some movie or the other. *Chinna
Thambi*, maybe, or *Idhayam*. Something piercingly soprano and
romantic. He was annoyed to find himself humming along.
When Priya glanced at him, he grimaced.

The last of the cows moved over the road with a flick of its
tail, sending a stringy cloud of flies wafting into the air. The car
was moving before its hindquarters had edged past the corner of
Sanjay's windscreen. The panicked urgency that had struck him
this afternoon hadn't released its grasp. Janani had been gone
now for over a week. Priya had reassured him that the baby was
due in two days' time, that they wouldn't be too late. Damned

if he knew anything about how often women gave birth earlier than their time, or how quickly, but here he was, unable to take a chance.

He'd come straight from his new job, stopping at home only to change into the clothes he'd purchased just for this purpose. The khaki fabric of the crisply new shirt was scratchy and stiff. The trousers were too big – the shop was too cheap to have consistent sizing – and the hem flopped over brown shoes that were thankfully Sanjay's own. It would be enough – shirt and trousers close, but not too close, to what a Madurai District police officer would wear. Enough, hopefully, to stall angry questions or worse.

It was an odd time of the day, evening bleeding into night, the lilac blush at the rims of the earth darkening like a bruise. When the thatched roofs and ramshackle buildings of Usilampatti finally appeared, he'd never been so happy to see them. He turned left down Usilampatti Main Road and sped past the tea stalls, the fashion shops and the looming government hospital. The winding, unnamed streets were a hive of activity that forced him to slow down. Children released from school played cricket with sticks of wood and home-made balls. A group of young girls were skipping with a heavy piece of coconut-twine rope, hauling on it and shouting encouragement to each other. Sanjay half-expected to see Lavanika's face. The thought of her tightened his chest.

Parking by the community hall, he and Priya hurried up the street. The stink of the village, animal dung and human urine mixed with food cooked out in the open air, was a welcome distraction. Sanjay thought about how he preferred this smell, now, to the heavy aromas of gasoline and rubber, dirty concrete and the sweat of too many people that permeated Madurai city centre.

The neem tree came into view, towering over the cluster of houses halfway up the street.

'It's that house, there,' he said, pointing at the tiny, thatch-roofed, mud-brick and concrete house.

'Come, then,' Priya said.

Without conscious thought, Sanjay's strides lengthened until his aunt was almost trotting to keep up. He forced himself to slow down. Running wouldn't help. It would just bring the wrong people down on them.

It was still only a few hours past sunrise. Although the day's heat wasn't as unbearable as it would have been a few months ago, in July or August, it was more than enough to leave large damp circles soaking through the cotton under Sanjay's arms.

He hadn't had a chance to look at Janani's home closely the last time he was here. Under its thatched roof, the house was painted a pale sky-blue beneath the grime of dirt, windows framed in a red border around the open-slatted shutters. The low double door looked bolted closed. As they made their way towards it, Sanjay was aware of eyes on him. A woman balancing a pitcher of water on her head stopped and stared with a foot over the threshold of her home. An old man watched them from where he squatted, half-hidden behind a coffee-brown cow and the flies gathered around its hindquarters. His protruding ears reminded Sanjay of the pujari at the family temple – he had to stop himself from calling out a greeting. There were other eyes too, peering from windows and through cracks in barely open doors, staring at his clothes.

Sanjay could feel curiosity in those hidden gazes, but no hostility. Not yet. He half-wanted a challenge. Maybe it would distract him from the blood thumping through him, the sound of his breathing in his ears.

The mosquitoes were coming out with the dusk; he swatted

at one taking a bite out of his forearm just as he raised a hand to knock on Darshan's front door.

'What if we're too late?' he asked.

Priya was glancing around, her face tight with tension.

'Stay positive,' she said. 'We have to try.'

'And if something's wrong . . .'

Priya hesitated. It shook him. His aunt always knew what to do, even when Amma was wracked with pain. Just having her here was a relief; she had agreed to come without a flicker of hesitation when he had asked her.

'What do you want to do?' she asked finally, into the silence that still emanated from the house.

He knew what he would do.

He knocked again. And again.

And finally the door clattered as the inner bolt was drawn, making him jump. After a hesitant moment of stillness, the right half creaked back, revealing a small, older woman squinting at them from around the slowly widening gap. Her dark hair was streaked with grey. She must have been in her early fifties, perhaps not much older than Priya, but life had added another decade to her face, stress and sun creasing it like a hazelnut's shell. The caution in her dark, crow-footed eyes turned to flat unfriendliness as she took in their clothes and the laminated identification card slung from a lanyard around Priya's neck. Sanjay became acutely aware of the prickle of sweat running down his chest as she squinted at him. *Stop it*, he thought. *She's never seen you.*

'Yes, sir?' she said to Sanjay's shirt.

'Vanakkam,' Priya said, as they'd agreed. 'My name is Nisha Subramaniam – I'm from the health centre. This is Officer Balan Rajendran.' She barely stumbled over the lies. Sanjay stayed slightly behind her and to one side. He nodded in greeting and thrust his shoulders back, trying to fill out the cloth over his chest. 'What's your name, please?'

The old woman's lips pursed. 'Vandhana.' The end of the word cut off like it had run into a brick wall.

Priya went on, steady as a bullock-cart driver on the national highway. 'I'm here to speak to . . .' She looked down at the clipboard in her hand. It held a sheet of paper with a list of random names and addresses, mostly family and Sanjay's friends, that he'd printed off that morning. 'Janani, Janani Adilaksmi. She lives here, no?'

'Why?' the old woman said, her voice sharp.

'Janani was due to give birth to a child recently, I understand,' Priya said. All her calm confidence seemed to do was have the old woman bristling like an angry street cat.

Vandhana flicked another look at Sanjay's clothes, braced her foot against the door and crossed her arms over her faded maroon sari. 'That's our business, not yours,' she said. The blue and pink flowers that dotted the cheap cotton looked comically at odds with her hostility. She was so tiny. Still, Sanjay could imagine her flying at them, those bony fingers curled into claws.

Priya looked as though she'd been carved out of granite, an aged version of a temple statue.

Sanjay cleared his throat. They'd agreed he'd stay a silent threat for honest answers. They'd agreed he might intimidate them if he spoke. But they were getting nowhere, he was worried, and he was roasting in this heat. 'We're here to help, Ma,' he said. 'Could you ask Janani if we can speak with her, please?'

The old woman's eyes moved to him. *See me*, he wanted to say. *I'm the damned police.* She opened her mouth to reply, then hesitated, her gaze travelling over his clothes once more. Pursing her lips, she opened the door wide.

'She's not here.'

Beyond the threshold, Sanjay could see a sprinkling of ageing toys – a plastic doll with thinning hair, a spinning top, a battered wooden cat – in one corner. Out of the way, but not yet out of sight. He felt his chest tighten. The rest of the room seemed clean as a shrine. Boxes used for storage were stacked and pushed flush against the concrete walls. He could just make out cooking utensils arranged neatly in the right corner, beside a second door that must lead outside to the back of the house. It was all about a third of the size of his own bedroom, and it was empty.

It struck him then that Janani probably knew his home as well as he did. She'd played in it since she could walk. She'd cleaned it every day for three years, mopped his bedroom, scrubbed the bathroom, dusted every surface. And yet, until this moment, he'd had no idea what her house looked like.

He rubbed a hand over his face.

'Where is she?' he asked and his voice grated in his ears.

'She went home to deliver the baby,' Vandhana said, glaring. 'Go there, if you want to find her.'

With a jerk of her head, she closed the door in their faces.

Distaste had twisted Priya Ammayi's face as they turned away. 'Poor girl,' she muttered in English. 'And poor woman.'

Sanjay turned to stare at her, face incredulous. 'What do you mean? She's an old bitch. Can you imagine how she treats Janani?'

'I know,' Priya said. 'But you saw her hands?'

He hadn't. There couldn't have been anything further from his mind.

'Oil,' Priya added quietly. 'Oil burns, all the way up her arms. Whatever happened, it wasn't an accident. Not enough dowry, maybe. Or too many girls.'

He hadn't noticed. He hadn't looked. All he'd seen was an angry, shrunken old woman before him.

At least she hadn't done the same to—

He was distracted by a small, scattered group of men – neighbours, perhaps, passing by – strolling across the road towards them. At least two had an aruval or a knife in hand, come from chopping sugar cane or breaking coconuts.

'Hoy! Who are you?'

The speaker was wearing a lunghi that needed a wash, a shirt tucked untidily into the waist. He held a solid-looking stick. As he drew nearer, he looked Sanjay up and down, and though he slowed his steps, he didn't stop.

'Why are you here?'

Sanjay was very conscious of his aunt, couldn't help adjusting his position so he was blocking her slightly. 'I am just—'

'Eh! Vanakkam!'

The shout was loud enough to make them all turn. An old woman was approaching him, silver hair pulled into a knot at the top of her head, shoulders slightly hunched. She looked vaguely familiar, but it wasn't until she was a few steps away that he recognised her.

The old midwife, standing outside her hut as a group of thugs ransacked it.

'He is here for his wife's sari,' the woman said. 'Go, go, you useless men.'

And they did, losing interest as easily as they'd caught it, hunters realising their quarry wasn't prey.

Sanjay took a much-needed breath. 'Vanakkam,' he said, bowing to the old woman. Beside him, Priya did the same.

She peered at them. 'You are Janani's Sanjay,' she said to him. It wasn't a question. He didn't reply. There was something about her pale eyes that disconcerted him, something very old, as though she'd seen a thousand lifetimes he couldn't imagine.

'We're looking for her, Ma,' Priya explained. 'To make sure she and the baby are well.'

'Do you know where she is?' Sanjay asked.

'You're asking at the wrong house,' the old woman said. 'I delivered her last night, at her parents' house. In Chellampatti.'

Pure relief flooded Sanjay. Vandhana had not been lying. 'She's well?'

'For now, yes,' the midwife replied. She wasn't smiling. 'I think you should go to her.'

He didn't have to think. 'Where in Chellampatti, Ma?'

Several minutes later, Sanjay was clambering back into the car. He waited, tapping his foot against the accelerator impatiently, as Priya Ammayi pulled herself in and clipped in her seat belt. No one wore seat belts.

He pulled a haphazard three-point-turn, knocking over a pile of empty baskets as he did so, then wove his way back towards the highway.

'Careful, Sanjay.' His aunt's fingers were wrapped around the handle above the window. 'No point in having an accident before we reach her.'

Chellampatti lay between them and Madurai. As he retraced their route, Sanjay hoped the cows were not being herded back across the highway. The road, however, stayed mercifully clear and he stepped on the accelerator. The jeep jolted forward.

He was so focused, it took him a while to realise the object on the left side of the road was a person. A woman. She carried a bundle wrapped in cloth in one hand, her other fist clutched around a linen bag. She looked like she was struggling, curled over, her shoulders hunched protectively and her steps uneven.

Sanjay wasn't sure what stopped him. The sari perhaps – had

he seen it before? Or maybe it was her posture, her movements, tugging at some thread of familiarity so deep he was barely aware of it?

Whatever it was, his foot moved to the brake before Priya called his name sharply. He didn't bother turning around. Pulling over hard, he parked the jeep with the left wheels up on a bank of grass and almost tumbled out of the driver's seat. Regaining his balance, he began to run, one arm waving pointlessly.

'Wait!'

The woman stopped. She turned, her movements slow, the arm holding the cloth bundle curling more tightly into her chest. Her head came up.

'Janani!'

He ran towards her and came to a knee-jarring stop before her. She was staring at him, eyes huge in her face. His gaze dropped to the bundle in her arms. The light was dimming, leaking away into the night, but there was enough to make out a little face, miniature features, eyes closed. One small hand unfurled from the cloth draped over it, the fingers reaching, before it settled back down.

'Are you all right?' he said, stepping forward. 'Let me take this.' He reached for her bag.

She flinched at first, clutching even harder at the baby, then let him take the bag.

'What happened, Janani? Where are you going?

A lorry carrying huge blocks of quarried granite passed them, bathing them in fine granite dust.

'I don't know,' she said, sounding exhausted, her brow folding in confusion. 'To Shubha's house? Kamala Amma?' Then her face cleared and she looked at him square in the face. 'I'm on my own now.'

The words told him nothing and everything. They spoke to him of something terrible. 'You've just had a baby,' he said. 'You should be in the hospital.'

She laughed. 'I'm fine,' she said, but she looked like she was going to wilt towards the ground like a dehydrated palm. It struck him how thin she was.

Priya had reached them.

'Janani, molé,' she said, and wrapped her arms around her and the baby.

Janani turned her face into Priya's neck.

'Come with me,' Sanjay said. 'Let me take you to Priya Ammayi's house.' He hadn't even asked his aunt. 'Just to rest for a while.'

Priya straightened, pulling away slightly. 'Yes. Yes, you come with us, molé.'

'Shubha. I want Shubha.'

She was paler than he'd ever seen her, and there was a sheen of sweat at her temple. He thought of her friend's house, that tiny, cramped, love-filled hut.

'I'll take you there,' he said. 'And then, come back with us.'

She looked at him a moment longer, then nodded.

He carried the bag to the jeep, his steps halved as he kept pace with Janani while Priya supported her with an arm around her back. The baby remained blissfully asleep and Sanjay saw long dark lashes brushing cheeks that should have been fuller, a tiny button nose, pink lips pursed in a crescent.

Two minutes later, they were back in Usilampatti. Sanjay felt himself accelerate as he drove past Janani's house, praying to Krishna or Ganesha or whoever was listening that no one had noticed his return.

When he reached Shubha's house, he saw that Janani had fallen into a doze, her head drooping over the baby. Leaping from the jeep, he knocked on the door, chancing glances behind him to see whether he had attracted attention.

An old man opened the door. 'Ah?' he asked.

'Shubha Ma?' Sanjay asked.

The old man gazed at him, understandably bewildered, and then Shubha appeared behind him. Her eyes widened.

'What is it?' she said.

He couldn't help but think how much more texture life had given her, to Janani, than there was to Diya. Or even himself.

'Janani,' he said. 'She's had the baby. She wants you.'

He stepped aside, and watched as her eyes darted to the jeep. 'It's a girl,' she said.

He nodded.

She was moving before he could think, darting back into the house. He heard the murmur of voices, and before he could try to catch the words, Shubha had reappeared with a cloth bag.

'Let's go,' she said.

Janani stirred awake as Shubha clambered in beside her. Sanjay pretended not to hear the gasp and the hitch of tears, or to see the women cling to each other, whispering over the baby, in the rear-view mirror. Priya was tight-lipped beside him.

They drove in silence, and the last vestiges of the day had bled away by the time they reached Priya's house. Sanjay pulled right up behind the Maruti.

Priya hurried to the front door before them, unlocking it with firm fingers, and then they were inside, into the comfortable yellow light of the small sitting room. His aunt settled Janani onto the floral couch.

'Food,' she said, 'that's first.'

She disappeared into the kitchen, just behind the small room where they sat. They could hear her clattering around, the heavy sound of full pots, the clang of steel plates, the smell of heating dahl and kadala.

Sanjay sat in an armchair opposite Janani and watched her watching the sleeping infant in her arms, the tiny chest moving, up and down, up and down, with her even breaths.

'Do you want to talk about it, Janani?' Sanjay said. 'About what happened?'

She looked up at him. In her eyes, he saw the same look that had shocked him more than a year ago, when he had first found her in the kitchen, when he'd first understood the reality of what she'd lost. The defiant, lava-hot rage. Her head moved just slightly, a tiny shake, and her attention went back to the baby.

Sanjay felt, rather than saw, Shubha's glare. He sat silent, feeling like an intruder, a voyeur into the intimacy of this mother and child and everything they'd experienced together.

Janani spoke. 'Having a daughter,' she said, 'is a curse. It's the same as watering your neighbour's plants and never your own.'

Shubha took her free hand.

Janani glanced at her, and then back up at Sanjay, and this time it seemed as though she were really looking at him. The anger had melted into a softness about her eyes that was nothing to do with the exhaustion that shadowed her face. They looked at each other for a long moment, and then she told him.

He listened as the whole story came out, about the permission she'd been given to travel home, about the comfort of her mother's arms, about how it was all a betrayal. An aching pain started in the heels of his palms and he realised that he was leaning forward, elbows on his knees, and his hands had curled themselves into fists so hard that his nails were digging into the skin. Unclenching them, he examined the deep crescent shapes in the skin.

Janani had stopped talking. Tears tracked down her calm, still face. Shubha's arms were around her – it looked like they were holding her upright.

'Ende Bhagavan,' Priya said. Sanjay looked back to see her standing in the kitchen doorway, arms folded, pity in her eyes.

The baby stirred, and her tiny cries chirruped into existence. She began to squirm, head turning left and right. Her ears were swirling flower petals, pink and perfectly formed.

'Oh,' Janani said, 'she's hungry . . .' She looked up, uncertain, embarrassed.

'Come, come,' Priya said, moving forward at once. 'I'll show you your room; Shubha, come too. Sanjay, bring their bags and then go away, give them privacy.'

Priya's house was small in comparison to the main family house, but lovely and neat. Sanjay followed the women to the smaller of the two bedrooms, the bed perfectly made up, a picture of Rama, Lakshman and Sita on one wall and a watercolour of the Golden Temple at Amritsar on the other. It smelled like fresh flowers.

Janani looked around her as though she were in a palace. The child seemed to sense it too, her cries fading as she settled slightly.

'I can't sit here, Priya Amma,' Janani said. 'I'm so dirty.' Her face crumpled.

Sanjay found himself stepping towards her, but thankfully Priya was in the way and reached her first, taking her and the wriggling baby in her arms.

'Don't be a silly girl,' she said. 'Sit back here –' she plumped up the pillows on the bed against the headboard – 'and feed the little one. There is a bathroom there.' She pointed at a door that led to the en-suite bathroom. 'We'll get the little one fed and Shubha and I can mind her if you'd like to bathe before we eat.

Sanjay,' she said, turning to him, 'go and finish heating the food and set the table, kutty.'

He nodded and left them. Closing the door behind him, he leaned against it and drew in a breath, filling his lungs, feeling his heartbeat slow. There were a few seconds when he considered succumbing to the mad desire to run outside and onto the street, to scream at the sky, to keep running until the energy pulsing through him had died and he was too exhausted to think and feel the maelstrom within him.

One more breath and he pushed himself away from the door to busy himself with the minor preparations for their dinner.

What they spoke about in that room, Sanjay never knew, but Janani stayed that night, the next, a third. Shubha flitted between her house and Priya's, his aunt's driver shepherding her back and forth. Priya told him that in between caring for the baby and sleeping in worn-out stillness, Janani was speaking, quietly, cautiously, openly. They had conversations about her life and Priya's, about their families, about the future. Priya hunted out old saris and salwars of her own to give to her, then sent Sanjay to the market with detailed, specific instructions for clothes for the baby.

Sanjay spent the early evenings after work at home, with Amma, reading or watching television, or talking. Until she told him to go, that she was tired, that he should make sure Janani was well. When he'd helped her to bed, he ran to Priya's house, ignoring his father's grimaces. Vijay didn't even notice, so absorbed was he in studying.

It took a while for Janani's reluctance to hand her new daughter to another person to fade. When Sanjay first held her, on the second evening, he had to sit down, and he felt like his arms were trembling. The little bundle was warm, the flecks of hair on her scalp light as feathers as she moved her head side to side against his arm in her half-sleep. He touched her soft cheek and one hand came up out of her swaddling. Minute fingers extended to wrap around his finger. He stayed like that for a long time. When he looked up, Janani was gazing at him, a half-smile on her face, almost dreamy. He was afraid that he had broken the moment, but her smile simply twitched upward, and then his eyes were locked to hers.

On the fourth night, they were waiting for him. The three of them, Janani, Shubha, Priya.

'I'm ready to go,' Janani said.

He looked between them, confused. Priya said nothing, her face grave.

'Go where?' Sanjay asked, confused.

She smiled. 'There is a shop I'm renting, remember?' Her smile faded. 'I'm never going back to them. To my mother and father. To Darshan and Vandhana. Never.'

She was holding the baby in her arms. It all seemed utterly impossible.

'I've told her she can stay as long as she wants.' His aunt smiled.

'You've been beyond kind, Priya Amma,' Janani said. 'You both have. But it's time I start my own life. My new life.'

'But . . . the baby . . .' Sanjay said. They looked so small, both of them.

'I'll take care of her,' Janani replied.

'Alone?' Sanjay asked.

The look on Shubha's face reassured him.

The two women looked at each other.

'How do you think I raised Lavanika?' Janani said. 'My mamiyar and Darshan were no help. Worse than no help.'

'And she won't be alone,' Shubha said. 'We are there.'

Janani smiled, the first real smile Sanjay had seen since he'd found her trudging down the highway with her newborn in her arms.

I'll help you, Sanjay thought, and then, *I love you*, and when the thought registered, in cold clarity, it was like being slapped in the face, or shaken awake, or being thrown into a pond on a hot day. He bit the inside of his lip so hard he tasted blood.

'Sanjay,' Janani said. 'I have some things, at . . . in Usilampatti. And my sewing machine, it's at Shubha's house still.' She smiled at her friend, a sweet smile that reminded Sanjay, with a wrench, of Lavanika. 'I can't carry them all. Please, will you come with me?'

'Of course,' he said. 'Whenever you want.'

'Of course,' Priya said, and she was smiling at him.

Chapter Twenty-Two

Now she is acclimatising to this alien world. She hears voices that were once muffled sounds. She teeters, still, on the edge of life.

Making the decision was the hardest part. To confront Darshan, or Vandhana – the fear that roiled in her gut at the thought. The thought of leaving Priya Amma's sanctuary. Leaving Sanjay. Of how close they were now. Of every conversation they had had. The stories Priya had told her of her own life, of the intolerant bore of a husband she had had, who had cursed her for not being able to bear a child, for every one of the eight babies that had ended in pain and blood and heartbreak before they had a chance to take a breath on their own. The sight of Sanjay holding her baby in his arms, half-terrified, half-fascinated, as her daughter curled her face into the crook of his elbow and slept, safe. The thought of being further from Shubha, her best friend, her companion, her sister.

But it was time.

And Janani knew, from the whispered, harried conversations, the nervous mentions of Radhakrishnan Aiya, that the time they had was short.

On the morning of the fifth day after she had walked away from her childhood home, Janani double-checked the contents of her bags. Priya had thrown away the old rice sack that had formed her bag and given her another two, proper, store-bought bags, lined and weighed down with saris that were old but still better quality than anything Janani had ever owned. On top of those were the baby clothes and cloth nappies acquired just in the last few days and, wedged between them all, small bags and containers of rice, lentils, vegetables, ground spices – rasam and sambar powders, cumin and turmeric, mustard seeds.

It was a Saturday. Sanjay would be driving them. He appeared early and the sight of him made Janani catch her breath – he was dressed in a lunghi, a checked shirt, as though he were a labourer in a field. She hadn't seen him in a lunghi since they were children. Part of her wanted to laugh.

'You look different,' she said instead.

He glanced down at himself and laughed. 'I don't wear this as often as I should,' he said. His eyes moved down to the baby, dozing in her arms. 'You like my outfit, little one, don't you?'

Her daughter yawned, a big, toothless stretch of her mouth, and kept dreaming.

Sanjay smiled, his dark eyes soft, and it hit her then, as suddenly and shockingly as though someone had poured a bucket of water over her head from behind, what this was, this clench in her chest that was so beautiful it hurt, that she loved him. She loved him. She felt the sliver of courage she was clinging to strengthen.

They drove in near silence. Priya came with them, sitting with Janani in the back seat, one hand on the baby's little foot. Janani felt that touch as though she were the one being soothed. She had barely been able to sleep, and a worm of nausea had been growing, thickening, all morning. The music from the radio flowed over her, and she had no interest in what it was. She could think of only two things: that Sanjay was sitting just ahead of her, his eyes visible in the mirror, and that they were moving closer to Darshan and Vandhana. Comfort and fear, but at least the first was the stronger.

The journey seemed to last a year, a year of familiar landscapes moving past her agonisingly slowly, the rice fields and restaurants, the university, the fields of cows. Still, it was too soon when they finally turned off the highway onto Usilampatti Main Road. The passed the government hospital and Janani saw Vandhana's face as though it were before her, twisted in anger at the knowledge that her next grandchild would be another useless girl.

And then they were there. The street was stirring from the quiet of early morning. Janani pressed herself back in her seat to avoid Ramya and Madhavi walking down to the pumps with their water buckets. Goats were being fed, cows led out to graze, wives on their front steps grinding rice and lentils for dosa and idli, vegetables being chopped, chickens being killed.

They stopped just ahead of the house.

'Are you ready, child?' Priya asked, and Janani nodded. She wasn't, but she was. She had to be.

They climbed out in silence. Priya took the baby from Janani as she emerged and Sanjay opened the boot of the car to lift out the bags. Janani pulled them on to her shoulders, waving Sanjay away.

'Stay here, please,' she said.

Sanjay opened his mouth to argue, then stopped. Janani saw his eyes flick to Priya, then back to her.

'I'll be right here,' he said. 'Watching. Call me if you need anything. Or wave to me. Look at me. I'll come.'

'Let me carry your bags,' Priya said. 'I can let them know we brought you safely and honourably.'

Janani looked at her, and her heart swelled as though air were being pumped into it, with love, with grief. Why could this not be her mother? She pushed the thought away and nodded.

They walked together towards the house, and Janani could feel Sanjay behind her, almost as strongly as the sun.

Janani could feel sweat pricking at her that had nothing to do with the heat. Her stomach roiled. She fought to ignore the clenching of her gut. She had no time for any of that now. She had to do this before she thought too much. She could feel the fear flowing through her like a river, threatening to burst its banks and overwhelm her, sweep her away.

Priya stopped walking several paces away from the front door. Janani looked back at her to catch her encouraging nod, then stepped forward to knock at the door. The heavy tread of footsteps sounded through the wood. She recognised them immediately. Pulling the baby more tightly against her body, she watched the door open, a jolting, uneven opening, to reveal first slivers and then the entirety of Darshan. He looked at her. Slowly some of the fog in his eyes cleared.

'Janani,' he said. His eyes dropped to the bundle in her arms.

The door opened further.

'Oh,' Vandhana said, her voice piercing through the gap. 'Finally, she returns.' Her unwelcoming gaze also fell to the baby. 'With another useless girl-child.'

They both stood there, looking at her. There was no attempt to step back, to let her in. To ask how she was. To reach for the child. Janani had felt more at home when she had arrived at Priya's house. In that moment's silence, all doubt died.

'I won't be here long,' she said. 'I'm just here to collect my things. Then I'll go, and you won't need to ever see me or this girl-child again.'

Darshan's jaw dropped. Fish-faced in disbelief, he turned to

Vandhana as though looking for guidance. Janani felt a wave of disgust ripple its way through her. Was there nothing he could do without his mother? Not even think?

Vandhana peered past her at Priya.

'You,' she said, frowning. 'What are you doing here?'

'I'm a friend of Janani's,' Priya said, her voice firm. 'I am here to make sure she is safe.'

Janani saw wariness creep over Vandhana's face as her gaze moved from Priya to scan the street. It was only mid-morning. Plenty of people were out in the open air. Those with no work to do – men, all of them – loitered, gossiping, with cigarettes or chewing tobacco, away from where their wives and mothers, sat on the threshold of their houses, preparing their afternoon and evening meals.

'Come inside,' Vandhana hissed. 'Stop making a scene.'

'Give me the child, Janani,' Priya said from behind her.

Janani turned. Seeing Priya there, calm-faced, dark eyes expressionless, she felt like wet cloth had been laid on any embers of her fear. She held out her arms.

They passed the sleeping baby between them. Janani kept hold of the empty bags Priya had given her just before they had left in the morning.

'She's not entering my house,' Vandhana said. 'She came here before. Lied to me.' She was frowning so hard that it seemed the pull of the earth was dragging her features down. It wasn't clear if she was speaking about Priya or her granddaughter.

'I had no intention of it,' Priya said coldly. 'I'll wait here.' She gestured to where Sanjay stood leaning against the car, arms crossed, gazing in their direction. 'So will he.'

Vandhana's mouth twisted like a child tasting bitter gourd for the first time. 'Get inside,' she said, moving away from the doorway.

Janani stepped into the house and Darshan closed the door behind her, shutting out Priya's concerned face.

'Have you lost your mind?' Vandhana hissed, just as Darshan said, 'What do you mean, you're leaving? Where would you go?'

She ignored them and managed to slip between them towards the bedroom.

'Don't just walk away!' Vandhana's voice rose as she forgot about listening ears from outside the house. 'Answer your husband! What are you doing, you little cow? You stupid bitch?'

Janani turned to face them in the doorway of the bedroom. 'I'm not staying here for you to take any more of my babies,' she said. 'To kill them. To scream at me, and hit me. To take the money I work for.' She took a breath. 'I'm leaving.'

Vandhana moved towards her, her face contorted. Janani was reminded of the sculpted rakshasas in the temples, their eyes bulging into semi-spheres, their mouths agape and teeth bared. 'How dare you?' she screamed, her hand raised.

Janani caught it as it came down towards her face, her hand around her mother-in-law's wrist. Her fingers closed completely around it and for the first time she was aware of how fragile Vandhana was, her birdlike bones pressing against soft skin loosened with age. Now she looked at Janani, her mouth open in shock.

'It's best for us all,' Janani said. 'You don't want me here.' She looked at Darshan. 'You don't want me here.'

Her heart was pounding. Darshan was no delicate-boned old woman.

But he simply looked baffled. 'What about the baby?' he asked. 'She's my daughter.'

'Do you want her, Darshan?' Janani felt herself trembling. 'Do you? Another girl-child? I won't be here to take her to school and brush her hair, feed her, teach her in the kitchen, work to give her a dowry. Will you send her to school, Darshan? Will you drink less, so you can buy her clothes and schoolbooks? Will you?'

He scowled at her, then shrugged. She saw his eyes flicker sideways and she followed his gaze. A bottle of some brown liquid stood on the floor beside the plastic chair. It was half-empty.

'Where will you go?' he asked.

'Yes, where?' Vandhana said. 'Will your parents take you back? The divorced, shamed daughter, to be a burden on them in their old age? And with a girl-child?' Her voice dripped with spite.

'It doesn't matter,' Janani replied. 'I'll starve, rather than stay here with you.'

Even Vandhana seemed taken aback by that.

Janani turned, walked into the bedroom and closed the door behind her, leaving them standing motionless. Sun shone through the window, drenching the unmade bed, the cotton sheet in a tangle that draped to paint in the dust on the floor. Even open to the outside air, the room smelled like days of Darshan's musk trapped in a container. Janani wrinkled her nose and hurried to the cupboard. To her relief, the key was in the lock as usual. The aged, warped wood creaked as she opened the door.

She rummaged for her saris, all of them pushed back into the corner of one of the shelves behind Darshan's shirts and trousers. Some were so old she would need to discard them, now that she had Priya's gifts, but for now she piled them all into the bag, not caring to sort through them. She didn't want to leave anything behind.

The most valuable of them, the sari wrapped tightly around her money pouch and every rupee she had saved, sat at the very bottom of the bag, a comforting weight to it.

Squatting down to the bottom shelf, she pulled out her

nighties and underwear, noticing as she did so that they were unfolded and stuffed in a jumbled pile.

Someone had riffled through them.

She shouldn't have expected any less, but still, tears of anger made the bottom of her eyelids prickle.

Her comb and pins were still on the bedside table, along with the small box that contained the meagre pieces of jewellery Vandhana had allowed her to keep. Stuffing them into her bag, she turned to the old chest that stood pushed against the wall at the foot of the bed. Wedged against it, leaning into the corner of the room, was Lavanika's bamboo mat. Janani felt the tears prickle harder before one escaped her right eye and meandered slowly down her cheek. She dashed it away and went to the chest.

It was locked.

Janani frowned at it. Inside this was her dowry jewellery. Her share of the inheritance from her parents, her bride-price.

She tugged at the lock with no real hope that it would budge. It didn't, and when she let it go, its heavy weight clattered against the wood. She hit it with her fist and pain speared through her wrist. There were more tears streaming down on her face now. Straightening, she kicked at the lock with her bare foot, then kicked it again. A second ache twinned with the pain in her hand.

The door to the bedroom slammed open.

'What are you doing?' Vandhana said.

Janani turned to her, breathing hard. 'This chest is locked. There's something in here that belongs to me.'

Vandhana's nostrils flared. 'What are you talking about, you stupid girl? That chest belongs to me. Everything in that chest belongs to me. Take your things, and if you've decided to leave, leave.'

It didn't matter, Janani thought to herself. She had never had anything she hadn't worked for. She knew how to live that life. And she felt so betrayed now, by Amma and Appa, that she wasn't sure she even wanted to see the jewellery they had given her.

But if there was one thing she felt certain of, it was that her parents' money did not belong to Vandhana. It didn't.

'My jewellery is in here,' she said, fighting to keep her voice calm. 'My family's wedding gift. I would like it back, please.'

'Just get out,' Vandhana snapped, her voice rising.

'I'm not moving until you open this,' Janani said, 'or you drag me out.' She was shaking. Every part of her body hurt. She was hardly thinking anymore. It was the twisting, burning sensation filling her gut that drove her now.

Vandhana took a step towards her. Janani had to fight back a flinch, and that instinct was fuel to the fire of her rage. She felt her own free hand come up. It was clenched, balled into a tight fist. It shocked her, how ready she was to swing, to hit out, to do something she had never done before. The feeling must have bled onto her face. Vandhana flinched, as though she were acting the part of Janani's reflection. They stared at each other over the chest.

Finally, Vandhana stepped forward, fumbling at her sari. On a cord tied around her waist were hung a few keys. She untied it and retrieved one. Bending slowly, she reached to insert the key into the lock trapping the chest shut. She fiddled with it for a while, her arthritic fingers or the arthritic lock reluctant to yield. Suddenly, there was a click and Vandhana fumbled the lock off the chest. She threw it open and straightened, her lips drawn tight with hatred.

The smell of musty dust and stale sweat emanated from the chest like steam from a cooking pot. It was barely half full. All

Janani could see was the top layer, a green silk sari Vandhana had worn to a wedding the previous year. Janani had stitched the blouse herself.

She reached down and pulled back the sari to reveal another, in pale yellow. And yet another, below it, blue crepe silk. She lifted them out, one at a time, placing them on the end of the bed.

There was no hint of the glint of jewellery. No gold, no silver. Just yards and yards of sari.

And at the very bottom, on the worn wood, lay her wedding sari. She remembered it well, the scratchy hot weight of it brushing against her skin, slowly getting warmer in the heat of the morning sun and the wedding fire. It had faded slightly now, the red silk lightening towards the gold-embroidered hem. On top of the bright cloth lay a set of glass bangles, red and gold to match. Janani ran a gentle finger over them, listening to them clink. Two had snapped; she lifted the pieces out carefully, encasing them in the palm of her left hand.

And that was all. No sign of her gold sari belt, of the thick chains Amma had draped around her neck that had reflected the sun and puja flames into her eyes, the heavy, dome-shaped, intricately embossed earrings that had pulled at her lobes until they bled, the bangles thick as rope, the delicate nose ring, all of them heavy, soft gold – all gone.

She stood up and met Vandhana's eye. Her mother-in-law held her gaze squarely.

'Where is it?' Janani asked.

'What rubbish are you speaking?' Vandhana retorted. She didn't hesitate – it was a natural reaction, the bounce of a ball thrown against a wall.

'My dowry,' Janani said. 'Where have you put it?' She was surprised to hear her voice emerge so calmly, but it did, as though what she had found were completely reasonable and her questioning was just an afterthought.

Vandhana seemed to take heart from her quiet reaction. 'It's gone,' she said. 'I've used it for what it was meant – sold it, to pay to look after you and Lav—' she wavered. 'Your daughter.'

Janani looked at the pile of saris on the bed, then at the bag that contained the few possessions she'd thought worth taking with her. Without a word, she turned around and walked to the corner of the room where the rolled-up sleeping mat leaned against the wall. At its base sat Lavanika's few toys – her doll and pink rubber ball, her anchangal stones. She picked them all up, one by one, and placed them in her bag atop her clothes. Then she swung the bag over her shoulder.

Vandhana hadn't moved. Janani left the pile of saris on the bed and walked past the open chest. She looked down as she stepped towards the door and found her foot alongside Vandhana's – almost the same size, silver rings encircling both of their second toes.

We could have been the same, Janani thought. *We could have loved each other.*

'Iraivan will thank you,' she said, 'for what you have done.'

She walked out without waiting for any sign her words had hit their mark.

Priya was hovering outside, swaying side to side with the baby. She looked up and smiled, relief evident on her face, as Janani stepped out of the house for the last time, into the comfort of the sunlight.

Janani reached for her daughter. Priya handed the sleeping infant to her and eased Janani's bag from her shoulder.

'Eh,' Darshan said behind her.

Janani turned. The baby stirred in her arms, her little lips parting.

Darshan looked down at the child, then back at her. 'Amma's going to find me someone else,' he said. 'A woman who can give me sons. I'm going to divorce you.'

Divorce. That word of shame and dishonour. That herald of a life that could end in a shack by the side of the road, alone, despised by all.

That ring of freedom.

'Best of luck,' she said. 'Don't worry. You won't see me again.'

As Janani turned away, she heard him shut the door firmly behind her. A breeze was kicking up, caressing her wet cheeks. The pain in her legs and stomach was making itself felt again, just flickers on the outer edges of consciousness.

Priya's arm was around her shoulders.

Janani looked at her, and managed to force a smile.

'I'm ready to go,' she said. 'I'm ready to never come back.'

They walked away from the house, to where Sanjay waited, arms crossed against his chest, his hair shining in the sun like a raven's wing.

Chapter Twenty-Three

Madurai, 2019

We leave Usilampatti for tomorrow.

Radhika and I escape the house together almost as soon as we return from Chellampatti. I want to get drunk, alone, but instead we go window-shopping and stop for ice cream that will likely leave me with diarrhoea. We talk about anything – anything except today. I have no idea how much she knows. From the way she acts, she knows nothing. If it's true, I'm thankful. If it's not, I'm grateful.

I don't know what's been said when we get home, but I suspect that what's known is everything. How I manage to get through dinner, I don't know, but as I begin to rush to bed, Kochachan challenges Radhika and me to a game of caroms and doesn't take no for an answer. We haul out the heavy rosewood board and put it on the Taj Mahal table in the drawing room. After watching sullenly from a corner of the room, Arjun joins in, taking the fourth side of the table between me and Radhika. At first, we play in silence, but after the first round, when Kochachan miraculously sinks the Queen and a white coin with one shot, we're laughing and insulting each other's technique. Arjun catches my eye, and I see in his gaze a frank, sheepish apology. I smile, reach out and steal one of his counters.

Radhika swaps out for Acha, and Kochachan for Manju Ammayi, and we play on. It's like nothing's changed.

We play and play until there's a yawn every second shot, and still I want to keep going. There's a mindlessness to caroms, a deep, pleasant, alert calm. And finally, it's just Acha and me, the coins sounding their sharp crack as they hit the side of the table, until it's past midnight and Acha has beaten me again.

We're silent as we reach for the coins, sorting them back into their box.

'You know, Nila,' Acha says, 'that you are my daughter. Mine.'

He's not looking at me as he says it. But the coins rattle, and I can see his hands are shaking.

I stand and cross over to settle on the couch beside him. Slowly, I rest my head against his shoulder.

'Why didn't you tell me?' I whisper.

'It was your amma's story to tell,' he says. He picks up one of the black coins, rolling it between his fingers. 'I knew she would have to tell it someday. I told her that, many times.' He sees my surprise. 'Oh, yes. But your amma is a strong woman. I knew she would wait until she was ready.'

'But you're my acha,' I say, and I have to bite back, *right?* 'You have just as much a right to tell me about your story. And that includes Amma.'

He chuckles. My cheek vibrates against his shoulder. 'Very true,' he says. 'But those sections of my life – your amma and you – she has more right to. I never had to fight for you like she did. You just came to me, a gift from God.'

I have to turn, wrap my arms around his chest and bury my head in his shoulder. I'm very tired of crying – my head is pounding with the effort and dehydration.

'I'm sorry, Acha,' I say. 'First Achacha. And now this.'

'I wish,' Acha begins, 'that you could have known your

achamma. She loved your amma. Accepted her, immediately. And I wish you could have seen what a good man your achacha was. In spite of everything.'

'I do,' I reply. 'They brought you up.'

He looks at me, and gives me the first real smile I've seen in days. 'Goose,' he says, and he puts his arm around me, leaving a smear of talcum powder on my arm.

At two a.m., I'm in bed, but I'm still awake. The mattress has moulded itself to my back as I stare at the ceiling and think about Rohan.

Not my brother. My half-brother.

Part of me screams that it changes nothing between us, while another part wails in grief, as though I've lost a limb.

They're so far away, the people I want to speak to. My brother, my best friend, the person I love. They'll be on the way to work, to class.

The urge to hear their voices is overwhelming, enough for me to reach out for my phone and squeeze it, its edges digging hard into my palm.

Instead, I text them. The same message, flying across the world, through cable and ether.

Miss you. Love you

My head is tight with lack of sleep as we drive down the Madurai–Theni highway once more the following morning. Despite my nerves, the heat has me dozing off. Warped images play behind my eyelids. An imaginary father, and grandmother.

Birth father. Biological grandmother.

In my half-dream state, their mouths move, speaking unintelligible words. Their faces are shifting, twisting shapes and colours.

My head drops forward and I jerk back into the physical world.

The only thing I notice on the way to Usilampatti is a roadside shrine, gaudy with colour, of a man riding a white horse, its saddlecloth decorated with blue flowers.

'Turn here, Shankar,' Amma says.

The streets here are as narrow as those of Chellampatti, but far more densely packed. Scooters and motorbikes whip around us like fish around a whale. I see groups of schoolchildren walking together, girls in dark maroon skirts, their hair braided, boys in shorts and collared shirts. They turn to stare, frowning into the glare of the sun, as Shankar navigates carefully around them.

We pass a sweeping banyan tree. A cluster of men huddle beneath it, casual in their lunghis, some standing, others perched atop the huge roots veining the ground. They watch us pass by. There's a chicken running ahead of us, a woman following, shouting, her green sari flapping behind her. Her neighbour is laughing.

I don't hear what Amma says to Shankar, but suddenly the car is slowing, then stopping, by a row of pastel houses, the sun bearing down on roofs of red tile and thatch.

Veliamma and I follow Acha out into the complex village air. When I look back, Amma's still sitting there, in the suntrap that is the car.

For a moment, I don't think she's going to get out. In that moment, I realise I don't want her to, if she can't. I take a step back towards the car, but Acha is far ahead of me. He's jogging towards her – I haven't seen him move this fast in a long time. He opens the car door and squats in front of her, like a devotee in front of an idol. She looks down at him and even from here I can see her face soften. They stay there like that, exchanging words I can't make out.

Veliamma has come to stand beside me. She puts a hand on my shoulder.

I see Amma's feet emerge from the car. She takes the hand Acha holds out to her and slowly they walk towards me. The sun shines on Acha's grey hairs, turning them to quicksilver. I'm reminded then that they're getting older, getting old. That this experience might be one they've earned the right not to endure.

They reach us.

'Sanjay,' Amma says. 'You stay here. You too, Priya Amma. We'll go and come.'

We all stare at her.

'No,' Acha replies. 'I don't want you going there alone.'

I look between them. I don't understand this, and the frustration burns me.

'It will be OK.' Amma puts a hand on his arm. 'Who knows. Perhaps they will not be there. Perhaps . . .' She looks at me, and stops. I realise then, that she hopes that they won't be. That perhaps she hopes they're dead. And now I am questioning if I even want to know.

Let's go now, a part of me says.

My history, my beginning, my life, says another.

I stay quiet.

'We'll wait where we can see you,' Veliamma says. Amma looks at her. Something passes between them, a knowing that only they have.

'If you take too long,' Acha states, 'I'll come to the house.'

Amma looks at him, and smiles. It's a special smile, softening her entire face, relaxing her shoulders, releasing the tension in her fingers. It's a smile that glows like warm candlelight. I sense I'm looking back on a time before I existed, a time I might never know or understand. It should leave me lost, confused. Yesterday, I might have been resentful. Instead, I'm glad.

Amma turns to me. *Let's go*, her head shake says.

We walk off together, down the road, towards the row of houses.

'When will we talk properly about all of this, Amma?' I ask.

She takes my hand. 'When we leave,' she says. 'When we're on the way home. We've got the rest of our lives to talk, isn't it?'

Amma's grammar. It makes me smile. It settles my nerves, a drop of oil on churning waters.

She leads me to one of the small houses, its walls painted a pale blue that doesn't look as if it's been fresh for years. Pieces of ragged cloth lie on the ground by the door, as do a couple of playing cards – the two of hearts and the four of clubs.

'It's smaller than I remember,' Amma says, looking around. Her gaze stops on something off to the right, past the house. I follow her line of sight and find a cluster of palm trees standing quite close to the house. Between two of them is strung a frayed-looking line of thick rope, with clothes hung out along it to dry in the hot sunshine. I can smell rasam, the strong fragrance of tamarind and fried mustard seeds, tomato and curry leaves.

The door stands slightly ajar. Voices drift from inside. They're too faint for me to make out what's being said.

Amma touches my arm with her other hand. 'I don't know if they still live here,' she says. 'Let's knock and see.' But her grip on my hand tightens.

I step forward, rap my knuckles on the wood.

The force rocks the door slightly and it squeaks on its hinges.

The voices within stop.

I wait a couple of seconds, then knock again.

The voices have begun once more, this time with a puzzled upward tilt. Then the sound of bare feet on hard floor, louder and nearer with each step.

I lean back as the door opens.

I find myself looking into the face of a middle-aged man, older than Acha. He has thick hair that's more grey than black and has begun to recede from the top of his forehead. He's hunched over, shoulders tightened with what looks like years of sitting behind a computer screen. Although his skin is still smooth, the melanin protecting it from years of soaking in the sun's rays, something else has weathered it. It looks stretched taut over the bones of his face. He's thin, but his belly protrudes in a way that suggests he's indulged in too much of something. With his scrawny arms and legs, the effect is that he looks like a spider, gangly limbs encircling a round centre.

I can smell something on him. Frying oil and sweat and whisky.

His eyes narrow, thick dark eyebrows lowering as he looks at me.

'Eh?' he says. 'Who are you?'

I hear Amma breathe beside me, a long exhale.

'Darshan,' she says.

His bleary eyes flick towards her.

'Yes,' he says. 'That's me.'

I don't understand his next sentence. There's a slight change in his posture, his shoulders rounding defensively. Wariness creeps into his puffy face.

I become aware of a swirl of nausea in the pit of my stomach. It starts to creep upward like smoke.

Amma's hesitant. I squeeze her hand and drop my head to her ear. 'We can go if you want,' I whisper.

Her head turns towards me, just slightly. Her fingers tighten on mine.

'Janani,' she says, pointing to herself with her other hand. 'Do you remember me?'

He stares at her as though he's seeing her for the first time. 'Janani,' he says. 'My God.'

He thinks he's dreaming. I can see it in his eyes, in the incredulous guffaw that emerges in a puff of whiskeyed bad breath.

'Darshan!' A voice emerges from inside, wavering, slightly shrill. 'Who is there?'

He calls back something I don't understand. Then he seems to realise my mother is not alone. He looks at me and his eyes narrow. 'Who is this?'

There's movement behind him and a moment later a small woman appears at the side of the man who must be my biological father. Her hair is a dull, featureless grey in the dimness of the house's interior. She wears a silver stud in her nose. Her sari's pink, faded but well cared for. Crows' feet branch out from the corner of her eyes. She peers at us, squinting into the brightness of the day.

'Janani,' she says, shaking her head.

Amma puts her palms together. 'Mamiyar,' she says. *Mother-in-law.* She's standing so close to me I have to brace myself to keep my balance. I lean into her.

'What are you doing here?' the old woman says. Her Tamil sounds harsher than I've heard before. My father's mother.

Before Amma has a chance to answer, Darshan – my father – speaks again.

'Who is she?' He's staring at me.

'My daughter,' Amma says. 'Nila.'

He seems a little more sober. His mouth is open. 'Your daughter,' he says. 'Lav—'

'No.' Amma's voice is sharp as a whipcrack.

'No,' the man, my father, says. 'No.'

There's a strained silence.

'The other one,' the old woman says.

354

'Yes,' Amma replies simply. 'She wanted to come here. To see you.' She turns to me, her whole body facing me. She says, 'Nila, this is your father, Darshan, and your grandmother, Vandhana.'

'She looks like her,' my father says.

Like my mother? I think.

'She looks like Lavanika.' My grandmother is squinting at me. 'She is pretty.' She turns back to Amma. 'Where do you live now?'

'Australia,' Amma says. I can feel the tension in her body, pressed against mine. It spills out, surrounding all of us.

Around us, the village street is busy, teenage boys passing us leading cattle, jeeps and autorickshaws and motorbikes filling the air with the shrill shriek of their horns, older schoolkids with bags hoisted high on their shoulders chattering and laughing. Curious glances are being thrown our way. We're clear strangers here. I'm aware of the weirdness of my being here, like wearing another skin. I feel like a disembodied spirit, watching other people's lives, completely detached from them.

'Australia,' my grandmother says. Her lips bare into the first smile I've seen from her. It looks strange on her face, as though she's forgotten how to do it. 'Your husband,' she hesitates slightly over the word, as though it's spiked, as though it will snag at her, 'he works there?'

'I work too,' she says. The hint of pride in her voice is contagious. 'I sew, and I teach sewing. I have my own business. And Nila has a very good job.'

My grandmother looks startled. Slowly, her head moves in the traditional, all-purpose nod. 'You work?' she asks me.

My spirit self is drawn back into the scene. It throws me, so that I have to hunt frantically for my meagre Tamil.

'Yes,' I say. 'I'm a . . .' I have no idea if there is an equivalent, so I say it in English, 'physiotherapist.'

She nods as though she understands.

'Well,' she says. 'It is good to see you after so long. Come inside. Have some tea.'

Amma opens her mouth to answer, then she stops and looks at me.

She's waiting for me to speak. To tell her that I want to go inside. That I want to stay.

My biological father lifts a bottle to his lips and takes a swig. It seems unconscious – he's staring at me, as though I'm a difficult crossword clue. Then he shakes his head like a wet dog.

'Come,' my grandmother commands, with that not-quite-smile.

'I don't want to,' I say to Amma in English.

She nods. Her hand is tight on mine.

Turning back, she says, 'We have to go, Mamiyar. There are people waiting for us.

'I have a new wife,' Darshan says. He chuckles, a weak, thin sound, like a coughing dog. I don't understand the next sentence. Then, 'I have two sons now. Two!' He looks at me, and the grimace of his smile fades slightly. 'And a daughter.' A hand goes up to rub his mouth, then his temples. Mumbled words emerge. 'Little bird,' I think I hear.

A frown furrows my grandmother's forehead as she darts a quick, sidelong glance at her son. 'He needed someone to look after him,' she says as though an explanation is needed. 'I don't know how much longer I'll be here, by the grace of God.'

Two sons. I have more brothers. I should want to meet them, to find out more, but I really want to go. These people repel me, as though there's a force encircling them, pushing me away. I wish Rohan were here, and I'm glad he's not. I wish Iphigenia were here too, and I'm just as glad that's she's far, far away.

Darshan has staggered back into the house. I can just make him out, sprawled in a plastic chair, limbs fanned out.

'We should go,' I mutter to Amma. 'They'll be waiting.'

I feel some of the tension leave her. 'You're right,' she agrees. 'Mamiyar,' she says to my grandmother, 'we need to go now.'

'Already?' the old woman says. 'You only just arrived. Will you come back another day?'

Amma looks at me. I keep my expression perfectly neutral. 'Perhaps, if we have time,' she replies.

'What's happening?' Darshan, my father, asks from where he lolls against the wall.

Vandhana turns and snaps at him. I grasp the second phrase, 'Get up, fool. They're leaving. They are going back to Australia.'

'Oh.' He stays motionless, a giant, alcoholic ragdoll.

My grandmother reaches for us, on hand to Amma, one to me. 'I'm happy you came,' she says. 'I am glad you're doing so well. I was wondering . . .' She looks between Amma and me. 'You know we have very little money here. Anything you could send us would be welcome. It would help us very much.' Her speech has slowed. It's deliberately careful, pitched to my child's understanding.

I feel like I've been punched. I'm aware my mouth's fallen open. My head swivels automatically to my mother.

I've barely ever seen the look that Amma now wears on her face. It's the look I once saw when a drunken middle-aged man with a rolling beer belly called us 'curry-munchers' after Australia Day fireworks as we walked home, my little hand in hers, Rohan asleep in Acha's arms. It was a look that frightened me and comforted me at the same time. Push me one step further, it said, and I'll break your nose.

'Mamiyar, we're not sending you anything,' she says. 'Not one rupee.' She adds something I don't understand, in a voice that's hard and harsher than I've ever heard.

Vandhana stares at her, and her face hardens. 'Ungrateful girl,' she snaps. I understand that line from an old Tamil soap that Amma watches one too many times. She turns to me. 'Will you help your father, and your old grandmother? Anything you can spare will help.'

The lump in my throat is pushing its way up further and I feel my face flush the way it does when I'm on the verge of tears. My heart's starting to pound; air seems like something impossible to reach.

Amma says something hard that makes Vandhana's eyes widen. She backs away, taking me with her. I'm aware suddenly of the heat of the sun, now almost at its zenith in the sky.

'You never even wanted her,' Amma says. 'You didn't want any of them.' Her speech becomes fast, furious, and I have to fight to keep track of even part of the conversation. *Ask*, I make out, and *money*. And *no right*.

'You know what life they would have had here,' my grand-mother says, and I realise I've fallen steps behind on the path of this conversation. She looks at me, then back to my mother. 'Did you tell her?' There's mockery in her voice. I recognise it because it's the same singsong quality I have, those very few times when I've surrendered to mindless rage, my version of a snarl.

Tell me what? I no longer care. The tone's enough I don't want to hear any more, not now. The ugliness of it all makes me want to scream. 'Come on, Amma,' I say in English, safe, secret English. 'Let's go.'

She looks at me and I see her eyes are bright. 'Yes, let's go.'

As one, we turn our backs.

And Vandhana says, 'Did you give money to the other grand-mother? Was she any better than me?'

Amma's fingers close like a vice around my arm. 'Let's go!'

We walk away. There's nothing but silence behind us, then the wooden *clack* of the door closing. Amma's grip on my arm doesn't loosen. Instead, she uses it steer me abruptly to the left, a sharp turn that almost has me stumbling.

'What are you doing?' I say. My mind's swirling too much to do anything but follow her lead.

She doesn't answer, too intent on leading me towards a cluster of palm trees to the far right side of the house. Washing hangs from the line like pennants, colourful yards of sari, interspersed with white lunghis. We keep going until we are standing in front of the shortest of the trees, the junior by perhaps a foot. There, Amma stops. She's staring at the ground. I look down too, not knowing what I'm expecting to see.

'Amma,' I say. 'We should go.'

'I had two more babies,' Amma says. Her voice is tight and drawn, as though she's forcing through a swollen throat. 'Girls. Your sisters. They are here.'

It's a long, silent moment before I understand her words and still I don't understand them. The ground beneath the tree is un-remarkable, as brown and stony and covered in dried remnants of palm leaves as that around it. Sisters.

'What happened?' I ask. Miscarriage. Stillbirth. Illness. What kind of grief has my mother been carrying all these years? My mind shies away from the thought of the wound I may have reopened.

Amma's arm circles my waist. She holds me tight against her. A shiver runs through me and doesn't stop. It makes her tremble too.

'Listen to me,' she says. 'I can only say this once, I think.'

She tells me, in quick sharp sentences, in a breathless mono-tone. She tells me under the broiling, grilling sun. As she speaks,

I squat down until I'm hovering over the ground under the palm tree. I can't help it. Stretching out a hand, I place it on the dirt.

Yes, I've craved knowledge, but this knowledge? I don't want to think about it. I don't want the images that come to my mind. I don't want to see the baby pictures of myself, of chubby cheeks and toothless smiles, flailing tiny arms reaching for pink, tiny feet, to imagine that they're other babies. Babies buried somewhere beneath the dirt under my palm. My sisters. And my grandmother has put them there.

I don't want to think about it, but my mind doesn't care what I want.

Amma falls silent. A crow cries out somewhere above us, and is answered by a long, mournful moo from a passing cow.

'And then,' Amma says, 'this'. She takes something from her handbag, holds it down to me. I turn, reach for the photograph she holds out to me, the faded colour photograph of not-me, standing curly-headed by a flowering bougainvillea, the dimple so like my own cratering the smooth skin above the left corner of her mouth.

It's the same photo, and not. It doesn't have the folded corner of the one I slipped from the dusty old Bhagavatam. It's aged in other ways, in the light of day.

'Your acha did take this photo,' Amma explains. She smiles, a slow, shy tilt of her lips. 'He never told me he had two prints.' A finger reaches out. 'Lavanika,' she says. 'Your oldest akka. Your chechi. You looked so much like her, when you were little.'

I feel her hand on my head.

'In another life,' she continues, 'she would be here, too. For you. She would have told you her favourite stories. She would have rocked Rohan to sleep. She would be a bright, beautiful young woman, just like you.'

The air in my chest seems to have turned to cement. My face is wet, and all I can taste is salt.

'I'm sorry,' Amma says. 'I didn't want to tell you. I wanted to protect you. It's all I've ever wanted to do. And maybe that hasn't always been the best thing for you, but I cannot help it.'

Of course she can't. How could she, with all she's lost?

'I wish you never had to know,' she adds, so quiet she might be speaking to herself.

'But I do need to know,' I say.

And so does she.

My secrets, my fears.

They all seem like the greatest triviality as I crouch there, my hand on the grave of my older sisters' infant bodies, and feel my mother's story sink into my bones.

We return to the car in silence. As we approach it, I see two young men approaching us from the opposite direction. They're in their late teens. Their checked shirts and navy trousers are almost identical and they're laughing at some private joke. One of them is chewing paan, and it stains his lips and teeth red. I feel an urge to call out to them, they look so familiar. I must be staring because they fall silent as they pass, their gaze locked on us.

It strikes me then that they remind me of the alcoholic man slumped in the blue-walled house behind us. The similarity's bare now, given how his face has sagged and swollen and lined, but perhaps what he might have looked like, thirty years ago.

Amma seems to have reached the same realisation. She has stopped, too, and is looking back at the two boys. Together, we watch them walk towards the house we've just left.

'Do you want to . . .' Amma starts.

'No,' I say. 'Maybe some other time. But not today.' Today, I've found and lost three sisters

*

Acha's waiting for us by the car. He's clearly been standing there, at attention, for some time, because he relaxes visibly as we get closer. Veliamma is inside, fanning herself with a newspaper despite the aircon. I can see Shankar further down the road, carrying a plastic bag of what looks like several cans of Miranda.

'How did it go?' Acha asks, his eyes moving between us.

I stop and look at him for a long second. Acha. My father.

Two steps later and I'm in his arms, feeling the scratch of his beard against my forehead, smelling his aftershave, that familiar, soothing fragrance that's surrounded me every time I've needed comfort since before I can remember.

When I raise my head from his shoulder, I see my mother. I can just make out the feathered lines stretching from the corner of her eyes, sweeping upward from the furthest reaches of her lips. Her face is so much softer than that of the woman we've just seen, my grandmother. It's etched with love and smiles and care.

I step out of Acha's arms.

I take a deep breath.

And I tell them.

I had thought that at this moment I'd feel terrified, but now I'm just numb.

I see, rather than hear, Amma's intake of breath. There's a long, long silence. I'm aware of everything in this moment – the thick, soupy warmth of the air, the horns, the screech of crows, the whisper of leaves. Either everything is broken now, or nothing is.

Amma takes a step forward, then another. 'Why didn't you tell us?' she says.

My eyes are stinging. 'I just . . .' I say, but I can't find anything past that.

Acha's hand reaches upwards. Slowly, he strokes my hair.

'Oh, my child,' Amma says. 'You were afraid, weren't you? Of me.' She sighs. 'What kind of a mother am I, that my own child is afraid to talk to me?'

I put up a hand. 'No,' I say. 'It's not your fault. It's not. I just . . . didn't want to disappoint you.' I'm still holding the photo. It's beginning to crumple in my fingers, and I unclench them.

'Silly girl,' Acha says. 'You have never disappointed us.'

Amma's eyes shimmer. There's a slight twitch at the corner of her mouth. Slowly she reaches out and takes my free hand, her fingers threading through mine, tight, close.

Chapter Twenty-Four

Madurai, 1993

She sees less than ten metres in front of her face. Her head turns to the sound of her mother's voice.

Janani stepped inside. Afternoon light streamed through the windows lining the top of the walls. Small though it was, there was a comforting sense about her new home. Perhaps it had something to do with the smell of the room, a homely mix of rice and incense.

'From its days as a storeroom,' Sanjay said, when she mentioned it. He handed her the key to the roller shutter door. His fingers brushed hers and she almost dropped it. 'But it's all yours, now. What does a sewing shop smell like?'

Janani laughed. 'When I live in it too?' she said. 'Cloth and metal. Crisp cotton and silk. And spices. Cloth absorbs the smell of spices.'

She shifted the baby in her arms for a greater purchase of the key. It felt good to have the cool metal against her palm.

'Give the little one to me.' Shubha had appeared at her shoulder.

Janani smiled and relinquished the child.

It had been a week since she had walked out of her marriage home, a week in which she had realised how blessed she was to have friends such as hers. Shubha and Narendran had insisted she stay with them from the moment Sanjay had driven her to their doorstep and they had heard her story. She had expected they – or at least, Narendran – would be disgusted with her, a woman abandoned by her husband, who had abandoned her family. All she had hoped to do was to take the sewing machine and her work and go.

'And what do you have in your new house?' Shubha had de-manded. 'A bed? A stove? Gas? Silly woman, stay here until you have all those things. And when people ask questions, we can tell them to go to hell.'

Priya had nodded in firm agreement.

'You are very brave,' Narendran had said quietly. 'You'll suc-ceed in life, Janani.' He'd held the baby and tickled her foot.

So she had stayed. Not for long, of course – Narendran and Shubha had enough troubles, caring for the elders and for the children, as well as for themselves. But those few days were a blessing. Together she and Shubha pounded rice and cut vege-tables as the baby slept on a bed of folded sheets by them. And when Shubha went to work in the rice fields, Janani sat sewing. Word had spread, and women approached her every day. Yes, they'd come to her in secret, at dusk, probing her with questions, judgement in their eyes, but then they'd pressed on her material for saris, salwar kameezes, skirts, pattu pavadas. She measured them, or their little girls and boys. She lost herself in the Singer's rhythmic whirr and the feel of cloth being crafted beneath her fingers.

In the afternoons, Priya came in an autorickshaw to collect her. They went shopping for the building blocks that Janani would need for her new life alone – the pots and pans and buck-ets, the cook-stove and containers, a set of drawers for her few possessions, toiletries and a coconut-palm broom. Priya refused to let Janani pay. Every moment of that week was another step forward, and every evening she fell asleep with her daughter on a bamboo mat on the floor, smelling the soft, milky smell of her baby skin.

On the last day, Parvati Ma had come, her slight frame bent in on itself, leaning on Sanjay's shoulder. Together they had helped her sit on the couch, and Janani had laid the baby in her lap. Her daughter had kicked her feet and clenched her minute fist around Parvati Ma's finger. Janani had watched Sanjay's face, his eyes tender on his mother as she laughed, the lines of pain around her mouth lifting. She had watched as Parvati Ma glanced up at her, caught her gaze, turned to look at Sanjay. The smile on that thin, drawn face settled her more than anything had done since she had left her parents' home behind her.

Now here she stood.

And beside her stood Sanjay. He was dressed in cream trousers and a blue cotton shirt. She could feel the warmth of him, the lean strength in his body. It occurred to her that she always wanted to lean in towards him. How different he was to Darshan, from whom she was always angled away, as far as she could go.

Sanjay reached over and turned on the light. It washed the room in warm yellow, and Janani looked at her belongings, neatly set out, just as she wanted.

They had strung a curtain of heavy cotton fabric, dark blue, about halfway up the room. It hung suspended from thick rope, stretched from a nail in the top of one wall to the other. Behind it was a pillow and sleeping mat on one side, her cooking implements on the other.

'Janani,' Shubha said. She was frowning slightly as she rocked the baby. 'Will you be safe here?'

'Of course,' Janani replied. In truth, she had no idea, but she had no time for fear right now. 'Don't worry about me,' she said, laying a hand on Shubha's arm. 'This will suit me very well for now. I have everything I need. And you're not so far away.'

Shubha looked unconvinced.

'It's just for now,' Janani added. 'Soon I'll find a house to rent.'

'Yes,' Sanjay said. 'And, Shubha Ma, she'll be safe.' He grinned, a roguish grin that she remembered from a decade ago. 'I had a chat with the neighbours, when you were . . .' He swept an arm around the room. 'Now they all know you are the widow of a policeman, a friend of mine, and that the police are watching to make sure that you're OK. They've been told that if they do the same, it would be a real favour.'

The two of them looked at him. Shubha let out a laugh that made the baby startle, and Janani shook her head. Tendrils of her hair that had come free of her braid during the afternoon drifted over her face.

'You prankster, Sanjay Annan,' she said. 'You might need another of those uniforms, for all the policemen suddenly appearing in your life.'

His smile grew wider.

She couldn't help the impossible thought that might now be slightly less possible – that maybe, just maybe, there would be more days in her future when she could be this close to him.

Outside, the sun was lowering itself gently into the horizon, a ball of fiery orange. The jeep was parked by the side of the road.

'Shubha Ma, I'll drop you home,' Sanjay said. 'Why don't you go and be comfortable in the car?'

Shubha looked at them, her eyes flitting from one to the other. Nodding, she handed the baby back to Janani. Her daughter was starting to whimper, ready for her next meal.

They watched her go.

'This is good,' Janani said. 'A new life.' She hesitated. 'Although I'm afraid, too.'

'Of course,' Sanjay said. He ran a hand through his hair. 'But don't think you're alone. You're not.'

It was there, the warmth, a deeper, far more comfortable warmth than the heat of the evening.

'I know,' she replied.

He was very close to her. She should move away, every fibre of her being knew, take a step back to let the safety of distance come between them. And yet she stood there, savouring his nearness like the newborn rays of the sun. He reached out and brushed the stray strands of hair off her face, back behind her ear. His hand lingered for a brief second, then dropped. She loved his hair, she thought, suddenly, fiercely, the way it curled over his forehead, covered the tops of his ears, its thick, lush darkness. She felt her face burn, just as she saw the dark flush stain Sanjay's cheeks. He stepped back.

'I'll be here as often as you need,' he said. Suddenly he looked uncertain. 'But only if you want me to.'

The happiness she felt then was almost as painful as the grief for Lavanika that nestled like cold coal in her heart. She reached out and laid a hand on his.

'Please come,' she said, quietly. 'When you can.'

The baby had awoken, shifting, blinking her midnight-dark eyes, sounding her short, quiet cries.

'She wants you to come, too,' Janani said.

He grinned at her and they both looked into the round little face. 'Will you wait to name her?' he asked.

Janani shook her head. Perhaps she would be able to have a naming ceremony on her daughter's thirtieth day, but why not name her now? She had already escaped death. 'I've thought of a name,' she said.

Sanjay was quiet. He had held out his index finger to the baby's minute ones, and she gripped it, gazing up at him.

'Nila,' Janani said.

'Nila,' he repeated. 'It's a good name.' His mouth curled in a smile. 'Isn't it, little moonbeam?'

Again, that clench in her heart, agonising, beautiful.

Slowly, he detached himself from the little fingers.

'Tomorrow,' he said.

'Yes.'

She watched him walk to the jeep. He glanced back at her just before he opened the driver-side door and climbed in. She watched him wave at her as he turned onto the highway, watched him until he disappeared from view. Until tomorrow.

And he did come tomorrow. And the next day, and the next.

Until tomorrow was no longer soon enough.

Chapter Twenty-Five

2019

The last couple of days in Madurai pass in a blur.

We go back to Chellampatti, and promise Rupini Attai that we'll bring her to us to visit. And we visit Usilampatti once more. There, Amma visits the person she has missed the most, and I recognise the soft-faced, smiling woman named Shubha, who is swimming in a deep well of a family, grandchildren shouting and clinging to the folds of her sari. Her hair is grey, now, and wrinkles thread across her face, but she glows somehow. I stand back as they hold each other, laughing and crying. If what's passing between the two of them had been visible, it would have shone and trembled like molten gold.

As we take our leave, with Shubha's number stored in the depths of Amma's phone, a flicker of movement catches my eye. I look up the road to where a small hut stands, door open, empty, abandoned. The sun glints off something nearby and I see a silver-haired old woman turning away, her figure obscured by the shimmering mirage the heat has created. I think I see a smile, before she disappears around the corner of the hut.

We finally go to Meenakshi Amman, but we don't go into the main shrine. Instead, we walk in slow, leisurely laps around it, through the Hall of a Thousand Pillars, past the temple pond, through the grounds, and Amma tells me that the last time she was here, she had stood in front of the idol of the goddess with my older sister and prayed for a boy.

'I'd have prayed for a boy too,' I say.

'But Meenakshi Amman gave me what I really wanted,' she says. 'What I needed. She gave me you. My moon in the darkness.' She raises a hand to my face and her bangles chime as she touches my cheek. 'I would have done anything to protect you. And sometimes I try to do it in the wrong way, don't I?'

'Yes, Amma, you do,' I say, but my voice is gentle.

She smiles and puts an arm around me, and my chest burns with a fierce rush of gratitude to Meenakshi Amman, to fate, that I was born as I am, to the mother I have.

That I can make my own life.

And although I didn't know it until now, love who I want.

On the thirteenth day, two days before we leave, I watch as my father places his father's ashes in the Vaigai, another gem in Meenakshi's garland. The other women in his family stand with me, more of them now than at the cremation, family from Bangalore and Cochin, Mumbai and Delhi. All of us are at a safe enough distance to appease Achacha's traditional spirit. There's a freedom in it, for me. I feel as close to Manju Ammayi and Radhika, Priya Ammayi and Vijay Ammama and even Arjun, as I ever did. But there's no guilt about not knowing the rest of them. That's wafted away, leaving just the family I want to know.

'He never forgave me,' Acha says later, as we walk ahead of the others back towards the car. His voice is quiet. 'I was forever letting him down, from my teenage years. He treasured the respect he got, and he wanted his sons to be worthy of that. But I didn't do medicine. And then I married your amma. He saw her as a low-caste Tamil girl. The cleaner. But I loved your amma long before I understood what caste meant.' His eyes are distant, looking back, perhaps, on a boy and a girl playing a game of hide-and-seek or anchangal in the sunlit garden many years ago.

'He still loved you,' I say, remembering their gruff embraces all those years ago, how they used to sit up together, Acha and Vijay Ammama and Achacha, long after the rest of us had gone to bed. Remembering that frail, wavering hand, reaching towards Acha.

'He did,' Acha says. 'I think that's why he was so disappointed. And he could never quite accept your amma.' His jaw tightens. 'Or you.'

I wait for the sting of pain that should accompany those words, but it's muted, barely there. I link my arm through his. He turns slightly to kiss the top of my head. I have the love of the only family I need.

It's a quiet goodbye. Arjun shakes my hand solemnly and then hands me a tiny model of a black Labrador. 'So you don't miss Hercules between visits,' he says. 'Bring your partner next time. I might be married. We can go on a double date.'

I smile. I'd been worried about telling him, but all he had done was hug me, then clap me on the back, and I feel that something has healed between us.

Radhika gives me a crushing hug and when I tell her she must come and visit, her whole face lifts and lights and her smile is immense. She is volunteering, she tells me, with a charity in Usilampatti. They help families keep their baby girls. They help those girls get all the way through primary school into college, into work. I know, I tell her. I have their details and I'll be in touch.

When we get to Madurai International Airport, I pull out my phone and start a message. For another hour, as we wait for the boarding call to come, I read over it, amending, deleting, adding, adding more.

Amma leans over and nudges me. 'We're boarding, molé.'

I hesitate, close my eyes, and hit send.

The message flies over land and sea, and we follow it home.

A girl is a burden. A girl is a curse.

I read this in the articles and reports and books I've downloaded onto my phone. The flights, the hops from Madurai to Chennai, Chennai to Sydney, bring me no sleep. Instead I read until my eyes ache.

By the time we land, I am thinking of the millions of girls who are missing from India's population. Girls smothered and poisoned and drowned and buried alive. Girls that never emerge from their mothers' wombs. I think of the tightrope I'd walked from conception, balancing on the cusp of being here or not. Of Amma walking beside me the whole time, holding my hand.

I watch her sleep. When the captain announces we're landing, she opens her eyes, looking dazed with lack of rest. But when she sees me, she smiles. I lean forward and kiss her soft cheek.

G'day, mate, the signs through Sydney Airport greet us. *Welcome home.*

Amma's chanced bringing through some curry powders and pickles and bags of banana chips, but Customs only hold us for fifteen minutes before waving us on. As we walk out into the arrivals hall, my eyes are scanning the excited Saturday morning crowds. It's eight a.m. Families, friends, taxi drivers with name cards all stand shoulder-to-shoulder. Balloons and flowers abound. There's a giant inflated unicorn, the words 'Welcome Home' scrawled in silver cursive across its side.

A familiar voice bellows over the cacophony. 'Chechi!'

In the last few days, I've wondered what it would be like, to see him again. To know that, biologically, our fathers are not the same person. My chest has been burning with anxiety. What if this knowledge changes me, warps our relationship? What will it be like, to tell him? I'm frightened, of jealousy, of resentment.

It all melts away when I hear his voice.

I'm grinning before I can see him, using his follow-up cries of 'Amma! Acha!' to pinpoint his location. He seems to have grown even taller, towering over the family of three next to him, waving madly at us. His hair's grown; it flops across his face in an untidy mop that might be by design, and his angular cheeks, so like Acha's, are split with his smile. I wave back, bouncing on the balls of my feet.

'Rohan!' Amma yells back, as though she hasn't seen him in a decade. 'Rohan is there,' she says to Acha, clinging to his arm, and he nods, smiling at her, his eyes fond.

My eyes fall on the person standing beside my brother.

She's here.

Warmth rushes through me as I see her smile, her eyes gleaming.

'It was nice for Iphigenia to come,' Acha says.

I nod, not sure I'll be able to speak.

Amma hears him. She looks over at me and something about her dims, just slightly.

When we reach them, Rohan catches our parents in his long-armed embrace.

That leaves me with Iphigenia.

I'm very conscious of what almost seventeen hours of travel must make me look and smell like. My skin feels like it's coated in a thin film of grease and plane air. My eyes feel tight from tiredness.

Iphigenia is in jeans and a light floral blouse and she looks as though she's floated in on the autumnal morning breeze.

'It's good . . .' I start, and then her arms are around me.

'Welcome home,' she says. 'Missed you.'

'Me too,' I say. 'So much.' I squeeze my eyes closed, just in time.

We pull apart and look at each other. There are a thousand questions on her face.

'Hey, Chechi,' Rohan interrupts, hugging me as I turn towards him. His stubble grazes my temple.

When he lets go, I hold him at arm's length. The boy my mother prayed for out of fear, looking at me with wide, beautiful brown eyes. My little brother, who has just learned how to use a washing machine. His hair is gelled into its artful chaos. I ruffle it.

'Not the hair!' he says, ducking out of reach.

Iphigenia and I laugh, and I have to swipe at my eyes.

'Who wants a coffee?' Acha asks, arms wide, looking tired but happy.

He sets off towards the nearest café. My brother and mother follow him.

We're alone in the crowd. I reach for Iphigenia's hand. She looks at me, blue eyes rounded in surprise. Her mouth curves upward, slow as a sunrise, into a radiant smile. Her fingers twine around mine, slim and supple.

When we realised we loved each other, what feels like an age ago, she told me first, in Malayalam, calmly and quietly.

Now, I can feel my face burning, hear the blood pulsing through my ears. I've practised these words on the plane, facing the window, whispering the syllables under my breath at my reflection against the stars. Still I have to fight to stop the stammer as I say the words.

σ' αγαπώ.

I love you.

I see the tears in her eyes a heart thump before her lips are on mine.

Together, we walk after my family, our shoulders pressed together, fingers laced.

Amma is watching us. When I meet her gaze, I see her face soften, the lines smooth from her temples. She moves her head from side to side, ear to shoulder, in that all-meaning South Indian headshake.

Good, it says now. Good.

Glossary

Aachi Older sister (*Tamil*)

Acha Father (*Malayalam*)

Achacha Paternal grandfather (*Malayalam*)

Achamma Paternal grandmother (*Malayalam*)

Aiyan Older brother (*Tamil*)

Akka Older sister (*Tamil*)

Ammama Uncle (*Malayalam*)

Amma Mother (*Malayalam/Tamil*)

Ammayi Aunt (*Malayalam*)

Anchangal 'Five Stones', a traditional Tamil game, similar to knucklebones or jacks (*Tamil*)

Annan Older brother (*Tamil*)

Appa Father (*Tamil*)

Aruval A type of machete, used as an agriculture tool to cut coconuts or chop wood. Sometimes used as a weapon (*Malayalam/Tamil*)

Asura In Hinduism, a class of divine beings who are generally evil (*Sanskrit*)

Attai Aunt (*Tamil*)

Avial A South Indian vegetable dish, prepared with coconut oil, yoghurt and curry leaves (*Malayalam/Tamil*)

Channa A type of chickpea (*Hindi*)

Chechi Older siser (*Malayalam*)

Dosa/Dosai A savoury thin pancake made of lentil and rice flour (*Malayalam/Tamil*)

Idli A savoury, thick rice cake, made by steaming a fermented batter of ground rice and black lentils (*Malayalam/Tamil*)

Janeu The sacred thread (or strand of threads) traditionally worn by male Hindus of a certain caste (*Hindi*)

Kadala A type of chickpea (*Malayalam*)

Kasayam A general word for a traditional or Ayurvedic medicinal concoction (*Sanskrit*)

Kochachan Paternal uncle (*Malayalam*)

Kolam Decorative designs drawn freehand at the front door of houses during the Pongal harvest festival

Kulantai Child (*Tamil*)

Kutty Child (*Malayalam*)

Laddoo A sweet, made from gram flour or semolina, ghee and sugar, rolled into a ball (*A multitude of Indian languages, deriving from Sanskrit*)

Lunghi A type of sarong generally worn by men in the Indian subcontinent, tied around the waist and falling to the knees (*Malayalam/Tamil*)

Mamiyar Mother-in-law (*Tamil*)

Mamanar Father-in-law (*Tamil*)

Mayurkonrai 'Peacock flower' – the dwarf poinciana (*Tamil*)

Molé Daughter (*Malayalam*)

Moné Son (*Malayalam*)

Moru kutan A yoghurt-based or butter-milk based vegetable curry (*Malayalam*)

Mundu A Keralan sarong-type garment, usually white or cream, worn wrapped around the waist (*Malayalam*)

Nondi Hopscotch (*Tamil*)

Pallu The loose end of a sari, usually decorated *(A multitude of Indian languages)*

Parai An ancient Tamil drum made with a frame of neem wood and stretched cow hide *(Tamil)*

Pattu pavada/i A traditional South Indian outfit for young girls, consisting of a cone-shaped skirt with a contrast border and a blouse with styled neckline. Usually made of silk, and brightly coloured *(Malayalam/Tamil)*

Pavakkai thokku A tamarind-based bitter gourd curry *(Tamil)*

Payasam A sweet dish made with milk and vermicelli or jaggery *(Malayalam/Tamil)*

Periamma Aunt *(Tamil)*

Pottu A coloured dot or sticker worn on the forehead between the eyebrows, typically by Hindus, Sikhs, Buddhists and Jains, symbolising the sixth *chakra, anja*, where concealed wisdom is said to reside *(Malayalam)*

Prasadam A food-based religious offering to the gods, which is then consumed by worshippers *(Sanskrit)*

Puja Prayer ceremony or ritual *(Sanskrit)*

Pujari Priest who carries out a puja *(Sanskrit)*

Punnakai Smile *(Tamil)*

Rakshasa Demon *(Sanskrit)*

Rasam A South Indian soup dish, made with tamarind, tomato and spices *(Malayalam)*

Sadhya A traditional Keralan feast featuring a variety of vegetarian dishes and traditionally eaten on banana leaves *(Malayalam)*

Sambar A South Indian and Sri Lankan stew made with lentis, vegetables ,tamarind, herbs and spices *(Malayalam/Tamil*

Sharkara upperi A Keralan sweet – fried banana chips coated in jaggery *(Malayalam)*

Thayir sadam Yoghurt or curd rice *(Malayalam/Tamil)*

Thengai sadam Coconut rice *(Tamil)*

Tulsi Holy basil, a sacred Hindu plant *(Sanskrit)*

Ulli chammanthi An onion-based dip, served as a condiment for savoury dishes such as dosa or idli *(Malayalam)*

Upanayana The Hindu ceremony in which a boy is given his sacred thread *(Sanskrit)*

Vada/Vadai A savoury snack made from lentils, legumes or potatoes *(Malayalam/Tamil)*

Vanakkam Greetings *(Tamil)*

Veliamma Aunt who is older than one's parents (lit. big mother) *(Malayalam)*

Acknowledgements

I couldn't have written this book without a host of incredible people keeping me strong along the way:

My husband, Paul, who anchors me and makes me laugh.

My agent, Juliet Mushens, a force to be reckoned with – I'm so lucky to have her behind me.

My writing teachers and classmates, from the Australian Writers' Centre to the University of East Anglia, who challenged and cheered on and forged a better writer.

My editor, Rhea Kurien, for her wonderful support and always encouraging shaping of this novel.

Harriet Bourton, for championing me, at the beginning and throughout.

The Workshop Wizards, who make writing less lonely and, more importantly, are such wonderful friends.

My closest friends. You know who you are.

My lovely family in Madurai who gave me a home when I went to India to research this book.

Amma and Acha who raised me on books.

Suvarna, who has always been my number one cheerleader.

Mr Dharma Neethi and Logamani, the founders of the wonderful grassroots Women's Emancipation and Development Trust in Chellampatti, for their generosity in letting me spend a week following them like a shadow.

The women and children I met in Madurai. Thank you for sharing your stories with me.

And finally, thank you to my readers. I'm humbled that you're taking this journey with me.

Credits

Rajasree Variyar and Orion Fiction would like to thank everyone at Orion who worked on the publication of *Daughters of Madurai* in the UK.

Editorial
Rhea Kurien
Sanah Ahmed

Copyeditor
Jade Craddock

Proofreader
Sally Partington

Audio
Paul Stark
Jake Alderson

Contracts
Anne Goddard
Humayra Ahmed
Ellie Bowker

Design
Charlotte Abrams-Simpson
Joanna Ridley
Nick May

Editorial Management
Charlie Panayiotou
Jane Hughes
Bartley Shaw
Tamara Morriss

Finance
Jasdip Nandra
Afeera Ahmed
Elizabeth Beaumont
Sue Baker

Marketing
Katie Moss
Yadira Da Trindade

Production
Ameenah Khan

Publicity
Ellen Turner
Virgina Woolstencroft

Operations
Jo Jacobs
Sharon Willis

Sales
Jen Wilson
Esther Waters
Victoria Laws
Rachael Hum
Anna Egelstaff
Frances Doyle
Georgina Cutler

The
Daughters
of
Madurai

BOOK CLUB QUESTIONS

1. Discuss Janani and Nila's relationship. Janani has given up everything she knows for her daughter, and yet their relationship is fraught with tension. Why?

2. Janani tells Nila, 'Rohan will get married too, and anyway, he is a boy and boys are different.' To what extent do you think Janani holds this mindset by the end of the book?

3. What kind of character is Vandhana? Is she a villain or a victim of generational trauma?

4. 'A girl is a burden. A girl is a curse.' Female infanticide is just one localised symptom of a global issue. How could you map male bias in the western world?

5. 'Janani found herself wondering how very different her husband was from Sanjay, what she had done in her past life to deserve one and not the other.' Discuss the contrast between Darshan and Sanjay. How have their upbringings shaped them as men in this novel?

6. How does class impact the relationship between Janani and Sanjay, both in the past and present narratives?

7. Using Nila and Ipighenia's relationship as a starting point, discuss acceptance as a concept in *The Daughters of Madurai*.

8. Nila grows up in Australia, disconnected from her wider family in India. How does this distance shape her identity?

9. As some of the key female figures in Janani's life, Kamala, Shubha, Sanjay's mother and her own mother are all distinct characters. What differentiates them? What unites them?

10. The author intersperses Malayalam and Tamil words throughout the novel. What, if any, impact did this have on your reading experience?

11. There are many powerful and emotive scenes in this novel. What is one that has stayed with you?

12. This novel is about the imbalance of power between men and women in the society in which it is set. In what ways do women seek to address this imbalance? Are there any ways that women are able to wield the power to influence their own lives?

13. We hope you loved *The Daughters of Madurai*. If you were going to recommend this debut novel to a friend, how would you describe it?

Help us make the next generation of readers

We – both author and publisher – hope you enjoyed this book. We believe that you can become a reader at any time in your life, but we'd love your help to give the next generation a head start.

Did you know that 9 per cent of children don't have a book of their own in their home, rising to 13 per cent in disadvantaged families*? We'd like to try to change that by asking you to consider the role you could play in helping to build readers of the future.

We'd love you to think of sharing, borrowing, reading, buying or talking about a book with a child in your life and spreading the love of reading. We want to make sure the next generation continue to have access to books, wherever they come from.

And if you would like to consider donating to charities that help fund literacy projects, find out more at **www.literacytrust.org.uk** and **www.booktrust.org.uk**.

THANK YOU

*As reported by the National Literacy Trust